Connecting East Asia: A New Framework for Infrastructure

 ASIAN DEVELOPMENT BANK

 JAPAN BANK FOR INTERNATIONAL COOPERATION

 THE WORLD BANK

Asian Development Bank
6 ADB Avenue
Mandaluyong City, 1550 Metro Manila
Philippines
Telephone: +63 2 632 4444
Internet URL: www.adb.org
E-mail: information@adb.org

The International Bank for Reconstruction and Development/The World Bank
1818 H Street, NW
Washington, DC 20433
USA
Telephone: 1-202-473-1000
Internet URL: www.worldbank.org
E-mail: feedback@worldbank.org

Japan Bank for International Cooperation
4-1, Ohtemachi 1-Chome, Chiyoda-ku, Tokyo 100-8144
Japan
Telephone: 81-3-5218-3101
Internet URL: www.jbic.go.jp
E-mail: https://www.jbic.go.jp/english/opinion/index.php

ISBN-10: 0-8213-6162-7   ISBN-13: 978-0-8213-6162-7

e-ISBN: 0-8213-6163-5

DOI: 10.1596/978-0-8213-6162-7

Library of Congress Cataloging-in-Publication Data *has been applied for.*

Contents

Figures

Maps

Tables

Countries Covered by This Study

THIS STUDY FOCUSES ON THE DEVELOPING COUNTRIES IN EAST ASIA and the Pacific Region, which are members of the Asian Development Bank and the World Bank. These countries include Cambodia, China, Fiji, Indonesia, Kiribati, the Lao People's Democratic Republic (Lao PDR), Malaysia, Marshall Islands, the Federated States of Micronesia, Mongolia, Myanmar, Palau, Papua New Guinea, the Philippines, Samoa, the Solomon Islands, Thailand, Timor-Leste, Tonga, Vanuatu, and Vietnam.

Developing countries are low- and middle-income countries as defined in the World Bank publication, *World Development Indicators 2004*. The findings of this study are also relevant to other developing countries within the region and elsewhere in the world.

This publication follows the World Bank practice of reference to countries. In the Asian Development Bank, Hong Kong (China) and Taiwan (China) are recognized as Hong Kong, China and Taipei,China, respectively.

Foreword

INFRASTRUCTURE HAS ALWAYS PLAYED A CENTRAL ROLE IN THE EAST
Asian development model: to promote economic growth, to share the
benefits of growth with poorer groups and communities, and to
connect countries within the region and with the rest of the world. There
is little doubt that infrastructure development—by both the public and
private sectors—has contributed to the region's enviable record on
growth and poverty reduction.

At the same time, questions and concerns have often been raised about
the impact of infrastructure development on the environment and local
communities, about waste through corruption in public spending and private contracts, and about the appropriate roles of the public and private
sectors in infrastructure financing, ownership, and management. While
infrastructure can be a force for good, we also have to make sure it is done
well.

These questions are the motivation for this joint study by the Asian
Development Bank, the Japan Bank for International Cooperation, and
the World Bank. The report is organized around three main themes:
inclusive development, coordination, and accountability and risk management. It is aimed at senior policy makers and development practi-
tioners who have to look at infrastructure in the context of countrywide
policies and programs. It does not provide detailed recommendations
by country and sector. But it does provide a new way of thinking about
infrastructure issues, which is relevant to all countries in the region.

These three agencies support infrastructure development through
project financing and guarantees, as well as by assisting governments to
put in place policies to improve public sector performance and to attract
private investment. Therefore, this study is also relevant to our own operations. We will look closely at the implications for our technical assistance, capacity building, financing, and guarantee activities. Each
agency will follow its own operational strategy in each country. But we
hope this new framework will enable us to take a more coherent and consistent approach. We will also look for more opportunities to work
together—as experienced recently in Indonesia.

The recent Indian Ocean tsunami took many lives and devastated communities in its path. In Indonesia alone, the damages and losses are estimated at US$4.5 billion, of which about 20 percent would be required to rebuild infrastructure. This report is not about the tsunami. But many of the policy lessons—about coordination, community involvement, and accountability, for example—are also relevant to infrastructure reconstruction. Similarly, in the design of new infrastructure projects, we must take into account their vulnerability to natural disasters, to reduce the risk of future damage.

We offer this report as a contribution to the ongoing debates about the role of infrastructure in promoting growth and reducing poverty. We realize from our own consultations that policy makers in the region do not have to be convinced about the importance of infrastructure. They are keen, however, to learn from the experiences of other countries about how to better manage infrastructure. We hope you will find that this report provides a refreshing and provocative look at familiar issues—and sheds new light on the way forward.

Mr. Geert van der Linden
Vice President, Knowledge Management and
Sustainable Development
Asian Development Bank

中村誠一

Mr. Seiichi Nakamura
Director General, JBIC Institute
Japan Bank for International Cooperation

Mr. Jemal-ud-din Kassum
Vice President, East Asia and Pacific Region
World Bank

Acknowledgments

THIS REPORT HAS BEEN PREPARED BY A CORE STUDY TEAM LED BY Mark Baird and comprising Rita Nangia, Asian Development Bank (ADB); Yasuo Fujita, Japan Bank for International Cooperation (JBIC); and Jonathan Walters, World Bank. The principal author of the report was Jonathan Walters, with support from Adam Schwartzman. Additional contributions were provided by Marc Shotten, Elisa Muzzini, Philip Lam, Ivan Velev, Atsushi Iimi, Takuro Takeuchi, and Shigeki Furukawa. The core team was ably assisted by Evangeline Sucgang, Aggie de Sagon, Marivic de la Cruz, Motoko Kanamaru, and Melissa Morris. The study was prepared under the general guidance of Khalid Rahman (ADB), Toru Tokuhisa and Seiichi Nakamura (JBIC), and Christian Delvoie (World Bank).

Background papers for the study were prepared by Roger Allport (Halcrow), Shinji Asanuma (Hitotsubashi University), Michael Bennett, John Besant-Jones, Steven Burgess (World Bank), David Ehrhardt (Castalia), Sharon Felzer (World Bank), Yasuo Fujita and Shoichi Hisa (JBIC), Timothy Irwin and Hana Brixi (World Bank), Shizuo Iwata (ALMEC Corporation), Stephen Jones (Oxford Policy Management), Mahesh Kotecha (Structured Credit International Corporation), Zhi Liu (World Bank), Felipe Medalla (University of the Philippines), Shigeru Morichi (Institute for Transport Policy Studies), Lee Schipper and Wei-shiuen Ng (World Resources Institute), Alex Sundakov (Castalia), Yutaka Takamine (University of the Ryukyus), John Ure (University of Hong Kong), Liz Urquhart (Castalia), Jeremy Warford, Douglas Webster, Hiroo Yamagata (Nomura Research Institute), and Tito Yepes (World Bank).

Valuable comments on a draft of this report were provided by managers and staff of the ADB, JBIC, and World Bank, as well as by an external advisory group, including Joseph Anderson (Morrison and Forester), Dai Dongchang (Ministry of Communications, China), David Hawes (AusAID), Haresh Jaisinghani (AES Corporation), Takashi Kudo (Nippon Keidanren), Gilbert Llanto (Philippine Institute for Development Studies), Shigeru Otsubo (Nagoya University), Roel Ravanera (Asia-Japan Partnership Network for Poverty Reduction), Vijay Sethu

(ANZ Investment Bank), Frances Seymour (World Resources Institute), Bambang Susantono (Coordinating Ministry of Economic Affairs, Indonesia), Hidekazu Tanaka (Engineering and Consulting Firms Association, Japan), and Douglas Webb (Telecommunications Commissioner, New Zealand).

The study was supported by generous funding from the Government of Japan (Policy and Human Resources Development Fund [PHRD] and Japan Social Fund), the Public-Private Infrastructure Advisory Facility (PPIAF), the ADB, the JBIC, and World Bank. This funding enabled the study team, among other things, to organize consultations with government officials, private investors, civil society, academics, official lenders, and donors through three regional workshops in Manila (January 2004), Tokyo (January 2004), and Bali (June 2004) and a series of country visits. Some preliminary findings from the study were presented at the Asia Pacific Infrastructure Forum (Melbourne, December 2004) and the Indonesia Infrastructure Summit (Jakarta, January 2005). A draft of this report was launched in Tokyo on March 16, 2005.

Abbreviations and Acronyms

ADB	Asian Development Bank
APEC	Asia-Pacific Economic Cooperation
ARBAC	Bucharest Agency for Water and Sewerage Regulation
ASEAN	Association of Southeast Asian Nations
BAPPENAS	Badan Perencanaan Pembangunan Nasional
BOI	Board of Investment
BOT	build-operate-transfer
BRT	bus rapid transit
CALA	Cavite-Laguna Provinces
CDD	community-driven development
CoC	cost of capital
CoE	cost of equity
CPC	Communist Party of China
CPRGS	comprehensive poverty reduction and growth strategy
DAT	Department of Air Transportation
DEL	direct exchange line
DfID	Department for International Development
EAP	East Asia and Pacific
ECTEL	Eastern Caribbean Telecommunications Authority
EdL	Electricité du Laos
EDI	electronic data interchange
EGAT	Electricity Generating Authority of Thailand
EIA	environmental impact assessment
EKUIN	Coordinating Ministry for the Economy and Industry
EPA	extraordinary price adjustment
ERR	economic rate of return
ESB	Eastern Seaboard
FDI	foreign direct investment
GDP	gross domestic product
GMS	Greater Mekong Subregion
GNI	gross national income
GVRD	Greater Vancouver Regional District
HIPC	heavily indebted poor countries
ICD	inland container terminal

ICT	information and communications technology
IPP	independent power producer
JBIC	Japan Bank for International Cooperation
JICA	Japan International Cooperation Agency
JETRO	Japan External Trade Organization
KDP	Kecamatan Development Project
LAC	Latin America and the Caribbean (developing countries only)
LRT	light rail transit
MDGs	Millennium Development Goals
MEA	Metropolitan Electricity Authority
MIME	Ministry of Industry, Mines and Energy
MoF	Ministry of Finance
MoT	Ministry of Transport
MPI	Ministry of Planning and Investment
MRT	mass rapid transit
MWSS	Metropolitan Water Supply and Sewerage System
MWCI	Manila Water Company, Inc.
MWSI	Manila Water Services, Inc.
NDRC	National Development and Reform Commission
NEDA	National Economic and Development Authority
NESDB	National Economic and Social Development Board
NGO	nongovernmental organization
NPC	National Power Corporation
NRB	National Roads Board
NRW	nonrevenue water
NT2	Nam Theun 2
OBA	output-based aid
ODA	official development assistance
OECD	Organisation for Economic Co-operation and Development
PASO	Pacific Aviation Safety Office
PERPAMSI	Indonesian Water Supply Association
PDAM	Perusahaan Daerah Air Minum (Local Water Supply Enterprise)
PLDT	Philippine Long Distance Telephone Company
PLN	Indonesia State Electricity Utility
PPA	power purchase agreement
PPI	private participation in infrastructure

PPIAF   Public-Private Infrastructure Advisory Facility
PPP   public private partnerships
PPWSA   Phnom Penh Water Supply Authority
PSC   public sector comparator
PSTN   public switched telephone network
ROCKS   Road Cost Knowledge System
SAR   South Asia region
SEA   strategic environmental assessment
SEZ   special economic zones
SOE   state-owned enterprise
SPUG   Small Power Utilities Group
TEU   twenty foot equivalent units
USAID   U.S. Agency for International Development
UNESCAP   United Nations Economic and Social Commission for
            Asia and the Pacific
VoIP   voice over Internet protocol
WSS   water supply and sanitation
WUA   Water Users Association

Units of Measure

gw   gigawatt
km   kilometer
kWh   kilowatt hours
mW   megawatt
VA   volt-amp

Note: All dollar figures are in U.S. dollars, unless otherwise noted.

Executive Summary

THIS STUDY IS ABOUT EAST ASIA, AND IT'S ABOUT INFRASTRUCTURE. It's about poverty and growth, and it's about transport, water, sanitation, power, gas, and telecommunications—both the infrastructure, and the infrastructure services.[1]

Infrastructure is but one part of the development challenge, but its impacts are among the most important. In this study we show how. We look at the role that infrastructure has played in supporting East Asia's growth and poverty outcomes. We look ahead at what the challenges are for the future, and how to think of approaching them.

We will discuss these many challenges—in this summary and in the body of the study—but, in sum, they amount to this: responding to and shaping change.

Much of East Asia continues to grow rapidly, driven to a considerable extent by China. Urbanization is proceeding at a rapid pace. Demand for infrastructure services is increasing massively, particularly in cities. Much of the demand comes from the newly urbanized poor. Infrastructure has to meet the needs of this population, but also has to continue to provide the underpinnings for the region's growth.

The complexity of responding to these demands is greater than ever, and the cost of getting things wrong is high. Poorly conceived infrastructure investments today will have huge environmental, economic, and social impacts—and be costly to fix later. Neglecting the infrastructure needs of people remaining in poor parts of East Asia—particularly in rural areas and in isolated countries of the region—and failing to include them in growth will also be costly in human and political terms.

The "new framework"

In this study, we set out an approach around which to structure a response to these challenges. The approach is organized in four chapters, each of which discusses a different part of the infrastructure story.

Chapter 1 sets the scene. It's about infrastructure in East Asia today, and explains how the region got to this point. It tells five infrastructure "stories," each of which provides a different aspect of the context for the region's current infrastructure challenge: the economic story, the spatial and demographic story, the environmental story, the political story, and the funding story.

Chapters 2, 3, and 4 then set out what we have called the "new framework," picking up the key elements of the stories in Chapter 1 (see Figure 1).

Chapter 2 is about goals. It's about how infrastructure can reinforce East Asia's typically inclusive development. By *inclusive development* we mean improving the lives of all members of society, particularly the poor, by generating economic growth, sharing its benefits, and enhancing access to services. We organize the chapter around the idea of the connecting role of infrastructure. We see how this works at the regional and the country levels.

Chapters 3 and 4 are about what needs to be done to achieve infrastructure goals. We divide the issue into two parts. Chapter 3 looks at the big picture: the state's ability to generate strategic vision and translate that vision into infrastructure outcomes. This requires making trade-offs between multiple objectives, particularly when multiple actors are involved. Who makes those trade-offs is important, and how

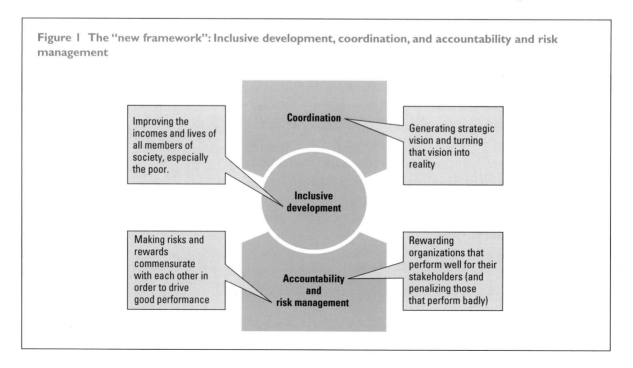

Figure 1 The "new framework": Inclusive development, coordination, and accountability and risk management

Improving the incomes and lives of all members of society, especially the poor.

Coordination

Generating strategic vision and turning that vision into reality

Inclusive development

Making risks and rewards commensurate with each other in order to drive good performance

Accountability and risk management

Rewarding organizations that perform well for their stakeholders (and penalizing those that perform badly)

leadership and participation are balanced in that process. This we describe as *coordination*.

Chapter 4 is about what happens lower down in the service delivery process. It's about the various players involved in service delivery—consumers, communities, service providers, regulators, investors, governments, and nongovernmental organizations (NGOs)—and how to ensure that their interactions result in the right infrastructure outcomes. We structure our analysis around two ideas: mechanisms that can be used to bring about *accountability*, by rewarding good performance and punishing bad; and the *risk management* required to ensure that potential costs and benefits are equitably and sustainably allocated.

Chapter 5 charts the way forward. It sets out 12 policy messages, answering to some of the key preoccupations of the region's policy makers, policy implementers, infrastructure service providers, civil society organizations, and other stakeholders consulted in the process of putting together this report. It also outlines the role that the official lenders, donors and development agencies can play in supporting countries to meet their infrastructure challenges.

Chapter I. The infrastructure challenge

In Chapter 1 we take stock of East Asia's infrastructure challenges in the context of five broader stories that have defined, and will continue to define, the region's development:

The "economic story" is about the role that infrastructure has played in underpinning poverty reduction, investment, and growth in the region—it's about levels of expenditure, stocks of infrastructure assets, access to infrastructure services, and infrastructure competitiveness, and what this implies for the future.

The "spatial and demographic story" is about the demands of rapid urban growth on infrastructure, and the contribution of infrastructure to that growth and to meeting the needs of urban areas. But it's also about the challenge of linking the poor in rural areas, both to services and to growth centers. And it's about the challenges of infrastructure on a regional level, supporting trade and spreading the benefits of growth across borders.

The "environmental story" is about dealing with the impacts of infrastructure on a range of environmental concerns—air quality, emissions, the availability of clean water and sanitation, and the function of ecosystems that provide livelihoods and other benefits. The environmental challenge is how to mainstream environmental issues, addressing environment not only at the project level but also more broadly in policy.

The "political story" is about who captures the benefits of infrastructure—who provides it, to whom, at what price, and at whose cost.

The "funding story" is about the scale of East Asia's infrastructure needs, and how to resource these needs. Ultimately, there are only two groups who pay for infrastructure—consumers and taxpayers. And there is another set that can finance it—the private sector, and official lenders and donors. What needs to be taken into account in structuring the roles of each? What can be expected of them?

The economic story

Regionally, East Asia has seen strong growth and strong poverty reduction outcomes. Output has increased by an annual average of more than 7 percent over the past 15 years, lifting 250 million people out of poverty in the past five years. Investment levels are generally high, averaging more than 30 percent of gross domestic product (GDP) since the 1990s.

Much of this investment has been to provide infrastructure services. A number of countries invest more than 7 percent of GDP in infrastructure (Table 1.2). Infrastructure stocks are increasing at a significant pace in a number of sectors. Energy generation capacity grew by more than 80 percent (and as high as 180 percent) in six countries throughout the 1990s, and road networks expanded at similarly impressive rates—by over 25 percent (and as high as 104 percent) in four countries over the same period (Table 1.3).

But there is great divergence behind these aggregate outcomes, and East Asia still has a long way to go. Half the countries in the region grew by less than 2.8 percent a year between 1994 and 2003. And there are still significant levels of poverty in many of the large, fast growers—close to 400 million in China; 40 million in Vietnam; and 100 million in Indonesia (Table 1.1).

Access to infrastructure services is similarly uneven. In approximately 40 percent of East Asian countries for which we have data, access to water supply is lower than the average for all low- and middle-income countries. The equivalent figures for sanitation, electricity, telephone, and Internet access range between 52 and 79 percent.

There are similar disparities between countries in East Asia: more than 90 percent of the population has water supply access in four countries; in three countries, it's less than 50 percent. Access to sanitation is 93 percent in Thailand, and 30 percent in Mongolia; access to electricity is 97 percent in Malaysia, and 15 percent in the Solomon Islands (Table 1.4).

What is the story behind these numbers? East Asian growth is largely driven by fast-growing urban agglomerations in coastal China, Indonesia, Thailand, Malaysia, and Vietnam. Connections between countries within the region have been important, with significant regional trade, much of it geared toward China's expanding markets (a theme we pick up in Chapter 2).

A number of the countries in the region have seen simultaneously high levels of growth and investment, a focus on infrastructure, and improved infrastructure performance outcomes. Malaysia and Thailand have achieved internationally competitive infrastructure networks (Figure 1.3). Other countries in the region are further behind, but in general, East Asia has provided the infrastructure underpinnings for economic growth better than in other regions.

High levels of investment have not necessarily meant efficient investment. China and Vietnam in particular (with investments rates of more than 30 percent of GDP, and investment in infrastructure at more than 7 percent of GDP) face the challenge of addressing efficiency, avoiding overheating, and managing a soft landing. A number of countries emerging from the Asian crisis of 1997—Thailand, Malaysia, Indonesia, and the Philippines—have restrained investment, in general, and infrastructure investment, in particular. Thailand and Indonesia are both placing renewed emphasis on infrastructure, and face the challenge of enhancing the investment climate, and increasing investment to underpin sustained growth.

In other East Asian countries—for example, Lao People's Democratic Republic (Lao PDR) and Cambodia—the mutually supportive relationship among growth, poverty reduction, infrastructure, and investment is less evident. Yet other countries and regions are landlocked, or isolated, and relatively unconnected to the major growth centers of East Asia—most rural areas, the outlying islands of Indonesia and the Philippines, Mongolia, and most Pacific island states. Infrastructure has an important role to play in all of these regions, forging connections to growth centers, and providing services to the poor.

The spatial and demographic story

East Asia's spatial and demographic story is dominated by urbanization. Levels of urbanization in East Asia are not high by international standards (36 percent of the population was urbanized in 2000), but these levels are expected to reach more than 57 percent by 2025 (Figure 1.5). By then, 500 million more people will live in urban areas.

Again, there are variations—Indonesia and the Philippines have high urbanization levels and high growth in urban populations; the opposite pertains to Thailand, where there are low levels of urbanization and low growth rates. Other countries span the range between these extremes (Table 1.5).

Cities drive East Asia's growth. Cities account for up to 70 percent of East Asian GDP growth. In general, urbanization has been associated with increasing incomes (Figure 1.6). The growth of cities has been associated with unprecedented prosperity (and growing inequality)—for example, the per capita GDP of Shanghai alone is about 11 times that of China's overall per capita GDP.

Densely populated urban areas have provided markets for outputs, inputs, labor, and other services and have allowed firms to profit from economies of scale and scope, specialization, and the rapid diffusion of knowledge and innovation. Agglomeration economies have been strong.

But urban growth brings with it a host of infrastructure challenges: increasing population drives increasing demand for infrastructure services. Gaps are emerging across urban infrastructure sectors, and these gaps tend to affect the poor (who are frequently found in peri-urban, informal settlements) more than the rest of the population (Table 1.6).

At the same time, infrastructure has an enormous role to play in maintaining the competitiveness of East Asian cities. Among the most challenging aspects of this role is to make infrastructure choices before land use patterns are established, thus avoiding the prohibitive costs of infrastructure retrofitting. Long-term planning and strategic vision are essential, as are mechanisms to deal with the cross-jurisdiction and cross-agency coordination challenges raised by decentralization. These issues are discussed in detail in Chapter 3, on coordination.

As important as the demands of urban growth are, 60 percent of the region's population (roughly 1.1 billion people) continues to live outside of cities. Poverty tends to be concentrated in rural areas, with a number of generally fast-growing countries, including significant pockets of rural poverty.

Rural economies depend on urban economies, but urban economies also depend on rural economies for human capital and agriculture products. While improving the livelihoods of rural people, the contribution of infrastructure to rural incomes, to health, and to education outcomes also has implications for urban areas—for example, in the supply of perishable foods or the productivity of future migrants.

But the unit costs of delivering rural infrastructure in sparsely populated areas are often higher than urban infrastructure, and striking the balance between urban and rural is difficult, particularly when budgets are constrained. Providing rural infrastructure as cost-effectively as possible is one of the key challenges. As in urban areas, delivery of rural infrastructure raises a number of coordination problems. Decentralization, if not carefully managed, may sometimes enhance rural isolation, rather than global connectivity.

Finally, the regional challenge for East Asia is to strengthen the connections between countries to spread the benefits of growth. In part, the challenge is to create the infrastructure required to connect isolated countries and areas of the region—the Pacific islands, land-locked Mongolia, and China's western provinces. And in part it's about the logistics required to facilitate trade (and lower costs through economies of scale where possible). These issues are discussed in Chapter 2, on inclusive development.

The environmental story

Infrastructure choices have important environmental impacts. Sometimes they are positive,[2] but frequently they are not. The environmental challenge is to take these impacts on board, and mainstream efforts to mitigate and limit negative environmental outcomes.

Project-level interventions have an important role to play. They can include environmental safeguards, measures to mitigate (or compensate for) environmental risk and cost, alternative projects design, or even alternative projects. But the underlying causes of environmental problems cannot be addressed at this level. Environmental considerations need to be embedded within national policy-making agendas.

There are a number of ways of doing this—for example, through environmental legislation, capacity building in environmental agencies, improved information and transparency, training at the community level and within infrastructure agencies, and the systematic use of strategic environmental assessments (SEAs) at the national and sectoral levels.

But mainstreaming environmental issues in this way is primarily a governance challenge, and a difficult one at that. Asymmetry in access to information, capture of the processes of information dissemination, and ease in manipulating environmental assessments all benefit powerful political groups. The ability to mainstream depends on the development of broader accountability, participation, and the existence of transparency mechanisms.

Environmental mainstreaming also poses significant policy and agency coordination challenges. Shifting from individual to mass transit may improve urban air quality, but this involves a host of interventions, from investment in urban rail to taxation on fuel and private vehicles to traffic management. And this is all the more difficult with the fragmentation of policies with environmental impacts across state agencies, and where the private sector and civil society are intimately involved. Coordinating across all these dimensions challenges government capabilities in any country.

The political story

The political economy of infrastructure is essentially a struggle over who captures the considerable benefits of infrastructure services and who bears the costs. Governments, consumers, and service providers (whether public or private) all have an interest. Tariff levels are the issue around which much of this struggle takes place.

The high economic benefits of infrastructure make a strong case for government intervention. So does the monopoly power that frequently accompanies the economies of scale required to deliver many infrastructure services. This intervention usually takes the form of tariff controls.

There are a number of reasons why this happens. Governments may want to protect a certain level of service, but they may be unwilling to allow tariffs to rise to levels required for cost recovery. Fiscal constraints may prevent them from providing subsidies to make up the difference. And the interests of those groups who benefit from lower prices—infrequently the poor, who are often excluded from formal services and thus remain voiceless—may provide a similarly binding constraint.

While public sector provision was the only service provision model in East Asia, the costs of low tariffs were absorbed by government budgets, quasi-fiscal loans from state-controlled financial institutions, capital consumption (that is, lack of maintenance and capital replacement), or by reducing operations. This began to change in the late 1980s when the private sector became an increasingly important force in East Asian infrastructure; however, in the process, they took on considerable political risk—much of which was realized after the Asian crisis of the late 1990s.

Addressing the political challenge has little to do with whether the public or private sectors deliver infrastructure. An environment that's lousy for the private sector is equally lousy for the public sector. Addressing the challenge depends on whether governments have long-term economic vision, can plan for the future, acknowledge the importance of efficiency incentives for infrastructure, and are intent on ensuring sustainable infrastructure financing mechanisms.

The funding story

East Asia's funding challenge is to resource estimated infrastructure needs of approximately $200 billion annually over the next five years. It is estimated that 65 percent of expenditure would need to take the form of new investment, with the remaining 35 percent channeled toward maintenance of existing assets—an equally and sometimes more cost-effective way of meeting service goals (Figure 1.10, and Chapter 1, Annex 1).

Ultimately, there are only two sources from which these needs can be funded: consumers (via user changes) and taxpayers (via subsidies). Financiers—whether in the private sector or in the development community—can change the requisite time profile of taxes or user charges, but eventually their contributions have to be repaid or remunerated (and if they aren't, the consequences will generally rebound on consumers or taxpayers at some later point) (Figure 1.11).

When consumers pay for infrastructure: Charging consumers for use of infrastructure services is common. The challenge is deciding the degree to which their contributions cover costs. The ability of infrastructure providers to cover costs varies by sector. In the water sector, for instance, it is unclear whether any East Asian water utilities have full recovered operational and capital costs (Figure 1.12). Non-cost-reflective tariffs may arise for a number of reasons: they may reflect excessively high costs of inefficiently run services, or they may reflect costs that are high for good reason. Sometimes tariffs are low for political reasons (as we saw above), and sometimes they are kept low to protect the poor. There is general consensus now that consumption of services by the poor can be subsidized, although there are considerable challenges in targeting the benefits of below-cost consumption.

When taxpayers pay for infrastructure: Subsidizing infrastructure from taxes raises micro issues, including ensuring that subsidies are channeled to expenditure with the highest returns, ensuring transparency, designing exit strategies, and balancing the emphasis on investment and maintenance. These issues are discussed in Chapter 4. Subsidizing infrastructure from taxes also raises macro issues, including whether too much subsidization of infrastructure threatens fiscal stability, or whether too little endangers economic growth and poverty reduction. These issues are discussed in Chapter 3.

When the private sector finances infrastructure: The private sector has invested approximately $190 billion in East Asian infrastructure since 1990 (Figure 1.8). This is a minor share of the region's needs, and a minor share of total infrastructure investment in the past. Since the Asian crisis, private sector investment has diminished significantly (although signs of upturn are now evident). A survey undertaken for this study, however, shows that private sector sentiment toward East Asia is optimistic, but varies by country, and is contingent on policy improvements and reduced risk (Figure 1.14). The key issue is not whether financing should be public or private, but how the public and private sectors share the risks and rewards in a way that works for both sides. Financing and ownership are secondary.

When official lenders and donors finance infrastructure: In purely monetary terms, the role of official lenders and donors has never amounted to more than a small percentage of total infrastructure needs overall (although this varies considerably by country). Official financing fell temporarily after 1997, but it is again on the rise, as the contribution of infrastructure to poverty reduction—indeed, of growth to poverty reduction—has been reappraised. In most infrastructure sectors there are activities in which private sector interest is likely to be limited, and others in which private interest needs external support. Official lenders, donors, and development agencies have an important role to play in both cases. The challenge is to maximize the role of those relatively small amounts of official financing—for example, by stimulating experimentation and innovation; supporting efficiency gains; mainstreaming environmental and social considerations; attracting private investors to share risks with the public sector; and building effective institutions to plan, coordinate, and regulate infrastructure services. We will revisit this topic in Chapter 5.

Chapter 2. Inclusive development

At the core of this study is the idea of the role of infrastructure in fostering inclusive development. Inclusive development is about improving the incomes and lives of all members of society, particularly the poor. It depends on generating economic growth, sharing its benefits with the poor, and enhancing their access to basic services.

Infrastructure is highly intertwined in our lives. Knowing that infrastructure is important per se is easy. Measuring the precise importance of a particular piece of infrastructure is difficult. But choices need to be made about infrastructure, and so we need to identify the impacts, understand how they are channeled, and recognize what they depend on.

We can look at this in a number of ways. This study primarily examines the ways that infrastructure connects. Conceptually, we can think about the role that infrastructure plays in a series of mutually reinforcing relationships that connect growth and poverty reduction—a subject on which the development world is coming to broad consensus.

Infrastructure provides people with the services they need and want. The absence of some of the most basic infrastructure services is an important aspect of what we mean when we talk about poverty. But infrastructure also has an important impact on poverty through growth. Infrastructure is an input into production and raises the productivity of factors of production. Through its impact on welfare, it provides people with the capabilities to fill (and create) jobs. Infrastructure connects goods to markets, workers to industry, people to services, and the poor in rural areas to urban growth centers. Infrastructure lowers costs, and it enlarges markets and facilitates trade.

In sum, infrastructure impacts on poverty in two ways: First, it supports the processes of growth on which much poverty reduction depends; and second it helps the poor access basic services, which can improve their lives and income opportunities. And at its best, infrastructure can draw poverty reduction, service provision, and growth into a reinforcing cycle (Figure 2.1).

A large body of empirical literature documents the impacts of infrastructure on poverty reduction and on growth. The specific impact of infrastructure on poverty, in particular, has been studied in a number of ways, and depends on how one defines poverty. The narrowest poverty definition focuses on the incomes and livelihoods of people living below the poverty line and is concerned with how infrastructure increases real incomes of the poor. But another body of literature looks at poverty more broadly, reflecting some of the key dimensions mentioned in the Millennium Development Goals (See Box 1). And broader still, a third strand focuses on enhancing social inclusion, human capabilities, and freedoms, focusing, for example, on the affect that transport and telecommunication services might have on people's ability to engage and participate in collective activities and access wider sources of information.

Impacts vary by each kind of infrastructure (Table 2.1). Overall, the literature suggests that transport, telecommunications, and electricity are important overall for growth and poverty reduction, and that rural roads, water, and sanitation are critical to the reduction of poverty among the poorest. Most important, however, it emphasizes that most infrastructure is effective only when combined with other interventions.

This does not imply, however, that everyone benefits from investment in infrastructure, nor even that the benefit are shared equally. Infrastructure undertakings—like all projects and sectoral reforms—have winners and losers. At the same time, there may be genuine choices to be made

---

Box 1 Infrastructure and the Millennium Development Goals

The Millennium Development Goals (MDGs)—the international community's agreement on the goals for reducing poverty—include eight objectives to be achieved by 2015. The goals are as follows:

1. **To eradicate extreme poverty and hunger—**

    Halve the proportion of people living on less than $1 a day.

    Halve the proportion of people who suffer from hunger.

2. **To achieve universal primary education—**

    Ensure that boys and girls alike complete primary schooling.

(Continued on the next page)

Box I (Continued)

3. To promote gender equality and empower women—

Eliminate gender disparity at all levels of education.

4. To reduce child mortality—

Reduce by two-thirds the under-five mortality rate.

5. To improve maternal health—

Reduce by three-quarters the maternal mortality ratio.

6. To combat HIV/AIDS, malaria, and other diseases—

Reverse the spread of HIV/AIDS.

7. To ensure environmental sustainability—

Integrate sustainable development into country policies and reverse loss of environmental resources.

Halve the proportion of people without access to portable water.

Significantly improve the lives of at least 100 million slum dwellers.

8. To develop a global partnership for development—

Raise official development assistance.

Expand market access.

How does infrastructure relate to the MDGs, and how is this relationship addressed in this study?

Poverty and infrastructure are at the core of the concept of inclusive development around which this report is written. In Chapter 2 we look at poverty from three angles, and consider how infrastructure in each of the sectors makes an impact. We look not only at income poverty (MDG I), but also the impacts of infrastructure on education, health, and the environment (with impacts on MDGs 2, 4, 5, 6, and 7).

Some of the channels through which impacts are felt are not as obvious as might be expected. It may seem intuitive that the ability of people to earn a living is increased when transport, information, power, and water are readily available. But infrastructure has some less obvious impacts—one study we refer to, for instance, examines the impact of transport and electricity on education. The impact of health services may be similarly affected by the ability of the poor to access facilities. A road or a telephone call can make an enormous difference.

Poor access to water and sanitation is an important part of the discussion about poverty, and this is addressed in the seventh MDG (environmental sustainability). But the role of infrastructure in the environment is much wider than this. In Chapter I, we focus on the challenges of mainstreaming environmental issues, although the environmental theme cuts across this study.

Finally, the role of infrastructure in creating livable cities and providing service to slum dwellers is a theme of Chapter I and is included in our discussion of urban management in Chapter 3.

between infrastructure investments that have an impact on growth, and those that have an impact on poverty reduction. Finally, institutions often face difficult trade-offs between the interests of different groups of poor and non-poor. Participation of affected groups in decision making is one measure that can help—a theme we pick up in Chapter 4, on accountability and risk management.

We can see how infrastructure fosters inclusive development at various levels. In this study, we examine this from the regional level and from a detailed country perspective.

Getting the goods to market has been the key to East Asia's prosperity. Trade has been crucial to rapid growth, and trade expansion (particularly exports to China) will continue to be important. The ability of poorer countries to share in this process will depend, in part, on their ability to develop an infrastructure that supports regional trade opportunities. For the most isolated and land-locked countries and regions, regional infrastructure cooperation will be crucial.

Superior logistics has played an important role in supporting this regional story. This is particularly so in the region's most advanced developed economies, but it is also true in a number of developing countries, including Malaysia, Thailand, China, and the Philippines (Figure 2.2).

East Asia's performance varies across countries (Box 2.5). On the whole, however, East Asia's logistics efficiency appears to be falling behind. Increased logistics costs stem from inadequate transport infrastructure, underdeveloped logistics and transport services, and bureaucratic (and sometimes corrupt) import and export procedures.

Issues of coordination—the subject of Chapter 3—feature prominently in the broad measures required to address East Asia's logistics challenges. This requires, in particular, coordination across national boundaries (in harmonization and simplification of customs procedures, for instance, or information sharing), and in urban management (most important, in the implementation of land use policies for the location of roads, ports, and other infrastructure related to logistics).

We then move from the regional to the country specific: Vietnam serves as a useful example of how infrastructure can support inclusive development. Over the last decade Vietnam has grown at an annual average rate of 7.6 percent, placing it among the fastest growing countries in the world. Economic development has been remarkably pro-poor, lifting around 20 million people out of poverty in less than a decade.

Infrastructure and investment have been important parts of that process, complementing the country's many targeted poverty reduction initiatives. Forty-four percent of government investment has been targeted to infrastructure. The impacts on poverty have been well documented for large- and small-scale infrastructure undertakings. Improvements to National Highway No. 5, linking Ha Noi and Hai Phong Port, for instance, are associated with significantly higher per capita incomes and poverty reduction in the Ha Noi-Hai Phong corridor. Studies of small infrastructure undertakings have revealed similarly impressive impacts, again most prominently in roads. One study found, for example, that the establishment of a new road in a village raised the per capita income of households by 30 percent between 1993 and 1998 (see Chapter 2 for details).

Chapter 3. Coordination

The East Asian experience demonstrates that the "big picture" is at least as important as the quality of a specific infrastructure ministry or service provider. The big picture is about generating strategic vision, and the state's ability to turn that vision into reality. This is what we mean by "coordination"—the focus of Chapter 3.

The advanced economy coordination model

Strong coordination is a prominent feature of the infrastructure stories in the region's now-developed economies—Hong Kong (China), Japan, the Republic of Korea, Singapore, and Taiwan (China)—as well as in the most advanced developing economy (Malaysia).

In these six advanced economies, political leaders and senior policy makers played a major role in creating long-term development visions, and the sectoral strategies that flowed from that vision. Each country had strong planning agencies to drive infrastructure development, and these agencies enjoyed considerable political influence—Korea's Economic Planning Bureau, Singapore's Economic Development Board, Malaysia's central planning agency and policy-making body in the Prime Minister's Office, or Japan's strong sector ministries and advisory boards. Sustained periods of high growth helped create the policy consensus behind the infrastructure investment needed to support that growth, while the discipline of needing to remain competitive injected efficiency into project choice and service delivery.

Sometimes infrastructure investment anticipated demand. But when investment was reacting to constraints—as was still largely the case—reactions were rapid and strategic. A number of bold infrastructure projects were undertaken—the Kobe Nagoya Highway in Japan, and the Seoul Pusan Highway in Korea—although inevitably there were some white elephants.

Sector strategies tended to adapt as production structures changed, as opposed to making piecemeal adaptations. Much of the workings of this approach was hidden from view, with individual accountability being largely internal to an elite, as long as the broader public was enjoying the benefits of growth.

By the 1980s, however, the strains and contradictions of the model were beginning to show. The model did not deal well with financial crisis or slowdown, revealing risks that had been hidden until then. Government-directed lending from the financial sector, lack of transparency, and corporate governance failures all began to prove problematic. In some cases, strategic investment proved to be supply driven, and cases of cronyism and corruption were not unknown.

As the state's role became more complex, and its objectives more diverse, its ability to squeeze efficiency gains from the existing system of public sector monopolies diminished. Greater complexity meant that the state, at the center, needed to focus more on the big picture and delegate more of the details to companies, regulators, local governments, civil society, and markets.

Key aspects of the developing country coordination challenge

A number of East Asia's developing countries appear to be pursuing similar models in their infrastructure development strategies. In doing so, they face a number of challenges—some of them new, some of them similar to those faced by the more advanced economies. They include the coordination challenges involved in getting levels of infrastructure expenditure right, of coordinating through decentralized government structures, and, in particular, of coordinating urban infrastructure.

Establishing the right infrastructure levels requires various kinds of coordination. One of the reasons that governments sometimes spend too much, or with unacceptably high levels of inefficiency, is poor coordination between planning and financing agencies. The separation of planning and financing functions is a common feature of planning frameworks in the region, and in a number of cases it gives rise to poorly and inefficiently resourced infrastructure undertakings (Vietnam and China provide good examples that we draw on in this chapter). These undertakings often have implications for fiscal and financial stability, as well as for related sectors—for example, the construction sector in Vietnam.

Other kinds of coordination failures may be responsible for expenditure levels that are too low, particularly in times of fiscal retrenchment. When budget deficits need to be cut, infrastructure projects are frequently a target—because they are large and lumpy, and their benefits take years to materialize. But infrastructure investments typically have high rates of return, and cutting such projects may jeopardize long-term fiscal solvency. Agencies responsible for fiscal adjustment therefore need to coordinate long-term fiscal policy with those responsible for infrastructure development spending. But liquidity crises can also force infrastructure reform. Central agencies need to coordinate with agencies in the infrastructure sectors to ensure that reform is promoted as much as possible, as well as ensure that liquidity pressures don't just shift state liabilities off-budget.

While the challenges of coordination to establish the right infrastructure levels are not new, the challenges of coordinating through decentralized government are. Twenty years ago East Asia was highly centralized. But today, subnational expenditure as a percentage of total expenditure ranges from 10 percent in Thailand to 70 percent in China.

Decentralization can bring significant benefits, by tailoring service provision to the needs of local constituencies. But it raises a number of problems for coordination. The first of these is managing spillovers in service provision—that is, cases in which projects bring benefits and incur costs outside of any single jurisdiction. Voluntary cooperation between local governments is unfortunately rare. Local governments largely lack the necessary short-run political incentives to cooperate, and governments therefore have to develop adequate coordination tools: Thailand's and Vietnam's matching grants are one example; the creation of special districts and regions in the United States and Canada present another model that might be adopted in the region.

Other inefficiencies that arise from poor coordination include excessive fragmentation (when municipalities are too small to provide services at efficient scale) and destructive competition (when local governments compete to build or upgrade prestige investments like ports or airports, rather than rely on facilities in adjacent jurisdictions). Central governments have an important role to play in filling in the "missing middle" of coordination.

These coordination problems are essentially challenges of horizontal coordination—coordination between jurisdictions. Similar problems present themselves in vertical coordination—coordination between central and local levels of government. Central governments have a key role to play in ensuring that local government infrastructure is in line with policy and regulatory frameworks. When fiscal and regulatory policies are poorly coordinated, and central governments provide financing, while local governments provide delivery, local governments have little incentive to achieve efficiency gains—and sometimes even to respect private sector contracts. This situation is exacerbated in the absence of effective reporting and expenditure tracking mechanisms.

A further important coordination challenge is the challenge of coordinating urban infrastructure—arguably the most complex coordination issue, given the pace of urbanization, and the number of functions that need to be aligned.

Effective land use management is the key to urban planning, but insufficient legal frameworks, deficient application of existing restrictions, and political intervention frequently hamper urban managers. Weak outcomes can be exacerbated by poor timing. When urbanization precedes the investment necessary for livable cities, the costs of improving infrastructure tend to escalate significantly, and retrofitted infrastructure solutions tend to be suboptimal. Coordination among multiple agencies, and across urban boundaries present additional challenges.

The state of play in the Philippines, Indonesia, China, and Thailand

How are the larger developing economies of the region addressing the challenge of coordinating infrastructure? The main theme of the Philippines' experience is that long-term vision and development plans are often undermined by short-term pressures within a fluid and fragmented political system, which in turn diminishes accountability and nurtures corruption.

The role of the Filipino planning agency, the National Economic and Development Authority (NEDA), is subordinated, in times of bust, to the goal of fiscal retrenchment and, in periods of boom, to pressures to support highly politicized infrastructure projects. Long-term development plans and budgets frequently bear little relation to each other.

While the formulation of the national development plan is highly consultative, with significant mainstreaming of social and environmental issues, there is a large gap between what plans say and how resources are allocated and policies are implemented. Civil society influences decisions not primarily through participation in planning, but through campaigns and protest at the permitting or implementation stage of infrastructure undertaking.

The effects of weak coordination present themselves across the Philippines' infrastructure sectors, with significant impacts on investment and competitiveness. The power sector, in particular, imposes significant financial pressure on the government and cannot fund needed expansion. Poor policy coordination has led to generally inadequate space for infrastructure expenditure and low levels of private investment: In 2002, total infrastructure investment was only 2.8 percent of GDP.

Indonesia's coordination story is that of an incomplete progression from autocratic technocracy to greater participation and decentralization. In the process, the country's planning apparatus has been largely dismantled. Under the Suharto regime, policy planning and coordination was centralized in two institutions that operated more or less in tandem, and had substantial ability to plan strategically and oversee the implementation of planning: Badan Perencanaan Pembangunan Nasional (BAPPENAS), which prepared national five-year development plans, and the Coordinating Ministry for the Economy and Industry (EKUIN).

Under the post-Suharto *reformasi* regime, the power of the planning agencies has been significantly diffused. Power has been redistributed downward to local government, and fiscal crisis shifted influence to the Ministry of Finance and the central bank. BAPPENAS is now left with a planning advisory role, and EKUIN's successor focuses mainly on short-term implementation issues.

Fiscal space for infrastructure has been limited in the last few years, and significant infrastructure backlogs have emerged. The state's ability to pursue growth and poverty reduction objectives through infrastructure provision has become highly constrained since the crisis.

Over the last 10 to 15 years, infrastructure service provision has been increasingly delegated to corporatized state enterprises or the private sector, with modest efficiency gains. However, this has been accompanied by little restructuring to allow for competition. Nor has the rule of law yet replaced the rule of a strong leader. The ability of the judicial system or of capital markets to bring better corporate governance, or encourage further private investment, remains limited.

The country's radical decentralization program has laid the foundation for greater government responsiveness to communities, but it also has created considerable uncertainty about interjurisdictional responsibilities and has limited fiscal space for central initiatives.

Since the onset of *reformasi*, civil society has flourished, and with it a new awareness of local and environmental issues in infrastructure planning and implementation. It has also given rise to experimentation with community-driven development in situations in which the state has failed to deliver—most notably in the Kecamatan Development Project (KDP). But the state's ability to mainstream these efforts into policies and programs is weak.

China's experience differs significantly from that of Indonesia and the Philippines. In China, authority has been extensively decentralized to the provincial and municipal levels, but the center remains substantially in charge and generates the strategic vision that binds the system. Accountability is essentially upward, and civil society's role is limited. Planning has become more strategic and flexible, and market forces play an increasingly important role.

China's principal planning agency, the National Development and Reform Commission (NDRC), remains powerful and—unlike BAPPENAS or NEDA—has not seen its strategic planning role undermined.

But infrastructure decentralization in China brings with it a number of coordination challenges. Central government is decreasingly able to control the infrastructure investment choices of the decentralized government. And the ability of provinces and cities to borrow from the state-owned financial sector for infrastructure investment, with limited credit assessment, has challenged the government's ability to exercise macroeconomic control.

At the same time, China is advancing with measures to strengthen the coordination of interjurisdictional infrastructure, with local municipalities beginning to group together in cross-jurisdictional infrastructure initiatives. China is also drawing on the experience of more advanced neighboring economies (as well as that of Thailand) in its development of special economic zones.

Like China, Thailand's record of infrastructure coordination is similar to that of the advanced economies of the region. Strategic long-term vision has played a major role, and coordination among technocrats has been effective. At the same time, participation has played a fairly limited role, although civil society is active.

However, the relationship between politicians and technocrats has been a changing one, with each taking responsibility for generating the country's development vision at different times. With coalition governments weakening the ability of the Cabinet to plan and coordinate for most of the 1990s, the country's principal planning agency—the National Economic and Social Development Board (NESDB)—played a preeminent role. With the Thai Rak Thai party's dominant control over government since 2000, the responsibility for setting the strategic vision shifted toward the Prime Minister's Office, with the role of the Ministry of Finance also increasing in importance. The role of the NESDB was uncertain for a while, although it appears to have regained some of its role in infrastructure planning, and involvement in the country's new infrastructure megaprojects.

Decentralization in Thailand has been limited. After perceived failures with decentralization to lower levels of government, decentralization has been focused on the 76 provinces. However, the provincial governors are appointed, rather than elected, and their role is more a deconcentration of central authority than a real decentralization. Stakeholder participation in infrastructure has made significant progress at the local government level. Nationally initiated large-scale projects, however, have shown less progress. Although environmental impact assessments are prepared, they frequently take the form of formal attachments to projects treated by their proponents as *faits accomplis*.

On the whole, Thailand's planning and coordination system has been flexible and adaptive. It has dealt well with crisis and long-term strategy. The system has evolved effectively as the political context has changed, and strategic vision has managed to play a central role.

Chapter 4. Accountability and risk management

Coordination is about the big picture. But we also have to think about what happens at the level at which services are delivered and outcomes achieved. In this study, we approach this in terms of two connected concepts: accountability and risk management (the focus of Chapter 4).

We think of accountability as a set of institutional tools that rewards organizations according to performance. Governments, communities, investors, service providers, and NGOs are all engaged with each other in dynamic tension, with their own goals and expectations, trying to hold each other accountable for delivery against those expectations. In doing so, they try to maximize their rewards and minimize their risks, subject to the constraint that everyone else is doing the same thing. This is what we mean by risk management.

Effective accountability and risk management are often most recognizable when they are absent. Most often this takes the form of poor service delivery. In its most dramatic form, we see it in financial collapse, as one stakeholder or another is shouldered with obligations they cannot bear. It also frequently takes the form of corruption.

While corruption arises for a variety or reasons, infrastructure has a number of peculiarities that make it a frequent target: The monopoly structure of supply can provide significant opportunity for rent-seeking. The political protection and intervention given to infrastructure often blurs financial accountability, and provides cover for a range of corrupt activities, including corruption in allocating scarce services, overstaffing, and excessively high wages. With difficulties in establishing the relationship between level of capital investment and service outputs, infrastructure providers can inflate levels of capital spending or hide underinvestment. The large scale of infrastructure often creates opportunities for large kickbacks associated with procurement. East Asian infrastructure is replete with examples of these kinds of practices.

Mechanisms to strengthen accountability

Active community participation, competition, and regulation each have important roles to play in avoiding these kinds of outcomes.

For some types of infrastructure services the best way to ensure accountability is to empower communities to plan and manage their own infrastructure, and ensure that once built, service delivery remains relevant to their needs. Indonesia's KDP is among the largest and best-known East Asian examples, but community participation in infrastructure is increasingly common across the region.

Community empowerment works best when infrastructure is small-scale. For large-scale infrastructure, however, sheer scale can make direct community management difficult. But this does not preclude community participation in aspects of infrastructure that affect them—Japan has useful lessons for the region about how community participation turned around the country's approach to environmental externalities.

Competition can also be used to hold service providers accountable. When competition exists, and customers are dissatisfied with a service, they can simply go elsewhere. Although most infrastructure networks cannot be provided competitively, services over those networks can.

On the whole, however, East Asia has not been in the forefront of introducing infrastructure service competition. In telecommunications, competition is still limited by international standards. In the electricity sector, East Asia has typically brought the private sector into generation through the least competitive means possible—that is, through a market structure in which a state-owned single buyer intervenes between private generators and customers.

Across the region, the choice of this model reflects some of the broader reasons behind the limited introduction of competition in infrastructure: the state's desire to maintain cross-subsidies for sociopolitical reasons, monopoly rent-seeking, the protection of incumbent state enterprises, risk mitigation for the private sector, and the political control of strategic assets.

Regulation is a further tool that can be used to hold service providers accountable. Independence and accountability are traditionally cited as key prerequisites to regulatory effectiveness. There are various ways of holding regulators accountable. Some relate to process and participation: clear statutes, judicial reviews, or subjecting the performance of regulators to independent audit. Others relate to transparency: requiring regulators to publish decisions, licenses, and benchmarked performance.

East Asian countries pursue these measures to various degrees. But infrastructure—in East Asia as elsewhere—is intensely political, and the accountability of the regulator cannot be divorced from broader institutions of political accountability. Nor can the ability of the regulator to hold service providers accountable be separated from the political context.

Moving toward regulatory independence is proving slow in East Asia, which is not surprising given the region's tradition of strong central control. Independence is difficult to measure, but in one survey of East Asian infrastructure regulators, less than 40 percent of the regulators described themselves as even nominally independent (see Chapter 4, Spotlight 3).

The key issue for East Asian infrastructure regulation is how to accommodate the evolutionary nature of independence. Ensuring that regulators are not given more discretion than the political culture can absorb is critical. One option is to delegate to a regulator the day-to-day application of a concession contract negotiated between investors and the government. Contracting out key aspects of regulation to third parties, until greater discretion can be allowed, is another. Granting regulators more discretion over time, and liberating them gradually from political pressures, could enhance predictability and reduce policy-based risk that currently is so high in East Asia.

Risk sharing, accountability, and managing government support

Issues of risk management and accountability arise with equal prominence in the relationship between government and service provider, in particular through the support that governments frequently give to service providers in the form of subsidies or guarantees.

Subsidizing the provision of services can be important for many reasons. Environmental protection and poverty reduction are the least controversial. It may also be politically important, however, to retain subsidies captured by influential, nonpoor groups, gradually phasing them out over time (particularly if reform eventually brings benefits that can be sustained without subsidies).

But subsidies have implications for risk and accountability. By weakening the incentive to provide services in the most efficient manner possible, they weaken the accountability relationship that binds providers and governments. And they can be highly risky: the more you get, the more you ask for.

There are various ways East Asian countries manage subsidies: reducing the need for them by addressing excessively high costs through competition, regulation, technology choice, or public enterprise reform; or reducing them directly by making them transparent (and thus subject to scrutiny), making them as one-time payments, channeling them through performance-based arrangements, or adjusting taxes or subsidies on competing products. Cross-subsidies are one option of maintaining accountability of the bottom line, although they come with other costs—primarily, lack of transparency and difficulties to introducing competition.

There are a range of less direct mechanisms besides subsidies that provide fiscal support and share risk—power-purchase obligations in the Philippines, for example, or Thai government backing for state railway borrowing. The accountability issues that these raise are all the more difficult given the contingent nature of the claims to which many of them give rise.

Addressing these contingent liabilities requires high-quality fiscal information and utilization of this information during the budget process. Ideally, governments should decide on an overall ceiling for fiscal risk, issue guidelines on risk assumption to sector agencies and local government, monitor risk, and require approval for the assumption of risk.

Many governments in the region have resorted to risk-sharing transactions with the private sector, rather than undertaking investment through the budget, to get an expenditure "off the books." But whether this improves solvency, as well as liquidity, depends on whether the transfer of risk to the private sector brings efficiency gains.

This depends on the accountability framework for service providers. In East Asia's electricity sectors, for instance, governments frequently have to provide guarantees, because they prevent private sector participants from competing for lucrative parts of the market. In this case, efficiency gains are likely to be limited, and governments are left carrying most of the risks.

Who in fact carries risk, however, is not always clear. Risk is hidden in certain arrangements and is more open in others. Additionally, risks are often reassigned in the lifetime of a concession contract, in response to shocks, but equally as part of a learning process involving both government and private sector providers.

And so to the eternal ownership issue: Are privately owned infrastructure service providers more or less accountable for performance than publicly owned providers? Accountability cannot be measured directly, but performance can be. Empirical evidence shows that private providers perform better, on average, when the incentive environment gives them a good reason to do so, but private ownership on its own doesn't seem to make much difference. When ownership is public, and markets are not competitive, accountability is a considerable challenge indeed.

In other words, ownership does not generally matter by itself. There have been plenty of disappointments in private provision in East Asia.

What does matter, however, is that private provision tends, on average, to respond better to competition and well-crafted regulation than does public provision. In short, it is easier to use incentives to hold the private sector accountable for performance than to do so for the public sector.

Outgrowing the top-down model means greater delegation and the use of decentralized incentive mechanisms. The more this happens, the more necessary it will become to attract the private sector, if infrastructure provision and efficiency are to keep pace with East Asia's needs. But this time around, private participation should come with competition and good regulation.

Chapter 5. The way forward

The framework set out in this study is analytical. It suggests a way of approaching problems, but is not a "tool kit" for implementing particular policies. Nonetheless, the framework has important policy implications. Here we trace 12 of them. These reflect key concerns articulated in the consultations undertaken in preparing this report, with the region's policy makers, policy implementers, infrastructure service providers, civil society organizations, and other stakeholders.

The 12 policy messages constitute an approach to strengthening infrastructure's contribution to inclusive development, as set out in Chapter 2. They promote the role of infrastructure in underpinning growth and poverty reduction. Infrastructure does not lead to inclusive development on its own—it requires actions that support the delivery of services to the poor who need them, and that underpin the growth dynamics on which improvements in welfare depend (Box 5.1). What do we need to think about to achieve this?

The discussion of coordination in Chapter 3 provides the basis for three of the policy messages arising from the framework. In Chapter 3, we saw how strategic vision has proved crucial for ensuring the effectiveness of infrastructure interventions. We also looked at a number of the challenges that arise in formulating and implementing this vision—coordination across financing and planning institutions, coordination across infrastructure and fiscal institutions, and coordination across decentralized government. The analysis set out in Chapter 3 gives us the following three policy messages:

1. The center matters—infrastructure demands strong planning and coordination functions

Infrastructure provides basic services on which survival and livelihoods depend; infrastructure is the backbone of economies and societies; infrastructure has major environmental impacts; infrastructure can bring powerful monopolies and foreign participation into areas of great sensitivity. As such, infrastructure is intensely political.

But infrastructure is also economically and technically complex, and has long-term implications. So the technocrats, too, have a critical role to play as they complement the role of politicians. This extraordinary blend of technocracy and politics places a premium on high-level, central institutions, which can articulate strategies that are politically sustainable and economically effective.

Institutions that can formulate those long-term strategies, and can coordinate the policies of different agencies to implement them, are essential to effective infrastructure service provision. Objectives that move beyond the purely economic, to mainstream environmental and social considerations, demand higher levels of coordinating capacity than hitherto. Sector ministries and local governments cannot work in policy-making isolation.

Old top-down models of detailed economic planning should be eschewed, but new models of strategic planning and central coordination need to evolve. This should underpin tendencies toward democratization, decentralization, independent regulation, private participation, and the commercialization of service providers.

2. Decentralization is important, but raises a host of coordination challenges

There has been substantial decentralization of government in East Asia, and this has often increased the responsiveness of infrastructure service provision to local needs. Decentralization has undoubtedly played an essential political role.

However, decentralization poses a number of coordination challenges, both vertically (between central and local governments) and horizontally (between various subnational institutions).

Decentralized governments have sometimes been isolated within their own jurisdiction. This is problematic because most network infrastructure has interjurisdictional backbones. Isolation can mean secondary or tertiary infrastructure lacks connections to primary infrastructure—in a sense, it goes nowhere. Some municipalities may be too small to achieve the scale necessary to deliver infrastructure efficiently. In competing with each other, municipalities may duplicate expensive infrastructure facilities, when such facilities, in fact, could have been shared. Avoiding these pitfalls depends critically on interjurisdictional cooperation—on filling in the missing middle.

Higher tiers of government need to encourage lower tiers to collaborate where primary infrastructure requires such collaboration. Matching grants to induce decentralized governments to participate in such investments, and institutional mechanisms to encourage cooperation in infrastructure planning will play a major role.

Central governments also have to ensure that they maintain sufficient capacity to monitor, manage, and coordinate in a manner that is in line with policy and regulatory frameworks. The inadequacy of such systems is a frequent cause of suboptimal service delivery and confused authority.

3. Fiscal space for infrastructure is critical

Ultimately, all infrastructure is paid for by users through tariffs or taxpayers through subsidies. Covering costs through user charges is a critical long-term objective. In the short term, user charges might be legitimately constrained by a variety of factors (see below under "subsidies") or large investment needs might require upfront financing to be recovered gradually from user charges.

Sometimes those financial shortfalls can be filled by the private sector, but sometimes private financing will be insufficient, unavailable, or unacceptably expensive. Even where the private sector comes in, it often requires risk-sharing with the public sector. In cases in which the private sector cannot or will not provide all the financing or bear all the risk, investments with adequate economic rates of return should be allocated fiscal space.[3]

Adequacy will depend in part on competing claims from noninfrastructure expenditures and from the need to keep fiscal deficits low. It will also depend on the veracity of the claim that user charges or private financing cannot fill the gap; sometimes it requires fiscal tightening to induce sector agencies to make reforms and seek other sources of funds.

In some East Asian countries, expenditure on infrastructure appears to have been less than optimal in recent years. Cambodia, Indonesia,

Lao PDR, the Philippines, and Thailand could be candidates for this list of countries. This may have undermined economic growth and poverty reduction, and even long-run fiscal solvency.

This does not mean that more fiscal space for infrastructure should be the first step in those countries. In several cases, fiscal tightening for macroeconomic stability and debt sustainability would take higher priority. In most cases, the possibility exists for stronger promotion of private financing in infrastructure and for higher user charges. And there can be opportunities for cost reductions, or better management and maintenance of existing assets. In some cases, strengthening public expenditure management should come before more public expenditure. If adequate institutions and controls are not in place, countries can easily veer from underspending to overspending.

But if and when those difficult preconditions are met, governments should allocate fiscal space based on long-run growth objectives and in pursuit of fiscal solvency. Infrastructure spending on worthwhile projects can create a virtuous circle: more growth, more fiscal revenue, more fiscal space. The challenge is to select the right projects—and put in place the policy and institutional frameworks that actually make them worthwhile.

**

Our discussion of accountability and risk management in Chapter 4 provides the basis for five additional policy messages. In this chapter, we looked at the a number of mechanisms through which accountability in infrastructure service provision can be strengthened—through the community, through regulation, and through competition—and how accountability and risk management arrangements can play out when governments provide support to infrastructure providers. The analysis set out in this chapter supports the following five policy messages:

4. "Subsidy" is not a dirty word—subsidies can be important, but are always risky, and should be handled with care

Infrastructure subsidies can be justified on a number of grounds, including environmental protection and poverty reduction. Although they would enjoy the environmental benefits, people often won't pay the full cost of sanitation, mass rapid transit, or renewable energy. In cases in which those benefits are external to consumers, subsidies may be needed to realize the benefits. Clean water or rural roads may have an important impact on poverty, but they may not be affordable by the poor. Such projects may require subsidies. And reform programs that help the poor or the environment may not be politically sustainable without subsidies for those with the power to derail the reforms. Similarly, transitional subsidies sometimes may be worth considering during short periods of economic crisis.

But subsidies can become open-ended and addictive, their fiscal impact can explode, they can undermine financial discipline and blur accountability, and they can postpone much-needed reform. Subsidies need to be employed with great care.

Subsidies should be a last resort after costs have been minimized through competition, regulation, appropriate technology and service standards, or public enterprise reform. Subsidies can be minimized through transparency, making them contingent on performance, or through subsidy bidding processes.

5. Competition is hard to achieve in infrastructure, but it's the best way to bring accountability

Infrastructure is quite often a natural monopoly, but institutional and technological innovation are expanding the potential for competition. It is now feasible to provide most infrastructure services (if not always the infrastructure itself) competitively. The most direct, and hence most effective, way of holding service providers accountable is through competition.

East Asia has been cautious about the introduction of infrastructure service competition; it has often preferred to "throw" more infrastructure at a problem rather than provide incentives for more efficient infrastructure services or address the political economy obstacles to competition.

This approach may have been effective when the basic infrastructure was being built, when economic objectives were relatively simple, and when top-down command solutions prevailed. But, as complexity increases, those approaches can be expected to work less well, and the role of competition will need to increase.

6. Regulatory independence matters more in the long run than in the short run

When competition is not yet firmly in place, regulation of monopolies will be needed. Regulatory independence from politics is an important long-term goal to ensure that service providers can cover costs and earn an adequate return on investments. However, regulators can establish their credibility with consumers, politicians, and investors only gradually. If regulators exercise more discretion than the political culture can absorb, a backlash can occur, creating unpredictability and instability.

Regulatory independence is a relative concept, and independence should grow step-by-step. New regulators should rely more on transparent rules than on discretionary power, and some responsibilities should be delegated to outside experts until in-house capacity can be built. Credibility, and hence independence, can be enhanced by transparency: Hearings should be public, as should contracts and licenses whenever possible. Accountability for regulators is key to their independence.

7. Civil society has a key role to play in ensuring accountability in service provision

Local communities within civil society can often manage local projects. They can participate in decision making about the large infrastructure networks that touch their community, or those aspects of large projects that affect them directly. They may need special protection, as long as the larger needs of society don't get lost.

Civil society can play an important role in accountability of infrastructure institutions through parliaments or through consumer participation in regulation. Civil society organizations and NGOs can provide small-scale infrastructure services, act as watchdogs against corruption and vested interest, and play an advocacy role for more sustainable infrastructure policies and services.

Advocacy NGOs face difficult choices between representing the interests of specific groups or issues, and representing the interests of society at large. How effectively and accountably they make those choices can have a significant impact on development outcomes.

8. Infrastructure has to clean up its act—addressing corruption is a priority

Infrastructure is often provided by monopolies, and can generate large rents. It often provides vital services, which are highly prized and highly political. As a result, financial discipline can be weak, political intervention intense, and rent-seeking prevalent. And the benefits of infrastructure can be easy to claim and hard to verify.

This combination of circumstances can create fertile ground for corruption. But that corruption discredits the very infrastructure on which it preys. This can undermine the political sustainability of infrastructure development, and deter those investors and financiers concerned about reputational risk and other costs of corruption.

Combating corruption is a long, hard struggle requiring strong top-down political commitment. Major reforms of the judiciary and civil service lie at the heart of any anticorruption effort. While these longer-term reforms are being put in place, significant progress can be made by removing rent-seeking opportunities and exposing transactions to public scrutiny.

***

Four additional policy messages derive from analysis developed across this study, although they all take their departure from what we described as the "funding story" in Chapter 1. Here we saw that infrastructure can only be *funded* from two sources: the resources of consumers, and the resources of taxpayers. But infrastructure can be *financed* by two other actors: the private sector (which may also include service providers), and official lenders and donors. The policy messages are as follows:

9. The private sector will come back—if the right policies evolve

Private investment in East Asian infrastructure peaked in 1997 and declined dramatically thereafter. It is now showing modest signs of recovery, but it still has not come close to matching the levels initially expected in the mid-1990s.

A perceptions survey was carried out for this study among 50 private companies active or interested in East Asian infrastructure investment. One survey response stood out above all others: A majority of investors said they were keen to invest, and would do so if policies were more predictable.

The private sector certainly has not disappeared from East Asian infrastructure; however, it is not actually making large investments. More predictable policies would bring it back. Moreover, if it came back, better regulation or more competitive market structures would help ensure efficiency gains from its return.

10. Public sector reform matters, but be realistic

In some places, the private sector won't come in sufficient scale, or will only do so on terms that are politically unacceptable (at least to specific groups with strong voice). This is likely to be particularly relevant in countries with small markets (population or purchasing power), those which are emerging from conflict, those where ideological opposition to private or foreign investment is particularly strong, or those where adjustment of large state-owned infrastructure is politically difficult because of employment effects. In some sectors, natural monopoly remains strong, so competition to induce the efficiency gains from private participation is not yet possible.

In sectoral terms, water and sanitation, large-scale hydropower and electricity transmission, some types of transport, and rural or cross-border infrastructure seem to have the hardest time attracting private investment, or using it to promote efficiency (although there are notable exceptions). In those situations, reform of the public sector may sometimes be the most feasible option for efficiency gains, at least in the near term.

But public sector reform is difficult to achieve, and even harder to sustain, so expectations should be modest. If the private sector can't be attracted because the state is unpredictable and lacks vision, or because tariffs and subsidies are below costs, then public sector performance is likely to be disappointing as well. Even if costs are covered, public resources may be better used in sectors other than infrastructure. The alternative of more thorough reform in the medium term to attract private investment should always be considered.

11. Local capital markets matter, but are not a panacea

East Asia's success is built, in part, on channeling high savings into domestic investment in infrastructure. The 1997 crisis underlined that domestic savings tend to be less footloose than foreign savings, and that domestic currency financing is less exposed to foreign currency risk. As domestic savings become more scarce, their efficient allocation becomes more necessary. As government functions become more complex, the delegation of resource allocation and risk assessment becomes more important. For these reasons, the contribution of the domestic financial sector to infrastructure development needs to grow.

Government will play an important role in regulating the domestic financial sector and encouraging financial innovation, as well as in promoting regional capital market initiatives. In countries where the policy—or quasi-fiscal role—of the financial sector has led to high levels of nonperforming loans to infrastructure, commercialization of the sector will be a priority in the near term. This will restore health to the financial sector and financial discipline to the infrastructure sector.

But to promote the financial sector's contribution most effectively over the long term, policies to improve the investment climate for infrastructure should take the highest priority. Trying to make a poorly designed infrastructure project work through financial engineering can have only limited effect; making it into a viable project through reform beyond the financial sector will usually have a greater impact.

12. Infrastructure needs reliable and responsive development partners

The development community is now reasserting its role in infrastructure in East Asia. But infrastructure is a long-term asset, and development partners need to stay for the long haul. Reliable partnerships—with quick response and harmonized procedures—are critical. Moreover, the nature of this partnership (financing, guarantees, policy advice, capacity building, and so on) will have to be tailored to country conditions. The needs of East Asia's large, middle-income countries are different from the smaller and poorer countries in the region.

Official development assistance (ODA) accounts for approximately 1 percent of gross investment in low- and middle-income countries of East Asia. However, aid financing plays a more significant role in the poorer countries of the region, accounting for more than half of gross investment in Mongolia and Cambodia. Aid flows also play a significant role in most Pacific island countries, Timor-Leste, Papua New Guinea, and Lao PDR. The level of aid, and how it is allocated (including the share for infrastructure), plays a big role in the public spending and investment priorities of these countries.

The case for official financing depends on how well it can be used, the availability of other sources of financing, and the overall debt position of the government. The level of aid usually declines, and the blend of loans and grants usually becomes harder, as income levels rise in recipient countries. However, even higher-income countries may see benefits in tapping official financing to ease the debt burden on their budget and to catalyze private sources of funds. The technical assistance embedded in aid-financed projects—for project preparation, environmental and social assessments, and procurement practices—can be beneficial for shaping the government's overall policies and procedures.

During the 1990s, some key development partners in East Asia focused their efforts away from infrastructure, at least from infrastructure on a large scale. These partners felt that poverty reduction should be more targeted or that the private sector should step in to finance infrastructure projects. This tendency was intensified by the 1997 financial crisis, as the creditworthiness of affected countries and many infrastructure service providers declined. Aid financing in crisis-affected countries shifted to program support, as budgets were cut and new investments in infrastructure were sharply curtailed.

The role of official financing for infrastructure is now being reappraised. It is acknowledged that growth is crucial to poverty reduction, that targeting complements growth, and that infrastructure is essential for both. The private sector did step in, then partly stepped out, and may now step in again. But even at its peak, the private sector was a relatively minor player in financing terms, especially in the poorer countries of the region, and official financing could be helpful to catalyze private investment. Some countries are now emerging from fiscal compression and need official financing to catalyze the private sector and provide more fiscal space for infrastructure spending. Support for more complex projects and new approaches can be particularly valuable.

As official financing for infrastructure increases again, it's important that it is used in a way that maximizes development impact. In the past, infrastructure projects have not always been well linked to a country's overall development and poverty reduction strategy. Aid must be used to support (rather than undermine) good policies. In some cases, this may mean funding sectoral programs, including recurrent spending for operations and maintenance and even subsidies. The broader impact of large-scale projects on government revenues must also be taken into account (as seen in the case of the Nam Theun 2 dam project, Chapter 4, Box 4.6).

Some official lenders and donors can provide instruments to back up government commitments to the private sector at a time when credibility with the private sector is still being established (for example, guarantees, insurance, official lending to the private sector). The overall case for the use of those instruments depends on a number of factors: first, the economic justification for the project; second, the proper allocation of risks between stakeholders and the ability to structure the guarantee to strengthen rather than dilute operators' incentives to deliver; and third, a robust budget framework for managing any contingent liabilities arising from government commitments.

However, in no case should such instruments be substitutes for good policies. Sound policies can reduce risks and demonstrate the government's commitment to reform. They are therefore more valuable to investors than official agency support per se.

Finally, official lenders and donors can provide important knowledge about what works and what doesn't in different countries and sectors. Some of this knowledge comes from higher-income countries that have been there before and learned from their mistakes and successes. It's therefore important that countries like Singapore and Korea stay engaged with the broader development community.

The type of knowledge needed will also vary by country—from basic institution and capacity building in poorer countries to more sophisticated market instruments in middle-income countries. For the latter, innovative ways are needed to combine private and public financing to extend maturities for long gestation projects. New approaches to developing financing mechanisms at subsovereign levels also need special attention.

1

The Infrastructure Challenge

EAST ASIA'S RECENT DEVELOPMENT PERFORMANCE MAKES FOR impressive headlines: As a group, the economies of the region have grown by more than 7 percent annually over the last 15 years. And the number of people living on less than $2 a day has fallen by more than 250 million.[1]

The story is similar in its infrastructure performance: Investment exceeds 7 percent of gross domestic product (GDP) annually in some countries, with a doubling of electricity generation capacity in only a decade in others, and increases in road networks of between 25 percent and 100 percent in still others.

Beyond the headlines, however, the story is more complicated. With large numbers of people surviving on less than $2 a day in even the fastest growing countries of the region, the remaining challenges are daunting.

And much of the aggregate growth and poverty reduction numbers are driven by a single country—China. Behind the aggregates, the developing countries of East Asia in fact differ vastly—by growth rates, wealth, population, and poverty incidence (see Table 1.1).

The group includes the most populous country in the world, and the Pacific island states, which have among the smallest populations in the world. It includes Malaysia, with a gross national income (GNI) per capita of more than $3,000, and Cambodia—the people of which enjoy less than one-tenth of that amount on a per capita basis. It includes the fast growers, like China and Vietnam, and a number in which growth is sporadic and slow. And, as we shall see, countries of the region differ too in their infrastructure performance.

Table 1.1 Growth, income, poverty, and population, East Asia

	Average annual growth, 1994–2003	Gross national income (current $, million), 2003	Population (million), 2003	GNI per capita (current $), 2003	Number of poor (million), 2005 projected
Malaysia	4.8	97,809	24.77	3,880	1.7
Thailand	2.8	140,277	62.01	2,190	11.6
Philippines	4.0	86,607	81.50	1,080	—
China	8.5	1,409,162	1,288.40	1,100	391.1
Indonesia	2.5	199,028	214.67	810	99.1
Vietnam	7.3	39,157	81.31	480	41.1
Cambodia	6.3	4,060	13.40	300	10.3
Lao PDR	5.9	2,084	5.66	340	4.3
Mongolia	0.1	1,252	2.48	480	—
Palau	3.0	130	0.02	6,500	—
Marshall Islands	−1.7	139	0.05	2,710	—
Fiji	2.7	1,955	0.84	2,240	—
Micronesia, Federated States of	0.1	261	0.12	2,070	—
Samoa	4.2	265	0.18	1,440	—
Tonga	2.1	161	0.10	1,490	—
Vanuatu	0.9	279	0.21	1,180	—
Kiribati	4.7	85	0.10	860	—
Papua New Guinea	0.2	2,739	5.50	500	4.1
Solomon Islands	−1.3	247	0.46	560	—
Timor-Leste	−3.05[b]	341	0.88	460	—
Myanmar	—	—	—	—	—

Sources: World Bank 2004d, 2004h.
Note: — = Not available.
a. living under $2/day, 2005.
b. annual average growth, 1998–2003.

There are a number of ways to tell the story of infrastructure in East Asia. In this chapter, we look at it from five interlinked perspectives. Each of these perspectives defines the context of infrastructure delivery in the region in different ways.

We start with the economic story, which places infrastructure squarely in the context of the region's remarkable growth performance, and its record in reducing poverty. Although growth and poverty reduction depend on much more than infrastructure alone (see Figure 1.1), the contribution of infrastructure to the region's macroeconomic story has been considerable. The context established here lays the ground for a

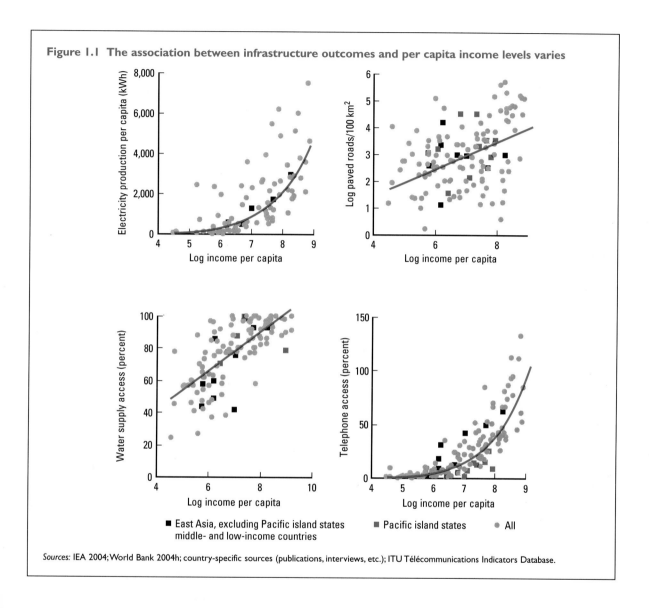

Figure 1.1 The association between infrastructure outcomes and per capita income levels varies

Legend:
■ East Asia, excluding Pacific island states middle- and low-income countries ■ Pacific island states ● All

Sources: IEA 2004; World Bank 2004h; country-specific sources (publications, interviews, etc.); ITU Télécommunications Indicators Database.

detailed discussion of inclusive development in Chapter 2—the *how* of infrastructure, growth, and poverty reduction.

We then look at the spatial and demographic story, in particular at the region's fast-growing urban areas, and the challenges of connectivity and coordination that this raises. Approaches to addressing these challenges are dealt with in Chapter 2 and, through the focus on coordination, in Chapter 3.

In our third story, we look at infrastructure from the perspective of the environment. Many infrastructure investments have a positive impact on the environment, most prominently water and sanitation. But other kinds of infrastructure undertaking entail significant environmental risks—risks that can be mitigated if the political will is present. But mainstreaming environmental concerns in the design and implementation of infrastructure raises difficult coordination problems, similar in nature to those that we raise in Chapter 3.

Our fourth infrastructure story is the political story, which provides some of the context for our discussion of coordination in Chapter 3 and risk management and accountability in Chapter 4.

And finally to the question of East Asia's infrastructure service needs, and how they can be resourced. This is the subject of the last of our infrastructure stories—the funding story.

The economic story

The economic performance of developing East Asia has been driven largely by fast-growing urban agglomerations in coastal China, Indonesia, Thailand, Malaysia, and Vietnam. It is associated with high investment, low or significantly decreasing poverty, and rapidly expanding output. The performance of these countries—particularly that of China—powers the region through an increasingly dynamic and complex web of trade, information, innovation, and investment links.

The forging of connections among countries in the region, as well as between East Asia and the rest of the world, has been an important part of the region's performance. Developing countries of East Asia have seen their share of world exports more than triple over the last 25 years (World Bank, 2005b).[2] East Asia intraregional trade now constitutes more than 7 percent of world trade (Ng and Yeats 2003).[3]

China has been central in this trade and growth equation.[4] Regional trade has allowed other East Asian countries to benefit from the remarkable expansion of the Chinese economy and markets. Since 1995, East Asia's exports to China have been growing at a rate of 11.5 percent annually (Ng and Yeats 2003). The role of logistical infrastructure—ports, roads, and rail—in supporting these connections is one of the themes of Chapter 2.

Within countries too, infrastructure has been an important part of the economic story. Investment has been sustained—in China and Vietnam, in particular, where gross fixed capital formation has averaged about

40 percent of GDP and 30 percent of GDP respectively over the last five years. And much of this investment has been in infrastructure (Table 1.2).

As a result, the faster growing developing countries of the region manage substantial infrastructure assets. In many cases, the stock of these assets has accumulated, and capacity to generate services has increased at remarkable rates (Table 1.3).

Sustained investment and efficiency in operations have helped some economies in the region—in particular Thailand and Malaysia—to achieve considerable competitive advantage across infrastructure sectors, both in international terms and when compared with the region's developed economies (a comparator group to which we shall return in

Table 1.2 Infrastructure investment, percent GDP

0–4%	4–7%	More than 7%
Cambodia	Lao PDR	China
Indonesia	Mongolia	Thailand
Philippines		Vietnam

Sources: Latest year available, based on available data from country-specific sources (publications, interviews); World Bank PPI Database 2005.
Note: GDP = gross domestic product.

Table 1.3 Total road network and electricity generating capacity, 1990–2000

	Total road network (km)			Electricity generating capacity (GW)			Annual average GDP growth (%)
	1990	2000	Growth (%)	1990	2000	Growth (%)	
China	1,028,348	1,679,848	63	127	299	136	10.1
Indonesia	288,727	355,951	23	13	25	98	4.2
Lao PDR	13,971	23,922	71	0	0	92	6.3
Philippines	160,560	201,994	26	7	12	81	3.0
Thailand	52,305	60,354	15	8	19	125	4.5
Vietnam	105,557[a]	215,628	104	2	6	180	7.6
Argentina	215,357	*215,471*	0	17	24	37	1.5
Brazil	1,670,148	1,724,929	3	52	69	32	4.5
India	2,000,000	*3,319,644*	66	72	108	51	2.7
Poland	363,116	364,656	0	27	29	9	5.5
South Africa	185,751	362,099	95	31	40	28	3.7
Korea, Rep. of	56,715	86,990	53	20	50	150	1.7

Sources: Country-specific sources; World Bank 2004h; U.S DOE; Energy Administration Information Database.
Note: Italics refer to data from prior year; GW = Giga Watts.
a. 1992 figure.

Box 1.1 The demographic dividend

East Asia has benefited greatly from its "demographic dividend." A baby boom has been traveling through the age structure of the region's population since the 1950s and 1960s. These young people began entering the labor force from the late 1960s and early 1970s (at around the same time as the proportion of births started to decline). The working-age population rose from 56 percent of the total population in 1965 to 66 percent in 2000. It is expected to reach about 70 percent by between 2015–20 (World Bank 2004e).

One of the distinctive features of East Asia is that the high working-age population has been combined with institutions, traditions, and policies that have encouraged high savings levels in that age group and that have channeled those savings into domestic investment (Figure 1.2). Infrastructure has been a major beneficiary of that phenomenon.

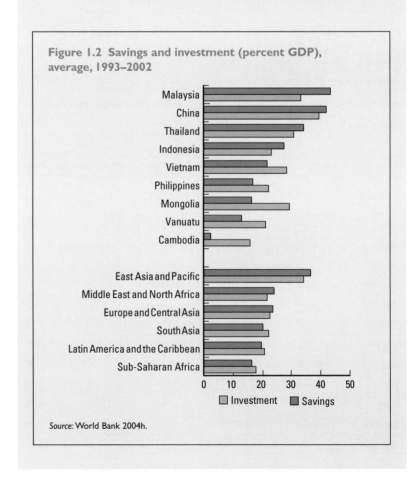

Figure 1.2 Savings and investment (percent GDP), average, 1993–2002

Source: World Bank 2004h.

Chapter 3). In other large economies in this group—China, Indonesia, Vietnam, and the Philippines—performance has been less impressive (Figure 1.3).

This overall impression is mirrored in the response of East Asian firms to World Bank Investment Climate Surveys, nearly 20 percent of which report that inadequate infrastructure service provision is a serious obstacle to the operation and growth of their business.[5] This is a lower percentage than in the rest of the developing world, but it is high enough to be of considerable macroeconomic consequence.

In short, East Asia has provided the infrastructure underpinnings for economic growth better than other developing regions (on average), but there is much room for improvement, and supply needs to keep pace with rapidly rising demand.[6]

In those countries in which infrastructure investment has been most sustained—China and Vietnam in particular—high levels of investment have not always implied optimal investment. Often efficiency in the selection and management of investment, in general, and infrastructure, in particular, has been lacking. Too much investment may be as dangerous as too little. The governments of these countries now face the challenges of improving efficiency, avoiding "overheating" by restraining excessive investment, and managing a "soft landing" with sustainable growth and investment—a point we pick up in our discussion of Vietnam in Chapter 2.

In the countries most affected by the 1997 crisis, growth has recovered (that is, in Thailand, Malaysia, and to a lesser extent Indonesia and the Philippines), but this has been driven primarily by domestic consumption and exports, rather than by investment. In the Philippines, physical capital per worker has been growing at barely 1 percent per year since the early 1990s. In Indonesia, Malaysia, and Thailand, capital per worker was grown by 4 to 7 percent per year before the 1997 crisis, but by less than half that rate since then (World Bank 2004d).[7]

Clearly, the postcrisis recovery in growth has come from increased capacity utilization and enhanced labor productivity and innovation; however, these factors will eventually reach limits without an investment recovery. In these countries, therefore, the challenge is to enhance the investment climate and increase investment to underpin sustained economic growth (while continuing to realize efficiency gains in management of assets).

Access to infrastructure services in Malaysia and Thailand, as well as the Philippines, and to a lesser extent China, is generally higher than that

Figure 1.3 Infrastructure quality ranking, *World Competitiveness Report*, East Asia

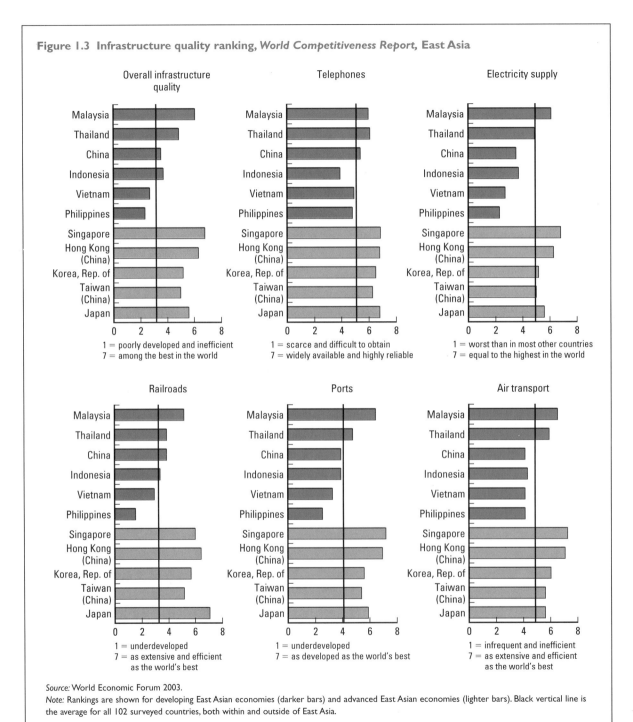

Source: World Economic Forum 2003.

Note: Rankings are shown for developing East Asian economies (darker bars) and advanced East Asian economies (lighter bars). Black vertical line is the average for all 102 surveyed countries, both within and outside of East Asia.

Table 1.4 Infrastructure access and stocks

Access to water, electricity, and telecommunications

	Water supply access[a]	Sanitation access[b]	Electricity access[c]	Telephone access[d]	Internet access[e]
Malaysia	93	—	97	62	34.4
Thailand	93	98	84	50	11.1
Philippines	86	83	79	31	4.4
China	76	39	99	42	6.3
Indonesia	78	55	55	13	3.8
Vietnam	49	25	81	9	4.3
Cambodia	44	22	17	4	0.2
Lao PDR	58	30	41	3	0.3
Mongolia	60	30	90	19	5.8
Palau	79	100	60	42	—
Marshall Islands	—	—	100	9	2.6
Fiji	—	43	80	26	6.7
Micronesia	—	—	45	16	9.3
Samoa	99	99	95	13	2.2
Tonga	100	—	85	15	2.9
Vanuatu	88	100	26	7	3.6
Kiribati	—	48	40	6	2.3
Papua New Guinea	42	82	46	1	1.4
Solomon Islands	71	34	15	2	0.5
Timor-Leste	—	—	22	—	—
Myanmar	72	64	5	1	0.1
Low and Middle Income	77	70	64	27	6.5

Transport networks

	Road network (km per 100 km²)	Percentage paved road	Rail network (km per 100 km²)
Malaysia	20	76	0.49
Thailand	12	97	0.79
Philippines	68	22	0.16
China	19	91	0.64
Indonesia	20	58	0.25
Vietnam	29	25	0.97
Cambodia	22	4	0.42
Lao PDR	14	15	—
Mongolia	3	8	0.15
Palau	—	—	—
Marshall Islands	35	—	—
Fiji	19	49	—
Micronesia	34	18	—
Samoa	28	80	—
Tonga	94	27	—
Vanuatu	9	24	—
Kiribati	92	—	—
Papua New Guinea	—	4	—
Solomon Islands	5	3	—
Timor-Leste	25	41	—
Myanmar	—	—	—
Low and Middle Income	38	41	1.70

Sources: IEA 2003; World Bank 2004h; country-specific sources (publications, interviews, and so on); ITU database.
Note: Shaded values above category average for low- and middle-income countries; — = Not available.
a. Percentage of population with access to at least 20 liters per person per day from "improved" water supply technologies from a source within one kilometer of the user's dwelling (see W1 in the Statistical Annex).
b. Percentage of population with excreta disposal system "under improved" sanitation technologies, adequate if it private or shared (but not public) and if hygienically separates human excreta from human contact (see W4 in the Statistical Annex).
c. Percentage of households with electricity access through commercially sold electricity, both on-grid and off-grid (see E1 in the Statistical Annex).
d. Telephone subscribers per 100 inhabitants.
e. Number of users per 100 inhabitants.

of its less wealthy (in per capita terms) neighbors (Table 1.4). Similar outcomes have been achieved in some of the tiny Pacific island nations, although—as we set out in more detail in Box 1.2—the context of this achievement is substantially different.

Box 1.2 Infrastructure challenges in the Pacific Island countries: A case apart

The nine Pacific island countries covered by this study stand apart from the rest of the region in a number of respects, with important implications for their infrastructure challenges.

Together, the nine islands have a combined population smaller than Jamaica's, in a total land mass smaller than Cuba's, spread over an area larger than China.

The challenging topography and the low population density clearly complicate the task of infrastructure service provision. The spread of the high fixed cost of infrastructure investment over a small customer base inflates unit costs and depresses revenues from service provision. Because of their remoteness and lack of economies of scale, the Pacific island countries, in relation to other East Asian countries, have a significant comparative disadvantage in attracting private sector participation and sustaining competition in infrastructure.

The Pacific island countries are lagging behind East Asian countries in terms of access and quality of service provision. A stunning 70 percent or more of inhabitants lack access to electricity. Telecommunications access is largely limited to urban areas. Because of a lack of transport alternatives, interisland shipping and civil aviation play a crucial role in a complex transport system serving hundreds of sparsely populated small islands. Nevertheless, airports and ports are characterized by low throughput on a per capita basis.

But poor performance in infrastructure cannot be attributed exclusively to geography and lack of economies of scale. The Pacific Islands have lower levels of access to telecommunications, electricity, and improved water and sanitation, than similar countries with the same level of income (for example, in the Caribbean). Policy and institutional choices also matter:

Poor coordination. Many Pacific island countries suffer from poor coordination in infrastructure policy and implementation. Hidden subsidies to corporatized utilities do not compete with other fiscal priorities in a transparent manner. Regulatory and policy frameworks are often not fully aligned or contradict each other—for example, Fiji adopted the "landlord" model for port operations, but contracted out stevedoring operations to a monopoly government-owned provider, thus diluting the potential efficiency benefits stemming from competition in service provision.

Low accountability. In most of the Pacific island countries, government-owned utilities are in charge of providing the service and sanctioning its quality. Most of the governments have now recognized that this model does not create an enabling framework for accountability to end users, and have moved toward more accountable institutional arrangements, through corporatization of state-owned utilities.

However, with only a few exceptions, accountability to end users has remained low, as corporatized utilities are often still subject to micromanagement by the government. When the prospect for private sector engagement exists, the imbalance between the public sector and the private utilities in terms of monitoring capacity can sometimes lend excessive power to the

(Continued on the next page)

Box 1.2 (Continued)

privatized utilities or lead to collusive outcomes, with little improvement in accountability.

Low capacity to manage risk. The risk management model in the Pacific island countries is often based on a model of government as absorber of risk—government-owned utilities are generally insulated from risk, as losses flow through to the government and are eventually born by taxpayers. The cost of government risk-bearing is often high, as the Pacific island economies are particularly vulnerable to external shocks (such as oil price shocks), which also tend to have an impact on the cost of infrastructure service provision. The total cost of risk-bearing could be reduced through more sophisticated project design, which would enable more effective risk-sharing. Consumers and service providers should be called on to bear at least part of the risk, to the extent that they are able to absorb it.

Notwithstanding the specific infrastructure challenges faced by the Pacific island countries, a few successful examples of corporatization (such as the Fiji Electricity Authority, Samoa Ports Authority, and Samoa Water Authority) and the positive performance of the private electricity and water utility in Vanuatu demonstrates that the possibility exists for improved performance and accountability through better management and commercial focus. The challenge is to design time-bound performance-based subsidies to encourage more efficient and inclusive infrastructure service delivery. The establishment of regional bodies (such as the existing Pacific Power Association) should be encouraged as the way forward to ease individual country capacity constraints and promote policy coordination among the Pacific island countries.

Sources: Castalia 2004b; Mellor and Jabes 2004.

The larger, faster growing economies also stand apart in the degree to which growth, investment, and poverty reduction have accompanied and supported each other. The poverty headcount in China has dropped from around 70 percent of the population in 1990 to close to 30 percent of the population today.[8] Vietnam has seen its poverty headcount drop from around 90 percent to 48 percent over the same period (Figure 1.4).

The risk of poverty, however, is much higher than the poverty headcount may suggest at any particular time. In all developing countries of East Asia, a far larger number of households fall intermittently below the poverty line than are permanently below it.[9] The 1997 crisis dramatically exposed this underlying risk, with lasting effects on policies and attitudes toward poverty, social stability, and vulnerability in the region.

In contrast to the region's best performers, a number of countries have been less successful in simultaneously nurturing growth and poverty reduction. In Cambodia—despite significant growth (albeit from a very

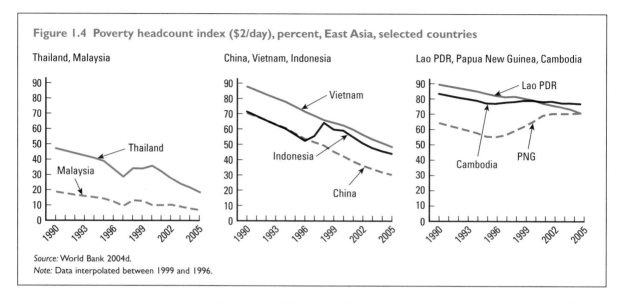

Figure 1.4 **Poverty headcount index ($2/day), percent, East Asia, selected countries**

Source: World Bank 2004d.
Note: Data interpolated between 1999 and 1996.

low base)—78 percent of the population is estimated to live on less than $2 a day. The corresponding figure for Lao People's Democratic Republic (PDR) is about 73 percent (World Bank 2004d). Infrastructure access, particularly those stocks that serve to connect and link (roads or rail), are significantly lower in Lao PDR and Cambodia (Table 1.4). And with investment levels at between one-third and one-half that of faster growing neighbors, a mutually supportive relationship between infrastructure, investment, growth, and poverty reduction is less apparent than elsewhere in the region.

Finally, other regions in East Asia remain isolated and relatively disconnected from the major growth centers of East Asia—most rural areas, the outlying islands of Indonesia, the Philippines, land-locked Mongolia, and most Pacific island states.

In the Pacific island countries, the poverty headcount is generally much lower, but economic growth rates tend also to be quite low and incomes are heavily dependent on aid flows, migrant labor remittances, or nonrenewable natural resources with volatile revenue streams. Populations in those countries therefore remain particularly vulnerable to poverty through slow economic growth and lack of economic diversity.

The spatial and demographic story

East Asia's spatial and demographic challenge plays out across three interlinked dimensions. The first is the urban dimension: Cities drive East

Asian growth, and as they do, their populations are expanding rapidly. Infrastructure not only has to keep up with demand for services, but also has to play a crucial role in maintaining cities' competitiveness.

The second challenge relates to rural areas, where poverty levels are at their highest. Infrastructure can help improve livelihoods; it also has an important role to play in spreading the benefits of urban growth.

And the third challenge is a regional challenge: to create regional markets; enhance trade and regional integration; and connect poorer, isolated areas to the region's growth centers.

The urban challenge

The urban agglomerations driving East Asia's growth have profound consequences for economic development. Cities account for 70 percent of the region's GDP growth. Urban populations are expanding rapidly. And with it come a host of infrastructure opportunities and challenges: challenges that entail integration and connection; and challenges that entail foresight and coordination. How to meet these challenges is one of the themes of our next two chapters.

The urban share of East Asia's population is not yet high by global standards, but it is rising exponentially. From 16 percent in 1960, to 21 percent in 1980, and to 36 percent in 2000, it is expected to rise to 57 percent by 2025 (Figure 1.5). By then, East Asia will have about 500 million more urban dwellers than it does now, mainly as a result of migration from rural areas (World Bank 2004c).[10]

From 2000 to 2015, the population living in cities with more than 1 million residents is expected to increase by about half (to 500 million) and the population living in megacities with more than 10 million residents will rise by a similar proportion (to 120 million).

The most rapid population growth is taking place in peri-urban peripheries. In Chinese cities alone, peri-urban areas will grow by about 250 million people over the next 25 years (World Bank 2004c). And increasingly, neighboring East Asian cities are connecting with each other and forming large urban clusters. These include large parts of China's coastal zone, Bangkok's Eastern Seaboard, the Philippines' National Capital Region, and the cross-border cluster of Singapore-Riau-Johor.

In general, urbanization in East Asia is correlated with increasing national income levels (Figure 1.6). Cities have driven growth. The rapid growth of cities has been accompanied by a striking change in economic

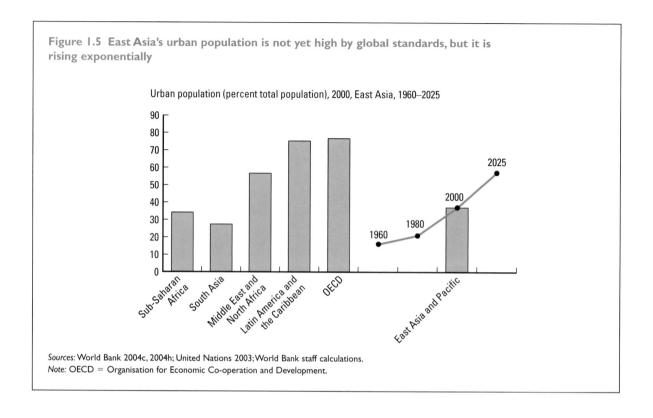

Figure 1.5 East Asia's urban population is not yet high by global standards, but it is rising exponentially

Urban population (percent total population), 2000, East Asia, 1960–2025

Sources: World Bank 2004c, 2004h; United Nations 2003; World Bank staff calculations.
Note: OECD = Organisation for Economic Co-operation and Development.

Table 1.5 There is significant variation in the speed and level of urbanization across East Asian countries

Level and rate of urbanization, percent total population, 2000, growth rate, 1995–2000

		Urbanization level		
		Low	Middle	High
Urbanization rate	Fast	Cambodia Lao PDR		Indonesia Philippines
	Intermediate		China Vietnam Myanmar	Malaysia
	Slow	Thailand		Mongolia

Source: UTCE/ALMEC 2004a, based on World Bank 2003e.
Note: Urbanization level: High >40%, 20% <middle<40%, Low<20%; Urbanization rate: Fast >6%, 2%<middle<4%, Low<2%.

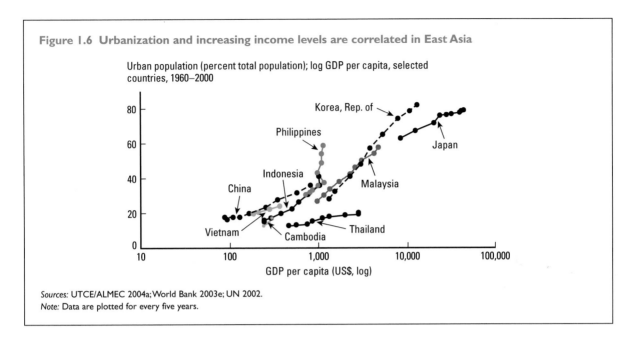

Figure 1.6 Urbanization and increasing income levels are correlated in East Asia

Urban population (percent total population); log GDP per capita, selected countries, 1960–2000

Sources: UTCE/ALMEC 2004a; World Bank 2003e; UN 2002.
Note: Data are plotted for every five years.

structure.[11] Densely populated urban areas have provided markets for outputs, inputs, labor, and other services and allow firms to profit from economies of scale and scope, specialization, and the rapid diffusion of knowledge and innovation.

Agglomeration economies have been strong in East Asia. Their impact is enhanced by the role of urban areas in the process of globalization. Cities such as Bangkok, Beijing, Hong Kong (China), Jakarta, Kuala Lumpur, Manila, and Shanghai are now major world centers. Beijing's selection for the 2008 Olympics and Shanghai's for the 2010 World Expo bear ample testimony to that evolution. The connection of East Asia's cities to global markets makes them centers for international trade, communications, employment of migrants, and foreign direct investment. Such cities are experiencing unprecedented prosperity as a result of their advantages. For example, the per capita GDP of Shanghai alone is about 11 times that of China's per capita GDP, and Ho Chi Minh City has three times the per capita GDP of Vietnam (Yusuf, Evenett, Nabeshima, Shotten, and Webster 2001).

But East Asia's urban growth brings with it a host of infrastructure challenges. Rapidly increasing and densely distributed urban populations impose increasing demands on infrastructure facilities and services, as well as the environmental and social risks of inadequate provision. Infrastructure gaps are emerging across urban infrastructure sectors (Box 1.3).

Box 1.3 Emerging urban infrastructure gaps in East Asia

In many East Asian cities, infrastructure provision is failing to keep up with rapid urbanization and demand on services. Figure 1.7 illustrates one example. It plots increasing car ownership against road extension per vehicle, which shows how, in major East Asian cities, rapid motorization has outstripped the capacity of city authorities to meet demand.

Figure 1.7 Changes in vehicle ownership and road lengths

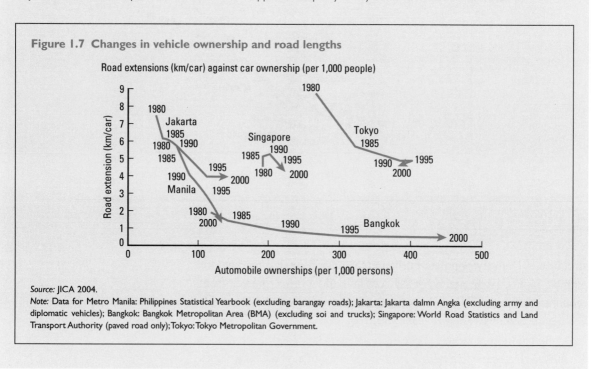

Source: JICA 2004.
Note: Data for Metro Manila: Philippines Statistical Yearbook (excluding barangay roads); Jakarta: Jakarta dalmn Angka (excluding army and diplomatic vehicles); Bangkok: Bangkok Metropolitan Area (BMA) (excluding soi and trucks); Singapore: World Road Statistics and Land Transport Authority (paved road only); Tokyo: Tokyo Metropolitan Government.

And these gaps tend to affect the poor, frequently in peri-urban, informal settlements, far more than the rest of the urban populations (Table 1.6). More generally, while cities have driven growth, and urban poverty is lower than rural poverty in every country in East Asia, urban poverty, and particularly inequality, is a real and potentially explosive problem. Densely populated cities can unleash new political risks and demands for government accountability, when the provision of basic services and the availability of jobs do not match popular expectations.

At the same time, infrastructure plays an enormous role in maintaining the competitiveness of East Asia's cities. Urban investment climates, and hence mass employment prospects, can depend critically on the quality of urban infrastructure.

Table 1.6 Inequality in access to infrastructure services in urban areas

Access to services, percent household with connection

		Piped water connection[a]	Sanitation	Electricity	Telephone	Access to water[b]
East Asia	Citywide	65.9	58	94.4	57.1	94.8
	Informal Settlements[c]	38.3	7.4	75.7	25.4	89.1
All Developing Countries	Citywide	75.8	64	86.5	52.1	88.9
	Informal Settlements[c]	37.2	19.8	59.1	25.4	57.6

Source: UTCE/ALMEC 2004a.

Note: a. Refers to percentage of households with piped water connection.

b. Portable water within 200 meters of the residence and includes water connections.

c. Data on informal settlement may contain inaccuracies as sample sizes are small and measurement is uncertain.

Among these challenges: connecting cities to hinterlands and international markets through enhanced transport infrastructure, telecommunications, and logistical services. Exploiting the region's comparative advantage in high-value services and high-tech industry by providing advanced communications and just-in-time delivery—the increasing tendency for integrated production chains to spread across a number of countries in East Asia, makes this all the more important.

Creating urban clusters in which innovation thrives. Providing efficient urban transport for people to travel between home, work, school, and leisure activities. Minimizing transport congestion and emissions. Ensuring environmental health through effective and affordable water and sanitation services. Making reliable energy services available to businesses and individuals, and managing environmental impacts.

And perhaps the greatest challenge in rapidly-growing cities, making infrastructure choices before land use patterns become so established that retrofitting infrastructure becomes enormously expensive. Long-term vision, strategic planning, and coordination are at a premium in East Asia's urban areas.

Most East Asian countries have responded to pressures on infrastructure services arising from urbanization by decentralizing substantial government responsibility to the local level. This has taken many forms, depending on the economic needs, political context, and institutional traditions of the countries concerned.

But in most cases, decentralization has brought with it numerous issues. These include how to coordinate efforts across different jurisdictions and agencies; how to restructure infrastructure service providers and how to regulate them; what the appropriate intergovernmental fiscal arrangements are; how to enhance municipal financing options; how much political autonomy different levels of government will enjoy and how accountability will work; and how to include greater participation by civil society and the private sector. These factors can profoundly shape the provision of infrastructure services.

We will take up these themes of strategic urban planning and management of infrastructure across decentralized jurisdictions in our discussion of coordination in Chapter 3.

The rural challenge

While East Asia is rapidly urbanizing, about 60 percent (or 1.1 billion people) still live in rural areas. Moreover, East Asia's poverty is overwhelmingly rural, and rural-urban disparities—across income as well as access to services—provoke political concerns and demands for inclusion in economic development (sometimes with an ethnic minority element).[12] A number of generally fast-growing East Asian countries include large pockets of rural poverty, most notably in western China, the Central Highlands and Northern Mountains of Vietnam, Mindanao in the Philippines, Northeast Thailand (see Table 1.7), and eastern Indonesia.

Rural economies depend increasingly on urban economies—for markets, financial capital, and migrant employment. But urban economies also depend on rural economies for human capital and agricultural products. The contribution of infrastructure provision to the health of rural economies can therefore have major economic and political impacts in both rural and urban areas. For example, the provision of rural

Table 1.7 Even in fast-growing Thailand, regional income and access to infrastructure can diverge significantly

	GDRP per capita (baht million)	Number of telephone lines per 1,000 people	Car ownership per 1,000 people[a]
(1) Bangkok	228,921	31.6	348.3
(2) Northeast Thailand	25,367	2.16	34.9
Ratio (1)/(2)	9.0	14.6	10.0

Source: UTCE/ALMEC 2004a.
Note: GDRP = gross domestic regional product.
a. Data as of 2000, including cars, vans, and trucks.

feeder roads can allow the supply of perishable foods to high-value urban markets, and the income generated can be invested in health and education to improve the productivity of eventual migrants to the cities. Rural infrastructure is not always just for the benefit of rural populations.

But rural infrastructure is also comparatively more expensive to deliver than urban infrastructure. Policy makers are often ill-equipped to strike an appropriate balance, given limited resources. Thereafter, the challenge is how to provide infrastructure as cost-effectively as possible. This can involve making appropriate choices about technologies and service standards: decentralized solutions, such as small-scale solar or diesel generation, water pumps, septic tanks, and satellite-based telecom-munications, can be preferable to network utility access. Furthermore, the external economic benefits of rural infrastructure need to be captured and channeled back into rural infrastructure financing.

There are also major challenges in reconciling those objectives with the desire to decentralize infrastructure responsibilities or to create space for community-based initiatives. Coordination between communities or local governments, or with higher levels of government, can be lacking. Decentralization, if not carefully managed, may sometimes enhance rural isolation rather than connectivity with the wider world (UTCE/ALMEC 2004b). After all, rural roads do need to connect with major highways, and common resources (such as watersheds) need to be managed in common.

The regional challenge

Just as rural and urban economies need connection, so do countries and large provinces. Regional integration is a high priority for large swathes of East Asia and the Pacific, and has been responsible for much of the region's economic success. Growth in Japan, the newly industrializing countries, and now China has successively led to growth in the rest of the region.

Western China's poverty reduction and social stability depend on enhanced integration with coastal China, and coastal China needs to draw effectively on its rural agricultural hinterland. At the other end of the scale, Pacific island microstates could share some resources and coordi-nate relevant policies (indeed, because some states include literally hundreds of islands, internal integration is also an issue), and outlying islands of Indonesia and the Philippines need to be included in the benefits of national economic growth.

In between, the Greater Mekong Subregion (GMS) has great opportunities for integration of transport, water resource management, energy, and telecommunications.[13] And as China emerges as the growth engine of the region, connecting with its markets becomes a high priority. Regional integration is an economic matter of realizing economies of scale, spreading risk, and exploiting comparative advantage, but also of cementing stable relationships in postconflict situations and including ethnic minorities in mainstream society. We shall pick up these themes in our discussion of inclusive development in Chapter 2.

The environmental story

Choices relating to many kinds of infrastructure—roads and road networks, power generation, solid-waste incineration, water supply, and sanitation—have potentially significant environmental impacts. Often these are negative.[14] (Although they may be positive too—sanitation plants, after all, can be key to reducing water pollution; some infrastructure can help encourage sustainable agricultural practices or create financially viable alternatives to exploitation of natural forests.)

High rates of economic growth and urbanization drive the environmental agenda in many countries in the region. And infrastructure, as we have seen, helps drive growth and urbanization. For many years, there was a widespread perception among policy makers in the region that environmental protection could wait, or at least take a back seat, to allow economies to grow without constraints.

However, in recent years, perceptions have started shifting, perhaps best exemplified by China's publication in 1994 of the "White Paper on China's Population, Environment, and Development in the 21st Century" (China's Agenda 21, 1994). This paper analyzed the environment as a resource whose exhaustion would constrain growth, rather than seeing environmental protection as primarily a constraint on growth. In parallel, there has been a gradually increasing focus on the quality of life, not merely on material living standards.

This shift in philosophy conditions policies relating to infrastructure and choices of infrastructure investments. Infrastructure policies and projects are increasingly judged by whether they improve the environment, or at least minimize environmental risks. Environmental priorities gaining strength in the region's agenda include improving urban air quality, reducing emissions affecting greenhouse gases, increasing the availability of clean water and of sanitation services, and maintaining the functioning of ecosystems that provide livelihoods and other benefits.

Interventions at the project level can be important, ranging from environmental safeguards, to measures to mitigate (or compensate for) environmental risks and costs, to alternative project design, or even to alternative projects: One can deselect projects if environmental costs are likely to outweigh other positive economic impacts. One can conserve the remaining parts of affected habitats. One can decide to use small-scale hydrogeneration rather than alternative, more polluting technologies, or design urban transport to minimize car use. One can even try to avoid catastrophic flooding by protecting watersheds and their associated hydrological functions, rather than build expensive and potentially damaging downstream hardware.

But the underlying causes of environmental problems cannot be addressed at the project level. The challenge, rather, is to effectively mainstream environmental concerns within national policy-making agendas.

There are a number of tools at the policy maker's disposal: Adequate environmental legislation can be adopted, and efforts focused on building capacity related to traditional responsibilities of social and environmental agencies. Improved information and transparency can go a long way—about the magnitude and incidence of environmental damage related to infrastructure, the costs associated with infrastructure projects, their direct and underlying causes, and remedial measures. Training measures can be taken to better inform communities about environmental issues. Awareness about cost-effective technologies can be raised within infrastructure-related agencies and enterprises. (Box 1.4)

In the medium term, measures can be taken to encourage the systematic use of environmental impact assessments, not only at the project level, but at the sectoral and national level too. Environmental objectives can be costed into pricing and other policies in key sectors such as energy, water, agriculture, and transport.

Box 1.5 outlines the use of the Strategic Environmental Assessment (SEA), referred to above, using the example of urban infrastructure development in Bali, Indonesia. SEAs can identify links and trade-offs, as well as institutional responsibilities for coordinating and implementing key elements of a program.

Box 1.4 Indications of the high cost of environmental pollution in China

Many analyses of the environmental damage in the region are based on China's experience. There is enormous variation in the results of the many studies conducted to express this in monetary terms, but even the lowest estimates indicate significant impacts of environmental degradation on GNP.

One major study estimated that environmental damage from pollution alone cost an equivalent of 7.7 percent of GDP, when willingness-to-pay valuation methods are used, or 3.5 percent of GNP when a human capital approach is taken (World Bank 1997).

In human and physical terms, estimations of costs are equally sobering, and include the following:

- 178,000 premature deaths in major cities each year, because of air pollution that primarily is generated by the consumption of high sulfur coal.

- 6.4 million work years lost annually because of air pollution–related health damages.

- 52 urban river sections contaminated to such an extent that they are not suitable even for irrigation.

- 10 percent of land areas threatened by acid rain.

- More than 1.5 million km^2 affected by soil erosion, losing the equivalent of twice the national production of fertilizer.

Source: Warford 2004.

Fundamentally, however, the challenge of mainstreaming is a governance challenge. And the challenge is difficult indeed. Measurement of environmental risks, costs, and benefits, for instance, is fraught with uncertainty, and hence value judgments play a major role. This means that data can easily be manipulated and even corrupted. The politically powerful can exploit their influence over information dissemination and decision-making processes to exclude the interests of politically marginalized groups, who tend to be affected disproportionately by environmental degradation. The economic interests of the powerful therefore will tend to override environmental concerns, unless broader accountability, participation, and transparency mechanisms can evolve to counteract that tendency.

Perhaps more benign than political asymmetry, but nonetheless very difficult, is the sheer coordination challenge posed by mainstreaming environmental issues. For example, improving urban air quality may require a shift from individual to mass transit. This can involve

> **Box 1.5 Strategic environmental assessments: The Bali urban infrastructure project**
>
> The Bali Urban Infrastructure Project was designed to improve urban infra-structure services throughout the island of Bali, Indonesia, and included major subprojects in urban roads and traffic management, water supply and sanita-tion, drainage, and flood control.
>
> Although not legally required, a Strategic Environmental Assessment (SEA) was conducted to help address the most critical environmental issues in Bali, given the threat to water catchments, forests, and cultural property posed by population growth, industrial development, and tourism. The SEA was designed to ensure that urban infrastructure development would take place in the context of, and be sensitive to, these environmental issues.
>
> The SEA involved extensive public consultation at local levels, which led to several concrete recommendations relating to implementation of the sub-projects, as well as to the selection of priorities. It included detailed recom-mendations for institutional capacity building required to ensure proper exe-cution of the investment program.
>
> The SEA produced a comprehensive environmental profile of Bali and, in particular, a set of maps defining environmental zones. Subprojects and their potential impacts were assessed in relation to the different zones. This infor-mation was indispensable to determining appropriate land uses in different zones and to helping avoid adverse environmental and social consequences of urban infrastructure development programs.
>
> *Source:* Warford 2004.

investments in urban rail, integration with other public transport systems, coordination with residential and commercial land use plans, taxation on fuel and private vehicles, fuel efficiency and quality regulation, regula-tion of user charges, urban road construction and traffic management, and many other aspects.

In a different context, a hydropower development program may have a negative environmental impact on water catchments, but a positive impact on carbon emissions, because it allows reduction of coal-fired generation. This involves complex environmental trade-offs and coordi-nation among many different actors.

More profoundly, policies with environmental impact may be deeply embedded in broader policy and institutional frameworks, and reform would be required on many fronts to make progress on an environmental issue. Reforming water prices to encourage water conservation, for example, might depend on parallel reforms in the enterprise, financial, and social sectors, as one study from China shows (Warford and Li 2002).

Finally, responsibilities for policies or programs with environmental implications will often be fragmented across many state agencies, and private sector and civil society stakeholders may be intimately involved. Environmental ministries may not have the political clout to coordinate effectively, and more powerful agencies may have other priorities. Decentralization may complicate the process, in the absence of good horizontal coordination, when externalities spill over from one jurisdiction to others (UTCE/ALMEC 2004b). Coordinating across all these dimensions challenges government capabilities in any country.

The political story

The financial and economic challenges of delivering infrastructure on the scale required in East Asia have an important political dimension. Among the most important (and discussed) aspects of this political dimension are the ideological battle over public versus private participation in infrastructure and the interplay of ownership, regulation, financing, planning, and policy making.

In infrastructure sectors, investments often have an economic impact well beyond the revenue recouped by the service provider—that is, economic rates of return frequently exceed financial rates of return by a substantial margin. This creates an a priori case for some form of government intervention to supplement the workings of markets. At the same time, economies of scale in infrastructure can yield substantial market power over often essential—and, hence, highly politicized—services. Such market power generally induces governments to control prices tightly in infrastructure sectors to protect against abuse of consumers. This control can be effected indirectly through regulation or directly through public provision.

Where infrastructure provision is potentially private, the existence of tight price regulation creates substantial political risk. Infrastructure is typically large and immobile; massive capital costs are sunk and cannot be salvaged. After investments have been made, governments can undertake creeping expropriation of investors' assets, but those investors are likely to continue operating as long as their variable costs are covered by revenues. An investor threat to withdraw in the face of such government behavior is often not credible. In short, any bargain struck with a government to give investors rights to a revenue stream that gives an adequate return on capital employed can obsolesce rapidly once the deal is struck.

In industrial countries, private firms created a substantial portion of the initial infrastructure, but over time this led to underinvestment in the face of political risk or lack of competitive pressure, and to some abuse of market power. After World War II, an ideological shift in favor of public ownership encompassed infrastructure also, and public provision became the dominant model. This occurred within a political environment that favored centralized economic planning—often of a highly dirigiste nature. This model was subsequently exported to developing countries, many of which were newly independent and were seeking to expand their infrastructure rapidly. In many cases, this preference in developing countries for public provision of infrastructure was accentuated by a postcolonial antipathy to foreign investment, at a time in which private domestic capital for large-scale investment was almost nonexistent.

But public infrastructure performance was often below expectations. Prices were frequently kept below costs, and costs were often excessively high. Competition or other incentive mechanisms to reduce costs proved difficult to implement in the state sector, even when technological advance made it more feasible. Vested interests resisted performance improvements to retain the benefits of overstaffing or appropriation of monopoly rents for personal or political purposes. Accountability to customers or citizens for performance was generally weak. Supply-driven or corruption pressures led to white elephant investments and an inherent bias against funding maintenance. State-owned enterprises were burdened with many noncommercial objectives.

Low tariffs were often not targeted to the poor (who frequently didn't have service access anyway because of funding constraints), but instead were directed at middle-class groups with political voice. Sometimes the resulting deficits were funded from cross-subsidies, often from commercial customers (thereby effectively taxing production and employment). Sometimes they were funded by government budgets or quasi-fiscal loans from state-controlled financial institutions, often with poor repayment records. And sometimes the deficits were funded by capital consumption (lack of maintenance or capital replacement) or by reducing operations.

In the late 1970s and early 1980s, many countries started to undergo fiscal compression as a result of global recession, inflation, and commodity price shocks. This was compounded by an ideological shift in favor of

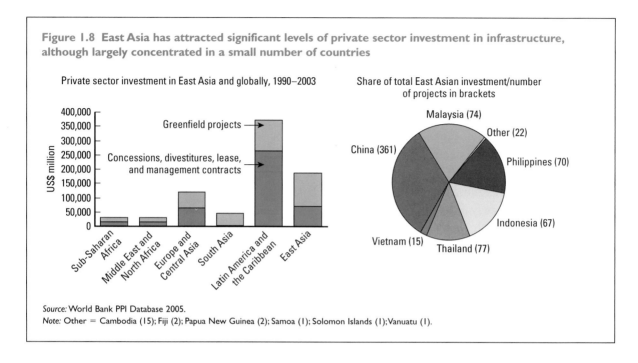

Figure 1.8 East Asia has attracted significant levels of private sector investment in infrastructure, although largely concentrated in a small number of countries

Private sector investment in East Asia and globally, 1990–2003

Share of total East Asian investment/number of projects in brackets

Source: World Bank PPI Database 2005.
Note: Other = Cambodia (15); Fiji (2); Papua New Guinea (2); Samoa (1); Solomon Islands (1); Vanuatu (1).

the private sector, and ushered in an era of fiscal conservatism and slimming down the direct economic role of government. An impetus toward private provision of infrastructure reemerged and, by the late 1980s, had spread to East Asia in a range of forms, from management contracts to transfer of ownership to the private sector. This trend accelerated in the early 1990s. Indonesia, the Philippines, Thailand, and Malaysia were initially at the forefront of this process, but China, Vietnam, and others were players also (Figure 1.8).

In many cases, private participation in infrastructure was pursued under fiscal pressure.[15] Subsidies were drying up, and infrastructure assets were seen as a potential source of public revenue if privatized. Poor performance resulting from underfunding increased public support for change. East Asia was growing rapidly, and was attracting investor interest; global costs of capital were cyclically low, appetites for emerging market risk were correspondingly high, and planning horizons generally short. Few actors had yet had bad experience—or indeed much experience at all—in private infrastructure in developing countries.

But the underlying political economy had not greatly changed. The political incentives remained for government to regulate prices tightly. In fact, years of subsidies to the middle classes had strengthened those incentives. Concession contracts or regulatory frameworks may have implied cost-reflective tariffs, but, politically, realities in countries where property rights can be fragile suggested otherwise. And fiscal conservatism meant that subsidies were often not available to cover the deficits that resulted from low tariffs (or subsidies were kept off the fiscal books, which made it hard to ensure that they would be honored in times of fiscal crisis).

Firms therefore wanted to push up tariffs, while governments wanted to keep them down (that is, to have firms fund the subsidies to the middle class that governments didn't want to pay for themselves). Lack of sector restructuring to accompany private participation meant that competitive pressures to reduce costs and improve performance were often not much greater than they had been under public ownership—so cost-reflective tariffs were high and politically contentious. Some deals created perceptions of corruption and cronyism. The warning signs for private infrastructure were in place.

And then, in the late 1990s, came financial crisis in emerging markets, rapid currency declines, the bursting of the bubble in global capital markets, and sectoral crises in the wake of the Enron scandal and the end of the telecoms boom. Several East Asian countries faced economic collapse, which plunged millions into poverty. In turn, this economic crisis brought in a period of dramatic political change—a wave of democratization has since been sweeping the region.

Under these pressures, many private infrastructure deals were renegotiated (voluntarily or otherwise), damaging investor perceptions. Many were cancelled (see Figure 1.9). Tariff adjustments to offset currency depreciation were highly unattractive both politically and economically in such a period. Governments suddenly found they had underwritten more contingent off-budget support for private infrastructure than they had realized or now felt they could afford. The role of capital flight and currency speculation in the financial crisis turned public sentiment against foreign investment. In some countries, democratization brought a flourishing civil society newly vocal in its criticisms of government policies, including those on private participation, financial management, and tariff adjustments. Private investor interest declined sharply, governments became more cautious, and civil society was decidedly skeptical. For a while private investment in infrastructure was out of fashion in East Asia. Nobody—government, private sector, or civil society—wanted to take the risk.

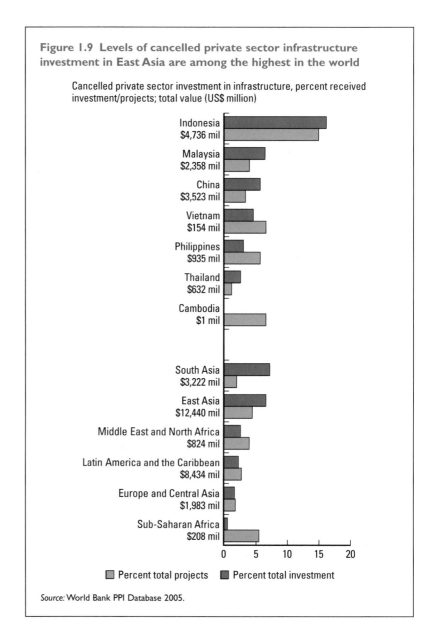

Figure 1.9 Levels of cancelled private sector infrastructure investment in East Asia are among the highest in the world

Cancelled private sector investment in infrastructure, percent received investment/projects; total value (US$ million)

Source: World Bank PPI Database 2005.

The economic crisis is now over, most countries have resumed high growth levels, and private investment, in general, is beginning to recover. But private investment in infrastructure is returning only very cautiously, and governments are sometimes tentative in their response.

The pendulum-swings between public and private provision of infrastructure reveal an underlying political reality: A policy and institutional environment that is lousy for the private sector is lousy for the public sector too. Governments that have long-term economic vision and plans for the future can acknowledge the importance of efficiency incentives for infrastructure and of ensuring sustainable infrastructure financing mechanisms, regardless of ownership. Those governments will have a conception of how infrastructure makes its macroeconomic contribution, how it will be financed, how policies should be coordinated, and how institutions should be developed.

Governments that live for the short term will be tempted to deprive long-lived infrastructure assets of adequate funding, and will be reluctant to undertake risky sector reforms—again regardless of ownership. In those countries, infrastructure development will be more piecemeal, financing more ad hoc, and institutions more fragile and fragmented.

The funding story

And so finally to the question of funding—that is, the scale of the resource requirement to address East Asia's infrastructure challenge, and how this requirement can be sourced. According to analysis undertaken for this study, to meet expected infrastructure service needs, East Asia would have to spend $165 billion a year over the next five years—or roughly 6.2 percent of its GDP annually—on electricity, telecommunications, water and sanitation, and major transport networks (see Figure 1.10).[16]

These estimates take into account both investment and maintenance of assets (an equally and sometimes more cost-effective way of meeting service goals). In meeting these needs, it is estimated that 65 percent of expenditure would need to take the form of new investment, with the remaining 35 percent channeled toward maintenance of existing assets.

In China alone, total needs account for almost 7 percent of GDP (and China's infrastructure needs account for 80 percent of the region's total). In low-income countries the needs are relatively greater than in middle-income ones. When other infrastructure needs are included (such as ports, airports, bridges, secondary roads, urban transport, and gas grids), the overall estimated need rises above $200 billion a year.

Moreover, these estimates do not incorporate any strategic decisions to invest in infrastructure ahead of demand, or to increase access for the poor in line with the Millennium Development Goals (MDGs) or other targets. But in East Asia, many national or local governments do indeed

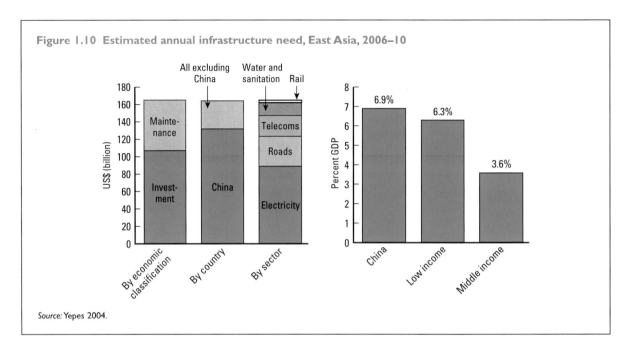

Figure 1.10 Estimated annual infrastructure need, East Asia, 2006–10

Source: Yepes 2004.

follow such policies: Thailand's Eastern Seaboard, Lao PDR's rural electrification, Shanghai's urban development strategy, and rural development policies in Western China are some striking examples of this approach. "Strategic" approaches to infrastructure investment can circumscribe financial discipline, and therefore bring risks of inefficiencies and corruption, but there are nonetheless plenty of regional success stories. Therefore, infrastructure needs in the region could legitimately be even higher than estimated.

Who funds infrastructure? Taxpayers, consumers, and the role of finance

How can East Asia achieve the resources required to meet these estimated needs? Ultimately, there are only two ways in which infrastructure is funded: by consumers (via user charges) and by taxpayers (via subsidies)—as shown in Figure 1.11. Financiers—whether the private sector, or official lenders and donors—can change the requisite time profile of taxes or user charges by providing financing in the form of loans or equity, but eventually those loans need to be repaid or remunerated (or, at least, failure to do so will generally rebound to taxpayers or, subsequently, to consumers through a higher cost of capital).

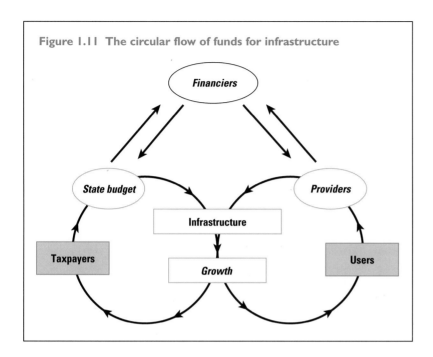

Figure 1.11 The circular flow of funds for infrastructure

This ability to change the time profile of taxes and user charges can be very important politically—effectively allowing a smoothing of tax or tariff increases. It can also be welcomed from the point of view of competitiveness for the economy or affordability for households, permitting time to adjust to higher tariffs levels. But loans and equity per se do not generally add to the total resources available to an economy over time.[17] In effect, they unlock the potential of other resources by allowing investment to take place despite economic or political constraints—taxes and user charges remain central.

Financiers of infrastructure can source their capital from domestic savings or foreign savings. At one level, the distinction does not matter: Savings are mobile internationally and will generally seek the highest return regardless of borders. In that sense, one could argue that East Asia's high domestic savings are irrelevant to the region's financing availability. However, in reality, savings are not entirely mobile: Regulatory barriers to capital mobility exist. In part, they exist for reasons of macroeconomic stability and, in part, to allow governments to direct domestic savings into activities they deem to be of a high national priority—a common practice in East Asia. In addition, holders of domestic savings (or their intermediaries) can have lower risk assessments of investment opportunities in their

> **Box 1.6 What about efficiency?**
>
> East Asia has seen considerable amounts of investment in infrastructure in the past. And equally large amounts are likely to be spent in the future.
>
> Delivering infrastructure services clearly requires resources. And this is why policy makers focus on expenditure levels (whether on investment or operations and maintenance).
>
> But the same level of spending can yield very different service outcomes. Efficiency of expenditure—getting the most service out of every baht, yuan, peso, dollar, or rupiah—matters enormously.
>
> In the framework we set out in this study, inefficiency is not a theme. It is an outcome that arises when the focus of policy is not inclusivity, when coordination is poor, when accountability is lacking, and when risks are badly managed.
>
> When we talk about costly environmental infrastructure impacts, we are talking about inefficiency. And likewise when we consider poorly aligned spatial and sectoral planning, infrastructure retrofitting, badly funded utilities providing poor services because consumers pay too little, taxpayers subsidize too little, or both (Chapter 1).
>
> Inefficiency also occurs when infrastructure has lower economic returns because the poor were not taken into account; when disabled access has to be funded postinvestment; when returns on infrastructure are lowered because regional coordination was not pursued; and when infrastructure did not link the right people, to the right market, at the right time (Chapter 2).
>
> Inefficiency also occurs when infrastructure investments are not aligned with long-term development strategies; when financing is out of synch with planning; when not enough emphasis is given to maintenance of existing assets; when spillovers across municipalities are poorly managed; where different jurisdictions engage in "destructive competition"; when scarce resources are fragmented; and when vertical coordination is weak (Chapter 3).
>
> And it also occurs when accountability breaks down, financial risks are realized, and corruption destroys value (Chapter 4).

home country than foreigners do. Those savings therefore demand lower returns at home and are more likely to be invested domestically. This makes the development of local capital markets an important component of infrastructure financing.[18] However, the returns still need to be there—financial engineering won't create them.

When consumers fund infrastructure

Covering infrastructure costs means charging consumers for the use of infrastructure services. At first sight, a simple proposition. But in reality, one that gives rise to a host of policy issues. How much of the costs of infrastructure provision should consumers pay, and how much should be subsidized by taxpayers? When are users unwilling to pay, and when are they are unable to pay? Should the poor pay less than the nonpoor? Is it preferable to provide a less expensive service at a lower rate? If costs are to be subsidized, which users capture those subsidies? And when is cost recovery a matter of low tariffs, and when is it a matter of inefficient service provision leading to high costs? These are just some of the many questions, to which the answers vary by sector, country, and policy regime.

In the water sector, for instance, tariffs are insufficient to cover even operating and maintenance costs of many of the region's water utilities (Figure 1.12). Taking into account capital costs, it is unlikely that any water utilities in East Asia (and few in the world) achieve full cost recovery.[19] This is not a situation that is evident in every sector (among infrastructure sectors, water most exhibits natural monopoly characteristics, and is least amenable to competition), but it is an instructive example nonetheless.

Non-cost-reflective (average) tariffs may arise for many reasons. They may reflect the excessively high costs of inefficiently run services, which consumers cannot reasonably meet. Sometimes costs may be high for good reason (reflecting, for instance, the cost of network expansion or natural supply constraints), but nonetheless unaffordable.

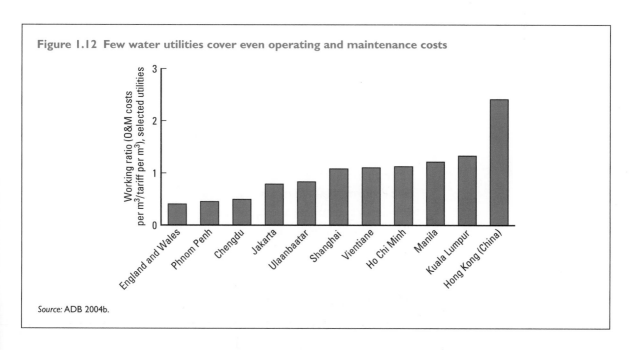

Figure 1.12 Few water utilities cover even operating and maintenance costs

Working ratio (O&M costs per m³/tariff per m³), selected utilities

Source: ADB 2004b.

Sometimes tariffs remain low when there is a case for raising them for political reasons: Infrastructure assets are often long-lived, and so infrastructure providers can be starved of funds before deterioration becomes noticeable. When politicians have a short time frame, the popularity of low tariffs is more important to them than the medium-term costs.

Sometimes policy makers keep average tariffs below cost recovery levels to protect the poor. And this is where many of the key policy questions we flagged arise. In fact, when government lacks good information about where the poor live, how they access infrastructure, and the decisions they would make if they could choose among different services and price options, keeping average tariffs low may not be an unreasonable position.

Although this too has a downside: Research over the past decade has repeatedly shown that it's primarily the relatively well-off who are able to connect to utilities networks that price below cost—extending services to the poor is too expensive for the utility. This leaves the poor to provide for themselves, frequently at much higher prices. In Indonesia, for instance, one survey suggests that people unable to access the services provided by the local utility, Perusahaan Daerah Air Minum (PDAM), paid between 33 and 122 times the price per volume paid by PDAM customers (World Bank 2004a).

There is now a growing consensus that subsidies can be used to meet the needs of consumers who are too poor to pay for services. The challenge is how to design instruments that most effectively target the most needy, while trying to ensure that average tariffs are as close to cost recovery levels as possible.

There are a host of options, but they basically work in three main ways (Estache 2004): by reducing bills, through, for instance, means-tested subsidies; by reducing the cost of services by improving efficiency; and by making it easier for the poor to pay their bills. But effective targeting is difficult. It requires data that are often unavailable (Gomez-Lobo, Foster, and Halpern 2000). And of course subsidies also bring with them economic efficiency and incentive cost problems—although recent analysis suggests that, in many cases, these costs are modest (Ravallion 2003).

When taxpayers fund infrastructure

The kind of subsidies we have been talking about frequently are transfers from taxpayers to infrastructure users. When taxpayers fund infrastructure, a number of important microeconomic questions arise. Is the tax revenue channeled into public expenditures with the highest rates of return? Are the expenditures transparent or are there contingent liabilities that are hard to monitor? In East Asia, with its high levels of directed lending from state-controlled financial institutions and revenue guarantees to infrastructure service providers (both, in essence, quasi-fiscal subsidies), this is a hugely important question. Are subsidies designed in a cost-minimizing manner? Is there an exit strategy to phase out subsidies? Is the balance between expenditures on investment and on operations and maintenance appropriate? Subsidies also have important implications for risk management and accountability—issues we shall discuss in detail in Chapter 4.

There are also vital *macro*economic questions: Is there too much public expenditure on infrastructure, thus jeopardizing fiscal stability (and hence also the investment climate)? Or is there too little expenditure, thus endangering economic growth and poverty reduction? This has become known as the "fiscal space" debate, and has arisen primarily as the result of a decade of fiscal austerity in Latin America (as mentioned in "the macroeconomic story" above), although it is of relevance to other regions.

In East Asia, the essential question is whether there are countries that have a sufficiently robust track record on fiscal stability, but that have such low levels of expenditure (public and private) on infrastructure that future economic growth and, hence, long-term fiscal sustainability are under threat. In Figure 1.11, the Circular Flow of Funds for Infrastructure, this would be manifested in two vicious circles: first, of low public expenditure leading to low growth, and second, of low growth depressing both user charges and taxes.

Higher public expenditure on infrastructure in such countries could instead yield two virtuous circles. In those countries, a balance of more vigorous promotion of private financing, tariff adjustment where needed, and higher fiscal space for infrastructure would be appropriate. This is particularly likely for lower-income countries, and for countries recovering from crisis, where infrastructure needs are high, and attracting the private sector may be only a gradual process. The challenge for countries is to ensure that they are fiscally sound enough to embark on this course, and to determine whether they have adequate coordination to achieve the necessary balance between fiscal space and other policies.[20] We pick up this theme in Chapter 3.

Box 1.7 So why didn't the private sector solve East Asia's infrastructure problems?

There are a number of possible reasons as to why the private sector did not live up to expectations:

(1) The initial expectations about levels of private investment were not realistic. The majority of infrastructure investment in the majority of countries—industrial or developing—is publicly owned and operated. It would take a long time for private investment to overtake public investment let alone displace it. Not all sectors are created equal—some are more attractive to private investment than others.

(2) There was a global downturn in capital markets, generally, and in the power and telecommunications sector, in particular. However, when those markets recovered, East Asian investment turned up only slightly. Clearly, local factors were more important than global ones.

(3) East Asia undertook only limited infrastructure sector reform, and minimal privatization of existing assets (most investments were greenfield). Competition and independent regulation did not play a major role. Most private investment therefore took place within more or less the same incentives framework as had previously existed, so performance could not really be expected to change much. Lack of reform meant that many private providers had only one customer—a state enterprise. This was risky.

(4) Government often proved to be unpredictable and property rights were difficult to enforce. Judicial systems did not always help much. Bargains obsolesced once investments were sunk. Market growth helped offset these political risks to some extent, but not enough.

(5) The subsidy framework was very unclear. Infrastructure services often enjoyed hidden subsidies that were reduced quite abruptly when the private sector came in. Consequent tariff increases created political backlashes against the private sector (particularly foreign investment). Sometimes tariffs increases came early, service improvements only later.

(6) However, some hidden subsidies remained, particularly in the form of guarantees where the state was the sole customer for the private provider (these guarantees usually went unrecognized in fiscal accounts). The 1997 crisis caused many of those guarantees to be called up: As a result, governments either faced unexpected fiscal pressure or reneged on guarantees. This discredited the concept of private investment.

(7) Contractual agreements with the private sector were not crisis-proof. Although currency crises can be expected to occur some time during the long life of an infrastructure asset, few contracts anticipated that eventuality.

(8) Too many private sector deals were tainted with corruption allegations. Few people made a comparison between the alleged corruption in those private sector deals and the corruption in public sector projects.

(Continued on the next page)

Box 1.7 (Continued)

(9) Determining how best to allocate risk between public and private sectors in infrastructure is an experimental process. What is initially seen as outright failure, can be seen as a learning experience after the dust has settled. And life can then move on.

When the private sector finances infrastructure

As for private financing of infrastructure, developments in East Asia have to be viewed against global trends. Private investors have invested approximately $190 billion in East Asian infrastructure since 1990.[21] But even at its mid-1990's peak, this represented only a minor share of total infrastructure investment in the developing world (20 to 25 percent) as well as in much of the industrial world.[22] And the private investment bubble of the mid-1990s has now burst throughout the developing world.[23]

However, annual private infrastructure investment levels in developing countries as a whole were still about 50 percent higher in 2001–03 than in 1990–95, while in the region they were roughly the same over those two periods (see Figure 1.13 and World Bank 2004f). In short, the

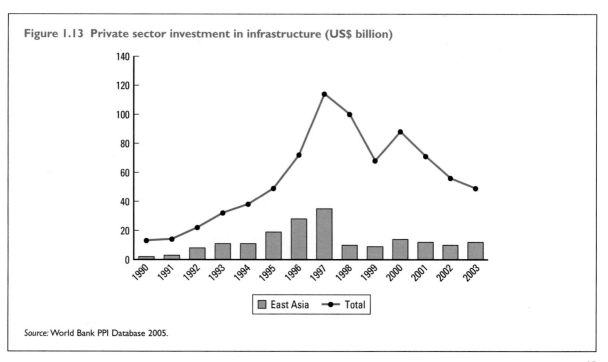

Figure 1.13 Private sector investment in infrastructure (US$ billion)

East Asia ■   Total ●

Source: World Bank PPI Database 2005.

current levels of actual new direct investment in East Asia appear to have stabilized at the levels of about 10 years ago, lagging behind the global average. Private investment appears to finance only about 5 percent of the region's total investment needs today, compared with perhaps 20 percent at its peak. Clearly these trends are partly an issue of movements in global capital markets, and partly a matter of the investment climate for infrastructure in the region.

A survey undertaken for this study shows very positive sentiment among potential private investors in East Asian infrastructure. But this sentiment varies by country and sector, and is contingent on policy improvements to reduce risk (see Figure 1.14).[24] East Asian investors are somewhat more optimistic than investors from outside the region, but a large majority of those surveyed—both in East Asia and the rest of the world—plan to "wait and see" whatever their origin.

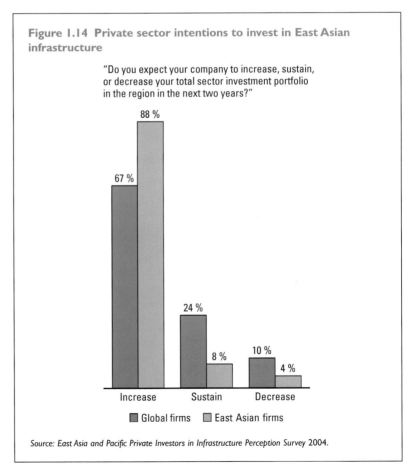

Figure 1.14 Private sector intentions to invest in East Asian infrastructure

"Do you expect your company to increase, sustain, or decrease your total sector investment portfolio in the region in the next two years?"

- Increase: Global firms 67 %, East Asian firms 88 %
- Sustain: Global firms 24 %, East Asian firms 8 %
- Decrease: Global firms 10 %, East Asian firms 4 %

■ Global firms   ■ East Asian firms

Source: East Asia and Pacific Private Investors in Infrastructure Perception Survey 2004.

Much needs to be done on the policy and institutional front to mitigate risks for the private sector—but most of the work needs to be done for the public sector too. In essence, the core issues are not public versus private, but about how they can share the risk and rewards in a way that works for both sides, and how the public sector harnesses the efficiency gains that the private sector can bring. The sources of funding and ownership are secondary.

When official lenders and donors finance infrastructure

And so to the role of official lenders and donors.[25] In purely monetary terms official development assistance (ODA) has never been more than a small portion of infrastructure financing needs. ODA and official aid accounts for approximately 1 percent of gross investment in low- and middle-income countries of East Asia, although these flows are more important in some countries than in others (see Table 1.8).[26]

In the mid-1990s some official lenders and donors reduced their financing of infrastructure on expectations of greater private investment, and because of a view by some that other sectors had more direct impact on poverty reduction. Official financing also fell temporarily in the aftermath of the 1997 financial crisis due to creditworthiness concerns.

Official financing of infrastructure in the region is on the rise again. The contribution of infrastructure to poverty reduction—indeed of growth to poverty reduction—has been reappraised. The depth of the policy and institutional challenge in infrastructure, and the long-term nature of reform, are now better appreciated. The emphasis has shifted away from the private sector's potential replacement of the public sector, toward a relationship of mutual support and partnership between private and public actors. And so official lenders and donors are repositioning themselves, and infrastructure now has a higher profile in the development community at large.

In most infrastructure sectors, there are activities in which private sector financing can help unlock resources. But there are others in which private sector interest is likely to be limited, in which private sector participation is more difficult to structure, or in which the private participation cannot demonstrate additional value. This includes most rural infrastructure, except where smart subsidies can be brought to bear; infrastructure with strong natural monopoly characteristics, like high-voltage transmission lines; most roads, except where traffic

Table 1.8 Aid dependency in East Asia and the Pacific, 2003

	Per capita income ($)	Aid[a] per capita ($)	Aid as percentage of	
			GNI	Gross fixed investment
Malaysia	3,880	4	0.1	0.5
Thailand	2,190	−16	−0.7	−2.7
China	1,100	1	0.1	0.2
Philippines	1,080	9	0.9	4.9
Indonesia	810	8	0.9	5.2
Vietnam	480	22	4.5	12.9
Mongolia	480	100	19.7	51.0
Lao PDR	340	53	14.3	69.2
Cambodia	300	38	12.5	54.1
Palau	6,500	—	19.7	—
Marshall Islands	2,710	1,076	40.6	—
Tonga	1,490	270	17.1	—
Samoa	1,440	186	12.5	—
Fiji	2,240	61	2.6	—
Micronesia, Fed. Sts. of	2,070	923	44.0	—
Vanuatu	1,180	154	11.6	—
Kiribati	860	191	21.7	—
Solomon Islands	560	132	24.4	—
Papua New Guinea	500	40	8.1	46.3
Timor-Leste	460	172	47.9	—
East Asia Average	1,070	4	0.4	0.9

Source: World Bank 2004h.
Note: East Asia Average includes Samoa, Cambodia, China, Fiji, Indonesia, Kiribati, Korea, Rep. of, Lao PDR, Malaysia, Marshall Islands, Micronesia, Fed. Sts. of, Mongolia, Myanmar, Northern Mariana Islands, Palau, Papua New Guinea, Philippines, Samoa, Solomon Islands, Thailand, Timor-Leste, Tonga, Vanuatu and Vietnam; — = Not available.
a. Includes both official development assistance (ODA) and official aid.

volumes (and willingness to pay) are high enough to justify tolls; and even potentially competitive elements of network utilities that are rendered uncompetitive by their small scale.

In these situations official financing plays an important role in unlocking a country's own resources to meet infrastructure challenges.[27] It may also play a role in leveraging private sector finance. (Some studies suggest that official finance—in particular concessional loans—may even encourage domestic revenue mobilization.[28])

However, the role of official lenders and donors is always going to be limited in comparison with the scale of East Asia's funding needs (although relative importance may vary by country). The challenge is how to focus those relatively small amounts of official financing so that

Box 1.8 Risk, return, and private investment in East Asian infrastructure

Given East Asia's large markets, and significant potential returns, it is difficult to imagine that private sector interest will not eventually revive.

While it is not possible to predict when this will be, we can be fairly confident about the conditions under which this return will take place: when the financial returns to capital exceed the perceived risks.

How, in this respect, does East Asia compare with other emerging and developing regions?

Evidence based on a sample of companies active in electricity, water, ports, and railways suggests that the average risk-adjusted cost of capital (CoC)—the hurdle rate faced by investors—has been significantly lower in East Asia over the period 1998–2002 than in any other region of the world (Figure 1.15).

And the same evidence suggests that East Asia is the only region in which returns on equity (RoE) are higher than the cost of equity (CoE), although just so (Figure 1.16).

One could speculate that market growth is the primary driver rather than policy reform, because East Asia has been slow to reform. But given that returns are just sufficient to compensate the CoC, policy reform could push returns high enough to lead to significant private sector investment. And with

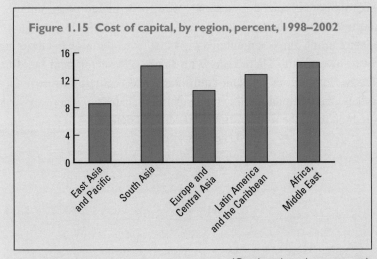

Figure 1.15 Cost of capital, by region, percent, 1998–2002

(Continued on the next page)

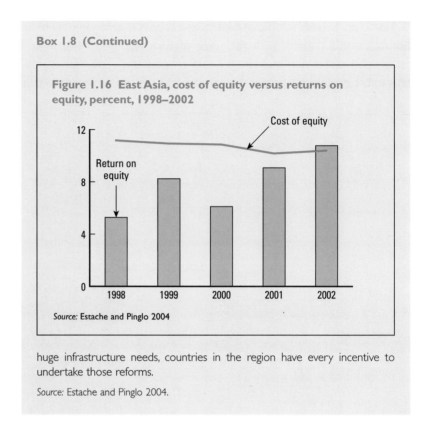

Box 1.8 (Continued)

Figure 1.16 East Asia, cost of equity versus returns on equity, percent, 1998–2002

Cost of equity

Return on equity

Source: Estache and Pinglo 2004

huge infrastructure needs, countries in the region have every incentive to undertake those reforms.

Source: Estache and Pinglo 2004.

their role is maximized in a variety of efforts, including stimulating experimentation and innovation; supporting efficiency gains; mainstreaming environmental and social considerations; attracting private investors to share risks with the public sector; and building effective institutions to plan, coordinate, and regulate infrastructure services. We will pick up this topic again in Chapter 5, where we look more broadly at the role of official lenders and donors.

Annex 1: Estimation of infrastructure needs

Overview of methodology

Developing economies in East Asia will need to spend an estimated total of $165 billion per year between 2006–10 in certain infrastructure sectors, namely electricity, telecommunications, major paved interurban roads, rail routes, and water and sanitation (compared with an estimated $147 billion per year in 2000–05).[29] This amounts to nearly 6.2 percent of the GDP for the region, comprising 4.0 percent for investment and 2.2 percent for maintenance. Furthermore, China alone is expected to account for 80 percent of infrastructure expenditures in the region. Among the sectors, electricity in China has the largest share (44 percent) of total annual expenditure in infrastructure in the region. See Tables 1.9, 1.10, and 1.11 for detailed breakdowns.

These predictions follow the methodology used in Fay and Yepes (2003). Infrastructure stock trends are obtained from a panel data estimation of the eight East Asian countries[30] for which adequate data were available using lagged dependent variables and controlling for economic growth and economic geographic variables. Projected stocks levels were then valued at best-practice costs. Investment expenditures are calculated as the increment in stock values over time, while the annual maintenance expenditures are estimated as a fixed percentage[31] of the stock value.

Projections for 12 other countries[32] were obtained by assuming the same sector expenditure as a percentage of GDP as for those countries in

Table 1.9 Investment and maintenance needs, East Asia, 2006–10, $ and percent GDP

	Investment	Maintenance ($ million)	Total	Investment	Maintenance (percent of GDP)	Total
Electricity	63,446	25,744	89,190	2.4	1.0	3.4
Telecom	13,800	10,371	24,171	0.5	0.4	0.9
Roads	23,175	10,926	34,102	0.9	0.4	1.3
Rails	1,170	1,598	2,768	0.0	0.1	0.1
Water	2,571	5,228	7,799	0.1	0.2	0.3
Sanitation	2,887	4,131	7,017	0.1	0.2	0.3
Total	107,049	57,998	165,047	4.0	2.3	6.3

Source: Yepes 2004.

Table 1.10 Investment and maintenance needs, China 2006–10, $ and percent GDP

	Investment	Maintenance ($ million)	Total	Investment	Maintenance (percent GDP)	Total
Electricity	51,668	20,739	72,407	2.7	1.1	3.8
Telecom	11,735	8,232	19,967	0.6	0.4	1.0
Roads	19,345	7,424	26,769	1.0	0.4	1.4
Rails	963	1,258	2,221	0.1	2.1	0.1
Water	2,097	4,090	6,187	0.1	0.2	0.3
Sanitation	1,830	2,644	4,474	0.1	0.1	0.2
Total	87,638	44,387	132,025	4.6	2.3	6.8

Source: Yepes 2004.

Table 1.11 Investment and maintenance needs, East Asia excluding China, 2006–10, $ and percent GDP

	Investment	Maintenance ($ million)	Total	Investment	Maintenance (percent GDP)	Total
Electricity	11,778	5,005	16,783	1.6	0.7	2.3
Telecom	2,065	2,139	4,204	0.3	0.3	0.6
Roads	3,830	3,503	7,333	0.5	0.5	1.0
Rails	207	341	547	0.0	0.0	0.1
Water	474	1,138	1,612	0.1	0.2	0.2
Sanitation	1,057	1,486	2,544	0.1	0.2	0.3
Total	19,411	13,612	33,023	2.6	1.9	4.5

Source: Yepes 2004.

the same income group within the sample of 8 countries. Estimates for Vietnam assume sector percentages equivalent to those in China. Collectively, these 13 countries for which direct data were not available represent only 2 percent of the GDP of developing countries in East Asia, so using the indirect estimation method described above does not introduce any possibility of serious bias in the overall results.

Note that the estimates do not capture any absolute measure of need, such as those developed in the MDGs, nor do they estimate what will actually be spent. Projections are only what expenditure would be at best-practice prices, and consistent with projected economic growth rates. The prices used are a mixture of global, regional, and country-specific prices.

Methodology by sector

Electricity Estimates for electricity include power generation capacity and associated networks for transmission and distribution. A model is used to project kilowatts of generation capacity per capita based on a dataset in five-year blocks covering 1960–2000. Physical stock is then valued at $1,000 per kilowatt of plant generation capacity plus $900 for the associated transmission and distribution networks (based on IEA 2003, which estimates that investment in generation in developing countries will account for about half of the total investments in the sector).

Generation capacity is a supply indicator and our estimations work with the assumption that governments provide it based on planned demand to avoid recurrent outages.

Telecommunications Estimates of infrastructure investment needed in East Asia are also strongly driven by demand from the telecom sector. This is expected to be the result of a rapidly expanding mobile market, which is already the biggest in the world. In China, the penetration rate for mobile phones is already up to 170 lines per 1,000 people in 2003 compared with 18 lines in 2000. For the region as a whole, there were approximately 230 million mobile phone users in 2003, and market analysts estimate the market to be growing at 4 million per month. Furthermore, unmet demand for landlines remains quite high in East Asia. The waiting period for telephone connections is more than 10 years in the Philippines, and about 2.6 years in Indonesia in 1993. Together these two factors—that is, growth in cellular phone usage and existing unmet demand—will contribute to a significant demand for investment.

Unit costs for telecommunications are particularly difficult to project given the high rate of technological progress in the sector. The cost projections are taken from Pyramid (see Ure 2004 and Yepes 2004) and World Bank sector specialists, but they are subject to a considerable margin of error.

Roads and rails Estimations for the stock of roads (and the investment required to maintain and add to the stock) refer to the paved networks, taking into consideration expressways and first- and second-class roads. These results do not include urban and county networks, and unpaved roads. Paved roads were divided into land area to capture country size differentials (the same has been done for all other sectors by dividing the stock by population). Roads as well as rails used five-year data blocks.

The unit cost for roads is the average of paving-type interventions available for the region in the Road Costs Knowledge System (ROCKS) database. The Chinese National Trunk Highway System, to be completed in 2007, was accounted for at an implicit unit cost of $150 billion for 35,000 km. The figures assume the level of highways in China to continue growing at the same rate after 2007.

Other transportation subsectors were not included because of a lack of historic information. Data on waterways—including any ocean or inter-island shipping routes, ports, or airports—are hardly available for this period and not likely to depend on the determinants that we use to project infrastructure stocks.

Water and sanitation Lack of historic and consistent information across countries is one of the main hurdles in water and sanitation analysis, because of considerable heterogeneity in supply mechanisms across countries. Even the definition of what is acceptable access to water or sanitation is fraught with differences. This report uses definitions currently used in the World Development Indicators. The definitions are as follows:

- Access to an improved water source refers to the percentage of the population with reasonable access to an adequate amount of water from an improved source, such as a household connection, public standpipe, borehole, protected well or spring, and rainwater collection. Unimproved sources include vendors, tanker trucks, and unprotected wells and springs. Reasonable access is defined as the availability of at least 20 liters per person per day from a source within one kilometer of the dwelling.
- Access to improved sanitation facilities refers to the percentage of the population with at least adequate excreta disposal facilities (private or shared, but not public) that can effectively prevent human, animal, and insect contact with excreta. Improved facilities range from simple but protected pit latrines to flush toilets with a sewerage connection. To be effective, facilities must be correctly constructed and properly maintained.

Comparable data for access water and sanitation are available only for 1990 and 2000. We estimate a random coefficients panel data model for those two years using 139 middle- and low-income countries across the world.

Multiplying projected access rates by projected number of households yields estimates for stock of connections available for each period in time. The estimated stock has then been valued at best-practice unit cost to yield sector stocks values that provide the basis to calculate the variation (investment need) and depreciation (maintenance need).

2

Inclusive Development

What is inclusive development?

Inclusive development is about improving the incomes and lives of all members of society, particularly the poor. It depends on generating economic growth, sharing its benefits with the poor, and enhancing their access to basic services.

As we shall see, infrastructure is essential to generating growth; to including communities, workers, firms and regions in that growth process; and to bringing services to those who need them most.

Development, inclusiveness, and infrastructure

As we saw in Chapter 1, economic development in East Asia has typically been inclusive, benefiting the poor, as well as the nonpoor. Integration among and within countries has fostered high economic growth overall, and the fruits have generally been shared. Inclusive development has brought political cohesion and social stability through mutual interdependence. Infrastructure has underpinned that interdependence, and has played an essential role in making development inclusive.

But there is no assurance that this will continue into the future. Significant income disparities have developed in East Asia: between low- and high-income countries in the region, and within countries. The structure of growth in many Asian countries has been changing. The divide between rural and urban areas is growing. Within rural areas there are some pockets of deep poverty, often with an ethnic minority dimension.

Coastal areas are prospering and are well-connected to global markets; remote and landlocked regions are lagging behind. Peri-urban areas are becoming a volatile halfway house for migrants, urban environments are under population pressure, and congestion is choking broad-based growth.

This chapter is about how infrastructure can reinforce inclusive development in East Asia. It is about what we can expect infrastructure to do for growth and poverty reduction in the region. And it's about what makes "good" infrastructure. As we shall see these are complex issues, and so we will have to address them in a number of ways.

This chapter has four sections. The first looks at what's so different about infrastructure—at what infrastructure is—and how this relates to the principal themes of this study. This has important implications for how we get infrastructure to serve the goals of inclusive development, and—as we see in Chapter 4—for accountability.

In the second section, we shift our emphasis. From looking at what infrastructure is, we consider what it does. Infrastructure connects. We look first at how infrastructure connects conceptually—linking growth and poverty reduction into a mutually reinforcing relationship. In the third section, we look at the role of infrastructure in connecting East Asia to the global economy and fostering regional integration. Finally, in the last section, we take our analysis to the country level and look at how inclusive development has played out in the case of Vietnam.

Box 2.1 Inclusive development with Chinese characteristics

When China's economic reforms began in the late 1970s, Deng Xiaoping coined the phrase *xiaokang* (or "well-off society"). Initially, *xiaokang* was defined solely by GDP per capita targets.

But in recent years, *xiaokang* has taken on a broader meaning. In 2002, the Sixteenth National Congress of the Communist Party of China established the objective of building an "all-inclusive" *xiaokang* society over the next two decades, in which prosperity is both created and shared. This concept also underpins Premier Wen Jinbao's statement that China's development strategy should be in accordance with "five balanced aspects": balancing urban and rural development, balancing development among regions, balancing economic and social development, balancing man and nature, and balancing domestic development and opening to the world (Wen 2004). Infrastructure has a central role to play in the balancing act to create the *xiaokang* society.

What is so different about infrastructure anyway?

Infrastructure is not like shoe factories, schools, or supermarkets—all of which can potentially contribute to inclusive development in different ways. Infrastructure, and the services it provides, have some rather peculiar features that shape its contribution: features that require specialized mechanisms to facilitate coordination, both vertical and horizontal (chapter 3); that give rise to a number of common risks; and tend to entail a particular set of institutions in the structuring of accountability relationships among the various actors involved in infrastructure (chapter 4). What are those peculiarities?

Infrastructure services tend to be capital intensive and exhibit economies of scale

The provision of large-scale electricity or transport services, for example, generally requires higher capital intensity than the provision of large-scale education or health services. Such infrastructure services can therefore suffer high risk, long gestation, and long payback periods—but enjoy substantial economies of scale. Including more users can greatly enhance the viability and affordability of the service (although this raises coordination and accountability challenges). In some cases, the inclusion of more users can even enhance the value of the service to each individual user (for example, I want as many other people as possible to be on my phone network, or as many locations as possible to be on my rail network). Indeed, it is often the network nature of infrastructure that brings the economies of scale.

Conversely, providing infrastructure services on a small scale can be expensive. But small can also be beautiful, because it may involve low risk, limited need for coordination, or a positive environmental impact—these factors can be worth the extra unit costs.

Infrastructure is usually lumpy rather than incremental

Infrastructure tends to come in lumps, and those lumps tend to form networks. To be useful, roads connecting population centers do actually need to go all the way and join other roads. A power plant with only 10 percent of a turbine is not a power plant, and a power plant without a transmission and distribution grid doesn't provide many people power. An urban water supply system can't function with only half a treatment plant, and a whole treatment plant needs an extensive water distribution system to be justified.

Of course, some infrastructure can be incremental—for example, a wind turbine, a borehole, a household boiler, a septic tank, or a feeder road. Such infrastructure can be crucial in particular circumstances, such as in rural or peri-urban areas, to realize environmental benefits, or to overcome financing and risk constraints. Or incremental approaches may facilitate community participation in governance (lumpy infrastructure has a strong association with top-down institutions). Incremental infrastructure can certainly be the best available option for a particular community of end users. But with current technology, lumpy infrastructure will usually be the cheapest way of providing for large-scale general use.

Infrastructure is long-lasting

After you've built it, it's probably going to be there a long time, even if inattention to maintenance reduces its useful life. A port, a street system, a sewerage network, mass transit, or a hydropower dam can last for decades. Once built, it can define for many years how and where people live and work. It can define which areas prosper and which stagnate, who accumulates wealth and who does not, who exercises power and who has little voice. In short, who is included in development and who is not.

Periods of rapid urbanization present massive opportunities and challenges, and can shape economies and societies profoundly. For some sectors, periods of rapid technological change can radically change what previously made sense.[1]

So risks are high, and infrastructure mistakes can haunt you for a very long time. Missing windows of opportunity can cost dearly, and so can locking in the wrong solutions. Long-term vision matters enormously.

Infrastructure is space-specific and use-specific

Shoe factories, schools, and supermarkets can change locations, or the space can easily be used for a different purpose. Some harbors have become leisure centers and power plants museums, but most infrastructure can't go anywhere else or do something new (and its scrap value can be low).

Infrastructure therefore makes a good hostage. With high sunk costs, revenues can be driven way down and operation will continue (as long as variable costs are covered, it's worse to stop than to carry on). At the same time, those sunk costs and space-specificity mean monopoly power is quite likely. A hostage with monopoly power can attract predators, particularly when the services it provides are politically sensitive. Consequently, infrastructure faces considerable political risk (and this is not just a private sector problem; public infrastructure can also be kidnapped by rent-seekers).

And space-specificity can bring local social and environmental impacts: Dams displace people living nearby, vehicles kill people where roads are located, airports bring noise to host communities, power plants emit noxious chemicals locally, and untreated sewage presents a health hazard for neighbors.

Infrastructure is complicated: It provides inputs for multiple purposes simultaneously—and does so along with multiple noninfrastructure inputs

Infrastructure is intertwined with the fabric of our economic and social lives, and connects us to one another. For example, water reticulation can simultaneously be the energy source for electricity, the provider of drinking water and sanitation to households, the source of fertility for food production, the source of steam for chemicals production, the carrier of heat for homes, and a medium of transport for people and goods. But that water helps produce chemicals, for example, only if there are skilled and healthy workers available, capital to fund the business, and a host of other services to help it operate and sell its products. Infrastructure is useless in isolation.

The fact that so much of our lives depends so intricately on infrastructure services makes their provision very important both economically and politically—but also intrinsically hard to value. A disruption to water or energy supply, or a breakdown in transport or telecommunication services, can have incalculable economic, environmental, and social reverberations. These disruptions can be very expensive to prevent. Correspondingly, reliable provision of those services can have benefits well beyond the revenues accruing to the provider of those services; but do we know what those benefits are worth?

Knowing that infrastructure per se is important is very easy; measuring the precise importance of a particular piece of infrastructure is very difficult. Our world would be unimaginable without electricity, but that doesn't mean it's the highest priority for every village. Choices are all the more complex when programs of infrastructure are involved. Infrastructure priorities are hard to measure and choices hard to make. But choices do need to be made about infrastructure, so we need to understand what impacts it has, how the impacts are channeled, and what they depend on.

Connecting growth, poverty reduction, and investment through infrastructure

This study is about the connecting role of infrastructure. We can think of this in a number of ways. Here we start with the connecting role that infrastructure plays in a series of mutually reinforcing relationships that link growth and poverty reduction—a subject on which the development world has come to broad consensus.[2]

In the first place, infrastructure provides people with services they need and want. Water and sanitation; power for heat, cooking, and light; telephones and computer access; and transport all make immeasurable differences in people's lives. The absence of some of the most basic infrastructure services is an important dimension of what we often mean when we talk about poverty.

Infrastructure also has an impact on the activities through which people earn their livings. It contributes to the health and education that people need to fill jobs, or create them. But infrastructure is also an intermediate input into production. Without power and water, all but the most basic production processes would grind to a halt. Infrastructure raises the productivity of factors of production—by generating the power that allows factories to mechanize, by allowing workers to get to work quicker, or by providing the networks through which information can pass electronically. Infrastructure connects goods to markets, workers to industry, people to services, the poor in rural areas to urban growth poles. Infrastructure lowers costs, enlarges markets, and facilitates trade.

In sum, infrastructure impacts on poverty in two ways: First, it supports the processes of growth on which much poverty reduction depends; and second it helps the poor access basic services that can improve their lives and income opportunities. And at its best,

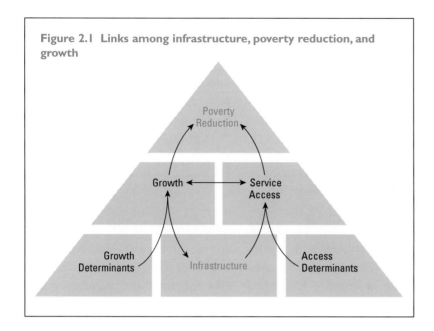

Figure 2.1 Links among infrastructure, poverty reduction, and growth

infrastructure can draw poverty reduction, service provision, and growth into a reinforcing cycle: More growth enables providers to expand services, while enabling users to afford these services. Further service provision encourages more growth. And stronger growth and better access to services both lead to greater impacts on poverty reduction (Figure 2.1).

What of the empirical literature on the impacts of infrastructure on both growth and poverty reduction? Of 102 studies conducted over the last 15 years into the impact of infrastructure on growth and productivity, a majority find positive impacts. In the case of developing countries, all studies show positive impacts (See Table 2.1, and Briceno, Estache and Shafik (2004) for more details). Using cross-country data, a number of studies have confirmed the significant impact on output of telecommunications and roads in particular (for example, Röller and Waverman 2001; Demetriades and Mamuneas 2000; Canning 1999 and Fernald 1999). Using a related approach, one analysis (Canning and Bennathan 2000) found that, in developing countries, rates of return to infrastructure are higher than for overall capital investment, while in industrial countries returns equalized. This implies that developing countries have underinvested in infrastructure (particularly in roads in middle-income countries and electricity in poor countries).[3]

Table 2.1 Distribution of study findings on impact of infrastructure investment on productivity or growth

Area studied	Number of studies	Percentage showing a positive effect	Percentage showing no significant effect	Percentage showing a negative effect
Multiple countries	30	40	50	10
United States	41	41	54	5
Spain	19	74	26	0
Developing countries	12	100	0	0
Total/average	102	53	42	5

Source: de la Fuente and Estache 2004.

Other studies found that public expenditure on transport and communications significantly raises economic growth (for example, Easterly and Rebelo 1993; Miller and Tsoukis 2001), although one study found a negative relationship between the share of infrastructure spending in total public expenditure and economic growth (Devarajan, Swaroop, and Zhou 1996).

The specific impact of infrastructure on welfare, especially of the poor, has been studied in a number of ways, and departs from how one defines poverty. The narrowest poverty definitions focus on incomes and livelihoods, measured, for instance, by the "dollar a day" poverty line. In terms of this approach, the impact of infrastructure on poverty is measured through the degree to which infrastructure increases the real incomes of the poor (for instance, by reducing the costs faced by the poor for services they use); the degree to which infrastructure opens up employment opportunities; and the degree to which infrastructure enhances the productive assets on which the poor depend (for instance, when access roads increase the value of land owned by the poor).

But poverty can be defined more broadly, reflecting some of the key dimensions identified in the MDGs (See Box 2.2). Here, research into the impact of infrastructure on poverty has examined the extent to which infrastructure improves access to education and health services (transport, communications, and power infrastructure are likely to play roles here) as well as the impact of improved water and sanitation services on health.

And perhaps the widest definition of poverty focuses on enhancing social inclusion, human capabilities, and freedoms. Such approaches might focus on the impact that transport and communications infrastructure have in improving people's ability to engage in collective

Box 2.2 Infrastructure and the Millennium Development Goals

The Millennium Development Goals (MDGs)—the international community's agreement on the goals for reducing poverty—include eight objectives to be achieved by 2015. The goals are as follows:

1. **To eradicate extreme poverty and hunger—**

   Halve the proportion of people living on less than $1 a day.

   Halve the proportion of people who suffer from hunger.

2. **To achieve universal primary education—**

   Ensure that boys and girls alike complete primary schooling.

3. **To promote gender equality and empower women—**

   Eliminate gender disparity at all levels of education.

4. **To reduce child mortality—**

   Reduce by two-thirds the under-five mortality rate.

5. **To improve maternal health—**

   Reduce by three-quarters the maternal mortality ratio.

6. **To combat HIV/AIDS, malaria, and other diseases—**

   Reverse the spread of HIV/AIDS.

7. **To ensure environmental sustainability—**

   Integrate sustainable development into country policies and reverse loss of environmental resources.

   Halve the proportion of people without access to portable water.

   Significantly improve the lives of at least 100 million slum dwellers.

8. **To develop a global partnership for development—**

   Raise official development assistance.

   Expand market access.

How does infrastructure relate to the MDGs, and how is this relationship addressed in this study?

Poverty and infrastructure are at the core of the concept of inclusive development around which this report is written. In this chapter we look at poverty from three angles, and consider how infrastructure in each of the sectors makes an impact. We look not only at income poverty (MDG 1), but also the impacts of infrastructure on education, health, and the environment (with impacts on MDGs 2, 4, 5, 6 and 7).

Some of the channels through which impacts are felt are not as obvious as might be expected. It may seem intuitive that the ability of people to earn a living is increased when transport, information, power, and water are readily available. But infrastructure has some less obvious impacts—one study we

(Continued on the next page)

Box 2.2 (Continued)

refer to, for instance, examines the impact of transport and electricity on education. The impact of health services may be similarly affected by the ability of the poor to access facilities. A road, or a telephone call, can make an enormous difference.

Poor access to water and sanitation is an important part of the discussion about poverty, and this is addressed in the seventh MDG (environmental sustainability). But the role of infrastructure in the environment is much wider than this. In Chapter 1, we focus on the challenges of mainstreaming environmental issues, although the environmental theme cuts across this study.

Finally, the role of infrastructure in creating livable cities and providing service to slum dwellers is a theme of Chapter 1 and is included in our discussion of urban management in Chapter 3.

activities, access wider sources of information and opportunity, or make time for both economic and noneconomic purposes (particularly for women in cases where they bear principal responsibility for water and energy provision for the household).

Empirical analysis sheds some light on the magnitude of infrastructure impacts on welfare, defined in these ways. Some studies show that water and sanitation access explains a substantial portion of the difference in infant and child mortality rates experienced by rich and poor, that better transportation increases school attendance, and that electricity access allows more study time (see Leipziger, Fay, Wodon and Yepes 2003). Another study (Calderon and Serven 2004) found that infrastructure quantity and quality—particularly water and sanitation—have a strong positive impact on income equality, as well as on economic growth. And a further study showed that enhanced access to roads and sanitation has been an important determinant in reducing disparities between the poorer and richer regions of Argentina and Brazil (Estache and Fay 1995). Studies of rural roads have shown they raise the productivity and value of land for poor farmers (for example, Jacoby 2000).

Rural roads have been found to have a substantial positive impact on overall poverty reduction in a number of other studies, but there are some interesting nuances. One found that rural roads were the form of public expenditure that reduced poverty most effectively in India (Fan 2003). For China, the same study found that they were the most effective form of public expenditure on infrastructure, but that expenditure on education and agricultural research and development was a more effective means of reducing poverty. A study of rural roads in the Philippines (Balisacan and Pernia 2002) found access to these roads is important for poverty reduction, and that the impact is increased if the roads are coupled with education expenditure. By contrast, this study found that the very poorest households lacked the minimal income and complementary facilities necessary to benefit from access to electricity.

Table 2.2 spells out some of the impact of infrastructure on poverty in more detail. Although precisely how any set of infrastructure undertakings would affect poverty depends very much on country context (Box 2.3). Most important the literature emphasizes that infrastructure is effective only when combined with other interventions.

None of this implies, however, that everyone benefits from investments in infrastructure, nor even that they benefit equally. While broadbased impacts on poverty may often be positive, the local socioeconomic

Table 2.2 Potential positive impacts of infrastructure services on the poor

Sector	Direct impact on poor	Indirect impacts on poor
Electricity	Mainly for lighting, TV, radio at low levels of income. Heating, cooking, appliances for self-employment at higher levels of income	Reduced energy costs for enterprises encouraging employment creation across wide range of activities. Improved health and other services (refrigeration, lighting, and so on). Improves ICT access
Piped Gas	Limited impact at low-income levels. Heating, cooking at higher levels of income	Reduced energy costs for enterprises encouraging employment creation (limited range of activities)
Roads	Access to employment and markets. Access to services (health, education)	Reduced transport costs and improved market access for enterprises and service providers, lowering costs of serving remote communities
Railways	Limited	Reduced costs and improved market access for enterprises
Urban Mass Transit	Access to employment opportunities	Employment creation from more efficient labor markets
Ports	Limited	Reduced transport costs for enterprises encouraging employment creation (for example, bulk commodities like agriculture)
Airports	Limited	Reduced transport costs for enterprises encouraging employment creation (high-value, low-bulk commodities and services)
Information and Communications Technology (ICT)	Better communication access, aiding migration, information on opportunities, access to knowledge, and potential engagement in wider communities	Employment creation through improved knowledge of markets, reduced management supervision costs, access to wider knowledge base
Water Supply	Improved health outcomes; time savings; lower costs	Limited
Sanitation	Improved health outcomes	Improved health outcomes (for example, reduced pollution by nonpoor households and others)

Source: Jones 2004a.

> **Box 2.3 The importance of infrastructure in particular poverty reduction programs varies**
>
> While infrastructure has an important part to play in addressing poverty, the nature of its role may vary depending on the nature of poverty in a particular setting.
>
> Where there is mass poverty, affecting large proportions of the population throughout a country, infrastructure investment may be an important part of a broader strategy for poverty reduction and economic growth, although precise priorities will vary depending on the context.
>
> Where poverty is highly location-specific (for instance, in remote highland areas) and clearly linked to geographic remoteness or poor access to key services (for instance, water supply and sanitation in urban slums), a targeted strategy of improving infrastructure provision to areas of high poverty concentration may be the single most important element of a poverty reduction strategy.
>
> In some cases, however, countries may choose to place significantly less emphasis on infrastructure investment in pursuing poverty reduction. This may be the case, for instance, when poverty affects a relatively limited proportion of the population and depends on factors other than those directly related to geographic remoteness—for example, factors like caste, histories of discrimination against particular ethnic groups, and cultural or other factors that present limited education attainment or employment opportunities for certain groups.
>
> *Source:* Jones 2004a.

impacts from infrastructure development can sometimes be negative, unless deliberately mitigated. For example, hydropower might provide inexpensive electricity to large numbers of consumers, yet displace people living and working in the vicinity of the hydropower dam, or negatively affect their agricultural land or fishing grounds.[4]

At the same time, there may be genuine choices to be made among infrastructure investments that affect aggregate growth and poverty reduction unequally: between investment with strong poverty-related impacts, but limited implications for short-run aggregate growth—for instance, rural water supply—and investments with strong growth focus, but limited poverty reduction impacts.

Institutions often need to make choices covering the trade-offs between the interests of different groups of poor and nonpoor, so that the two groups may share the benefits of infrastructure equitably. Participation of affected groups in decision making is one measure that can help—a theme we pick up in Chapter 4, on accountability and risk management.

Making the links: Infrastructure, trade, and logistics[5]

We can look at how these inclusive development issues play out both regionally, and within a particular country. As we saw in Chapter 1, trade and regional integration have helped distribute the benefits of growth. The role of infrastructure in sustaining this process, in particular that of logistics, is the subject of this section. In our next section, we'll trace some of the links among infrastructure, growth, and poverty reduction through a case study of Vietnam.

Getting the goods to market has been the key to East Asia's prosperity. Trade has been a crucial ingredient in the rapid growth of much of the region, and it is likely to remain so. Sharing in the region's growth, particularly for the poorest in the region, will depend heavily on countries' ability to carry out infrastructure investments and improve the efficiency of delivery of infrastructure services, in support of regional trade opportunities.

For some countries of East Asia—in particular, land-locked Lao PDR and Mongolia—effective regional infrastructure cooperation will be crucial. Box 2.4 sets out how the participation of Lao PDR in the GMS has enabled it to take advantage of its geographic location to pursue its development objectives through greater regional integration.

The case for regional infrastructure coordination is broader than just trade alone. Regional infrastructure coordination can play an important role in lowering infrastructure costs. It has been estimated, for example, that a full-trade energy scenario within the GMS would save the member states more than $10 billion over a 20-year period when compared with the other extreme of individual national self-sufficiency (Crousillat 1998). Interconnection could also significantly reduce future project-related environmental impacts throughout the subregion.

Superior logistics and low transport costs have been an important aspect of East Asia's outward-oriented growth. This is particularly so in the region's most impressive long-term performers—Hong Kong (China), Japan, Korea, Singapore and Taiwan (China)—but also in a number of developing countries—China, Malaysia, the Philippines, and Thailand (Figure 2.2).

Until recently, East Asia has been largely competitive (although performance varies across countries—see Box 2.5). Right now, however,

Box 2.4 Inclusive development on a regional scale: Opportunities for landlocked Lao PDR

Lao PDR is a land-locked country bordered by Thailand, Cambodia, Vietnam, China, and Myanmar. It is one of the poorest and least developed countries in the region, with per capita income estimated at US$320 in 1998. Despite growth achieved in the last decade, the social indicators of Lao PDR are among the worst in the region. There are few economic opportunities in Lao PDR with its sparse population to address development challenges.

The membership of Lao PDR in the GMS—which brings together five other neighboring partners (Cambodia, Myanmar, Thailand, Vietnam, and China's Yunnan Province)—has enabled it to take advantage of its geographic location to pursue its development objectives through greater regional integration.

Over the 12 years of its existence, the GMS has steadily evolved from a disparate collection of wary neighbors into a highly effective but informal collaboration that can now point to numerous successful cross-border infrastructure investments.

GMS members have identified nine priority sectors: transport, telecommunications, energy, tourism, human resources development, environment, agriculture, trade, and investment.

To focus on regional integration through infrastructure, individual subregional forums have been established for electric power, telecommunications, and transport.

One of the concepts favored by the GMS is that of the development of economic corridors, focusing on road investments to improve access, institutional and policy changes for trade facilitation, and transit policies to reduce logistic costs.

Traversing the subregion and reflecting primary transport routings, five economic corridors (two north-south, one east-west, and two southern) have been identified; several road investments are under way within these corridors, while feasibility studies are addressing prospective railway improvements. Plans for regional power interconnections and a telecommunications backbone have also been drawn.

These investments promote inclusive development for large remote areas of land-locked countries, such as Lao PDR and parts of China.

Among these undertakings is the Northern Economic Corridor project, which links Thailand and China through a short road link via northern and remote parts of Lao PDR.

In addition to hard infrastructure investments required to create a trade and transit corridor, the project included components that will benefit local communities along the road. A social action plan comprising community roads, small water and sanitation schemes, education and HIV/AIDS awareness programs, and local capacity building programs were integral parts of the project design. These components were planned in a participatory process involving large numbers of ethnic minority groups.

The project was funded through resources from two primary beneficiaries (Thailand and China) with catalytic support from multilaterals.

(Continued on the next page)

Box 2.4 (Continued)

    The multilateral role was three-fold: First, to help mobilize resources; second, to assist in project design to ensure not only greater regional connectivity, but also that isolated regions like Lao PDR would be included; and third, to promote pricing policies that would maintain newly created assets without undue fiscal burden on participating countries.

    A number of similar projects that seek to coordinate regional infrastructure are under way in the region. The development challenge is to ensure that they're able to replicate, and scale up, some of the features that are proving so important to Lao PDR. The challenge, in short, is to design infrastructure that truly promotes inclusive development on a regional scale.

Source: ADB 2002.

Figure 2.2 In the most open economies of the region, logistics costs are typically much lower

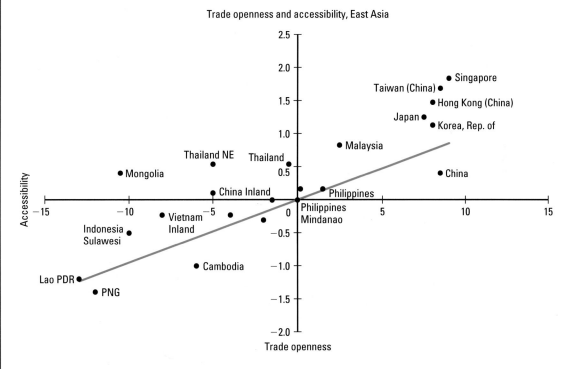

Trade openness and accessibility, East Asia

Source: Carruthers, Bajpai, and Hummels 2003.
Note: The measures of trade openness are based on those indicated in the *Global Competitiveness Report,* 2001–02 (World Economic Forum 2002). Values for countries not included in the *Global Competitiveness Report* have been added using World Bank assessment, in keeping with those of the World Economic Forum. All values have been normalized for the countries of East Asia. The measure of accessibility are based on the cost of transporting a standard TEU (twenty foot equivalent units) from the metropolitan region of the largest port to Hamburg. For inland regions, the land transport cost to the metropolitan region has been added. PNG = Papua New Guinea.

Box 2.5 East Asia's logistics challenge—country differences

East Asian countries differ in their logistics capabilities and their logistics challenges. One logistics study attempts to classify them into four groups.

Group 1 includes those that are outward orientated and highly accessible, that is, have low transportation costs and superior logistics. These include Singapore, Hong Kong (China), Korea, and Taiwan (China).

And then we have the developing countries that approach the Group 1 model to varying degrees.

Group 2 includes those countries that have open trade but face serious logistics challenges to inclusive development (Thailand, the Philippines, Malaysia, China, and Indonesia). In these countries, policies and institutions to encourage multimodal transport are at an early stage of development. Transport inefficiencies persist in some parts of these countries, particularly in rural areas. Penetration of third-party suppliers of logistics services (3PL) is generally low.

Group 3 includes the less open but accessible countries (Cambodia and Vietnam), while *Group 4* includes the land-locked and island countries (for example, Mongolia, Lao PDR, and Pacific island states).

The countries in Group 3 and Group 4 are either former socialist economies or are small island states dependent on a small number of commodities and tourism. History or geography largely explain the small role of international trade in their economies, although for some the situation is changing rapidly (for example, Vietnam).

In Group 3 and 4, countries lack adequate transport infrastructure. Roads are frequently closed or impose high vehicle operating costs, customs clearance is slow, border delays can be long, ports are often expensive and inefficient, and intermodal transport is generally poorly integrated. Government transport policies lack consistency and predictability, and policy coordination among different agencies and tiers of government is generally poor. Logistics services are rudimentary.

Source: Carruthers, Bajpai, and Hummels 2003.

the efficiency of East Asia's logistics is falling behind, with costs of transportation representing a high proportion of the final price of goods.

Higher logistics costs in East Asia stem from a number of factors: inadequate transport infrastructure, underdeveloped logistics and transport services, and bureaucratic (and sometimes corrupt) import and export procedures. Much of the problem is behind the border, and indeed beyond the port. The cost of internal access to ports is greater than the costs associated with the ports themselves or with maritime transport.[6] This has limited the spread of the benefits of trade-induced growth to areas beyond those adjacent to ports and has created congestion near the ports.[7] Reducing logistics costs is therefore crucial to inclusive development.

Significant benefits are likely to arise from improved logistics. Imported goods would become cheaper to inland consumers, raising real disposable income. A greater variety of goods would become competitive, raising living standards through increasing choice. Expanded input variety in manufacturing can also increase productivity. For exports, ex-factory or ex-farm prices would increase, as will the associated land values and wages. Exports of a wider range of products to a wider range of markets would become possible.[8] Increasingly larger areas of inland East Asia would be connected to international markets (and coastal domestic markets also).

Improvements in logistics would also reduce a number of risks to individuals, firms, and the economy as a whole, in a number of ways. For example, the product diversification just mentioned protects incomes against volatile prices for specific commodities. Similar arguments apply to market diversification. So too, in the case of agricultural commodities, efficient logistics allows surplus regions to sell to deficit regions, dampening price and income fluctuations. This is particularly important in countries where agriculture constitutes a large share of GDP and rural poverty is high (for example, Lao PDR, Cambodia, and Vietnam). Finally, improved logistics can also reduce uncertainty about delivery schedules, thus allowing producers and retailers to lower inventory levels, which they hold as insurance against late delivery. This, in turn, could lead to lower production costs.[9]

And countries that have good logistics are more able to participate in global production chains. In East Asia, this is particularly important for the electronics and automotive industries (see Figure 2.3 on Japanese auto manufacturing), in which the production process can include a number of countries. Participation in global production chains can help enhance the value of exports—an especially important development for those countries in which manufacturers are low skilled and low wage.

East Asia therefore faces a number of logistics challenges. As countries move progressively into more complex and higher-value manufacturing, and greater integration into global production chains, logistics requirements become more sophisticated. A greater premium is placed on short transit times, certainty of delivery schedules, careful handling of goods, certification, and standardization of product quality, and security from theft. The quality of freight-forwarding, warehousing, storage, packaging, and trucking services becomes more important, as does e-business use and the associated telecommunications infrastructure. Logistics

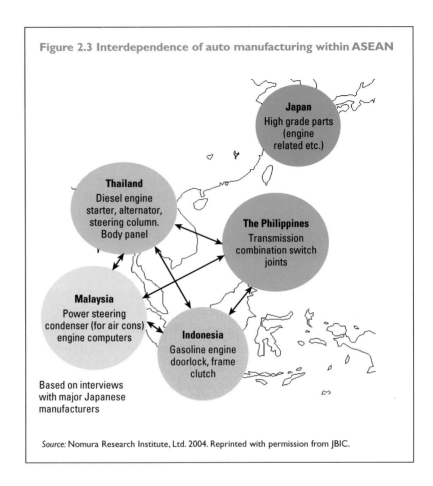

Figure 2.3 Interdependence of auto manufacturing within ASEAN

Japan
High grade parts
(engine
related etc.)

Thailand
Diesel engine
starter, alternator,
steering column.
Body panel

The Philippines
Transmission
combination switch
joints

Malaysia
Power steering
condenser (for air cons)
engine computers

Indonesia
Gasoline engine
doorlock, frame
clutch

Based on interviews
with major Japanese
manufacturers

Source: Nomura Research Institute, Ltd. 2004. Reprinted with permission from JBIC.

software issues are often as important as transport infrastructure hardware.

Rapid growth in containerized shipping represents a revolutionary technological change, but presents perhaps the major logistics challenge in East Asia. Regional ports are increasing their efficiency in container handling, but they are running out of berth space. Between 1980 and 2000, the capacity of the container fleet on East Asian routes increased by 20 percent a year, but the capacity of container berths increased by only 8 percent a year. However, expanding capacity requires greater land use, and municipalities are finding it increasingly difficult to accommodate the additional space requirements and the associated congestion in adjacent areas.

The solutions are multiple. In some cases, new ports can be built, or feeder ports currently serving hub ports can expand their direct services instead. In other cases, nonmaritime port activities (mostly value-added production and packaging services) can be moved closer to the industries they serve, and rail links can be built from those industries to the port to avoid road congestion.

In East Asia, containers are often used only for maritime transport, and are stuffed and unstuffed in the ports. But encouraging door to door movement of containers using multimodal transport could spread trade benefits across even larger areas. Here, remedial measures include adapting the rail and road vehicle fleet to carry loaded containers; contracting out logistics to 3PL,[10] regulatory reform to allow single trade documentation for all transport modes and clearance of containers away from port locations; effective communications systems for freight forwarders; and improved coordination among agencies responsible for different modes of transport.

Issues of coordination—the subject of our next chapter—feature prominently in the broader measures required to address East Asia's logistics challenge, in particular, coordination across national boundaries and in urban management.

Cross-border facilitation would yield major efficiency gains in East Asia (although less so for countries that are already both highly accessible and highly open—see Box 2.6). This requires coordination among countries and could be achieved through harmonization and simplification of customs procedures, information-sharing, customs modernization, establishment of transparent transit rules, and postentry compliance audit.[11] For all countries, streamlining and coordinating security procedures in the post-9/11 environment would enhance trade facilitation.

Additionally, urban governments need to implement land use policies for the location of logistics infrastructure and ports that internalize externalities.[12] This is not easy. Firms cluster together because it is to their mutual advantage. The positive productivity externalities they experience include the stimulus to innovation, information exchange, access to inputs, and specialized skills—the agglomeration economies. These become more important as production moves up the value-added chain, and they are a significant part of the high-growth story in East Asia. But, of course, firms do not take into account the effect their own move has on overall congestion and pollution—the negative externalities—that can ultimately choke growth and the urban environment. And so the urban management policy challenge is to trade off the positive and

Box 2.6 Integration of ports and land transport networks in Korea

Korea has one of East Asia's most developed land access networks to its ports, making use of road and rail links to the ports of Pusan and Kwangyang, the latter alongside a major steel mill and industrial complex and now in its second stage of development with a potential capacity of 2.4 million TEU (twenty foot equivalent unit, size of a standard container). Both Pusan and Kwangyang have been planned in conjunction with major road and rail links to Korea's major manufacturing regions. Pusan in particular has adopted a strategy of encouraging people to live and work in the city and, for this reason, has developed a new port area away from the downtown area to allow the original port area to be redeveloped for residential and commercial use. This has reduced traffic congestion and air pollution, and improved logistics efficiency has made the new port easier to reach from the city's industrial areas and the rest of Korea.

The Yangsan inland container terminal has been constructed to relieve port-generated traffic congestion and environmental problems resulting from the massive transport movements the port generates. Another inland container terminal (ICD) is under development in the center of the Korean peninsula to serve the growing industrial zones on the west coast and in the central region of the country. Together with the ports, the ICDs are part of a logistics system based on an advanced electronic data interchange (EDI) and information service. In this way, Korea will be able to maintain the competitiveness of its industrial base, while moving its manufacturing away from the existing congested urban areas and spreading its benefits more widely throughout the country.

Source: Carruthers, Bajpai, and Hummels 2003.

negative externalities for urban areas, and to do so in coordination with national or regional strategies for inclusiveness.

Focus on Vietnam: Infrastructure and inclusive development

In the last section, we looked at the connecting role that infrastructure plays across the region, enlarging markets and facilitating trade. In this section, we drill down a little further into the role of infrastructure in fostering inclusive development in one of the region's best performers: Vietnam.

Over the last decade, Vietnam has grown at an annual average rate of 7.6 percent, placing it among the fastest growing countries in the world. Economic development has also been remarkably pro-poor, lifting

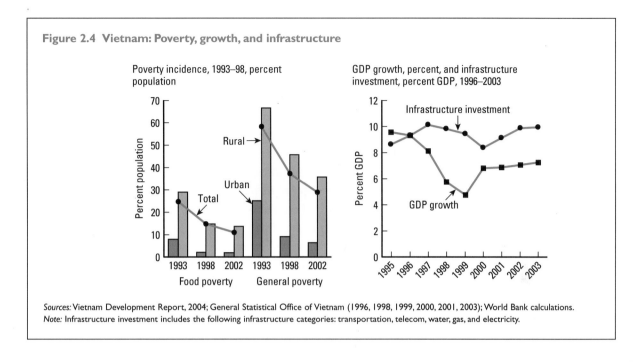

Figure 2.4 Vietnam: Poverty, growth, and infrastructure

Sources: Vietnam Development Report, 2004; General Statistical Office of Vietnam (1996, 1998, 1999, 2000, 2001, 2003); World Bank calculations.
Note: Infrastructure investment includes the following infrastructure categories: transportation, telecom, water, gas, and electricity.

around 20 million people out of poverty in less than a decade.[13] In fact, Vietnam is one of the best performers in East Asia in terms of elasticity of poverty to growth (4 out of 23 in an analysis of middle- and low-income countries), with one extra percentage point of GDP growth leading to a decline in the poverty rate by slightly more than 1 percent.[14]

Infrastructure and investment have been an important part of this story, complementing the country's many targeted poverty reduction initiatives.[15] Approximately one-third of GDP has been directed into capital investment (44 percent of government investment has been in infrastructure, both national and local). Infrastructure investment has risen as a percentage of GDP, to 10 percent in 2003, as GDP itself continued to rise significantly (Figure 2.4).

Since 1993, continuous economic growth, fueled in part by infrastructure investment, has been the main engine for poverty reduction, complemented by targeted poverty reduction programs. The mutually reinforcing relationships set out in Figure 2.1 are deeply embedded in the processes of inclusive development that characterize Vietnam's recent development experience. Let's look at some of the evidence.

Infrastructure has affected poverty in Vietnam through large-scale investments and through smaller-scale rural infrastructure. On the large scale, trunk infrastructure has played a critical role in creating links among growth centers and their surrounding rural areas. It has connected remote areas with power grids, trunk roads with feeder roads, and, in the process, generated opportunities for business and promoted income diversification and off-farm employment.[16]

One systematic exercise to assess the impact of large infrastructure investment on poverty reduction in Vietnam finds that investments in water and sanitation and transport, in particular, have a large positive impact on poverty reduction at the provincial level. It suggests that public investments in transport and in water and sanitation are highly progressive, lifting more people out of poverty in Vietnam's poorest provinces (Larsen, Lan, and Rama 2004)

Among the country's most important large-scale infrastructure undertakings is the improvement of National Highway No. 5, which links Ha Noi, the national capital, and Hai Phong in the Red River Delta Region. Together, these two cities comprise northern Vietnam's major growth center. With the improvement of National Highway No. 5 and the expansion of Hai Phong Port, the transport corridor has enhanced the access of Ha Noi to global markets by improving land and sea transport. Foreign direct investment (FDI) to major industrial zones has increased significantly, particularly since 2000, driving industrial and export growth in the north.

An interview survey with more than 70 FDI firm managers suggests that nearly 90 percent of new investments would not have been realized without the improvement of National Highway No. 5 and the Hai Phong port. The survey indicates that managers were attracted by cost reduction in transporting imported inputs, time savings in the delivery of raw materials and final products, and improved coordination of production and sales schedules.

Most of the provinces in the Ha Noi-Hai Phong corridor achieved faster growth in per capita income and reduction in the number of poor households compared with the average for the Red River Delta and the whole country (Map 2.1).

And growth has now spread to neighboring areas, particularly Hung Yen and Hai Duong provinces (located between the two economic hubs), with similar transformation of the rural economy. Rural households have diversified their agricultural production (from rice to fishery and poultry) and have been increasingly engaged in new business opportunities. More convenient transportation has also spurred demand for tourism in

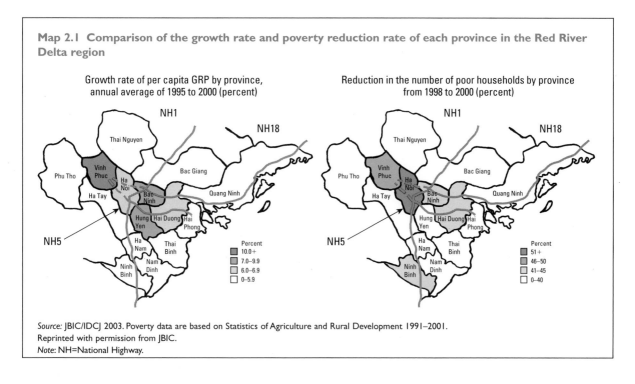

Map 2.1 Comparison of the growth rate and poverty reduction rate of each province in the Red River Delta region

Growth rate of per capita GRP by province, annual average of 1995 to 2000 (percent)

Reduction in the number of poor households by province from 1998 to 2000 (percent)

Source: JBIC/IDCJ 2003. Poverty data are based on Statistics of Agriculture and Rural Development 1991–2001. Reprinted with permission from JBIC.

Note: NH=National Highway.

Ha Long Bay, in effect, extending the corridor into a Ha Noi-Hai Phong-Ha Long development triangle.

But Vietnam has also concentrated on the small scale. Enormous investments have been made in rural roads—reducing the number of communes lacking all-season road access to district centers by more than 50 percent—with significant effects on poverty (World Bank estimates).

One study into these rural road investments suggests that the establishment of a new road in a village raised the per capita income of households by 30 percent between 1993 and 1998, after controlling for other factors, such as household size and education (Deolalikar 2001). Moreover, the spatial location of roads increased the household probability of moving out of poverty by 68 percent over the same period of time. It showed that rural roads expanded school enrollment of children at all levels and improved the utilization of public health services. And the spatial and economic benefits of rural roads were significantly larger in poorer provinces than in the richer ones.

Another study of the marginal returns in agricultural growth and poverty reduction to various kinds of government spending suggests that

Box 2.7 Inclusive development: Transport access for the disabled

Including individuals with disabilities is an important factor to consider during the planning and design phase of infrastructure projects. Equally important is rectifying existing infrastructure deficiencies, which may hamper the quality of life of disabled persons by denying them the ability to effectively use their surrounding environment.

One important means of inclusiveness is to address public transport design to enhance access and safety. Four major disability groups should be considered:

- Orthopedic: ambulant and nonambulant (wheelchair users)
- Sensory: visually impaired and hearing impaired
- Cognitive: mental, developmental, and learning disabilities
- Multiple: combination of any or all of the above

Individuals with orthopedic disabilities are generally those with locomotive disabilities that affect mobility. Wheelchair users face a particular challenge in developing countries—the spatial need of wheelchair users often exceeds that of people with other types of disabilities, and the need for provision of ramps, curb-cuts, and elevators is critical. Individuals with sensory impairments need visual signs and tactile clues, such as route finders, and adequate signage must be provided to increase directional clarity for the hearing impaired. Disabled individuals who are cognitively challenged and those with multiple disabilities need a combination of these provisions.

Some mass transit systems developed recently in the East Asia region do include full accessibility features—sometimes as the result of campaigns by disability advocacy groups during the project planning stage. The new Bangkok underground system, Malaysia's PUTRA mass transit system, and Beijing's new subway and light rail system under development include barrier-free components in their design.

Manila is betting on the bus rapid transport (BRT) system to dramatically improve the accessibility of persons with disabilities. The BRT uses buses linked by threes or fours with dedicated corridors running along a 22-mile highway that surrounds the city. These buses have low floors for ease of entry and exit, tend to move at a uniform speed, and stop only at designated stations. BRT systems are currently operating in various Asian cities, including Jakarta and Shijiazhuang, with a system under construction in Beijing, and in the planning stage in Shanghai, Bangkok, Chengdu, and Chongqing.

Whenever new infrastructure is constructed or new vehicles are bought, access features that serve most passengers who are considered disabled can be incorporated at relatively low cost. For example, elevator installation at 18 stations of the Bangkok underground system cost approximately 46 million baht (about $1.1 million)—out of a total of 105 billion baht (about $2.6 billion) in construction costs for the whole system—or roughly 0.0004 percent of total costs. However, retrofitting an existing system is much more expensive. The cost of installing just one elevator in an existing New York City subway station is approximately $2 million.

(Continued on the next page)

Box 2.7 (Continued)

Consequently, city planners need to incorporate access provisions in their planning at the earliest stages. Development banks can be helpful by adopting policies for universal and inclusive design for built environments and public transport in infrastructure projects they finance. These institutions can also provide specialist expertise.

Finally, one critical consideration concerning disability issues and infrastructure in East Asia is the emergence of an aging society. Disabilities—or degrees of impairment—increase with age, even in seemingly healthy individuals. Infrastructure planners have time now to plan for this demographic shift and to adequately provide enabling environments for all members of society.

Source: Takamine 2004.

the payoff of investment in roads is second only to that of investment in agricultural research. Returns to road investment proved even higher than those in education (Fan, Huong, and Long 2004).[17]

But as important as these achievements have been, Vietnam is in no position to rest on its laurels. Access to basic infrastructure services has not been equal, and the degree of this inequality is increasing. The percentage of the population in the lowest-income quintile with access to clean water is 22.7 percent, less than half the national average. It is also striking that only 2 percent of the population in the lowest-income quintile has access to hygienic latrines, compared with 70 percent for the top quintile of the population (Vietnam Development Report 2004).

Increasing inequality, particularly between urban and rural areas, raises new infrastructure challenges.[18] On the one hand, infrastructure can be used to continue to reach into those isolated regions whose inhabitants are cut off from services and economic participation. But rapid urbanization is also placing a significant strain on urban infrastructure and the capacity of urban managers to keep up with demand. New pockets of poverty are emerging in peri-urban settlements.

As the complexities of the infrastructure challenges multiply, and the scale of the risks increases, Vietnam will be increasingly unable to sustain the inefficiencies that characterize its coordination and delivery of infrastructure and infrastructure services.

3

Coordination

What is coordination?

Coordination is about the state's ability to generate strategic vision and its ability to turn that vision into reality. It requires making trade-offs among multiple objectives, particularly when multiple actors are involved. Who makes those trade-offs, and how leadership and participation are balanced in that process, are of considerable importance.

Infrastructure is hard to do

It's easy to build infrastructure. But building the infrastructure that delivers the right services to the right people at the right cost is difficult. So the quality of the institutions managing that delivery process is crucial.

The peculiarities of infrastructure discussed in Chapter 2 have major implications for institutional needs. The lumpiness and capital intensity, the long gestation periods, and the use- and space-specificity all imply that specialized agencies and local autonomy are needed for infrastructure. The risks, the complexity, the longevity of the assets, and infrastructure's intensely political nature all speak for centralized coordination and planning. In short, managing infrastructure is about balancing politics and economics, centralization and decentralization, leadership and participation, the big picture and the specifics.

And the East Asian experience demonstrates that the big picture is at least as important as the quality of a specific infrastructure ministry or service provider. What matters most is strategic vision. We need to look at how infrastructure fits with broader development strategy and political context, how that strategy gets formulated, and how it connects through service delivery to outcomes. This is what we call "coordination."

In this chapter, we look at the issue of coordination in three ways. We start with six examples of the region's most advanced economies, as well as the most advanced developing country case—Malaysia. We call these the "high-flying geese." The experiences of these economies give us useful illustrations of one broadly successful East Asian model of coordination. These examples are also proving useful to a number of the developing countries in the region, as they struggle with coordination in their own contexts.

From here, we turn our attention to coordination issues proving most important for the developing countries in the region. We look at three issues. We first consider the challenge that governments face in establishing the right level of infrastructure spending. Often, in times of economic expansion, poor coordination among the agencies responsible for investment and financing leads to too much or inefficient infrastructure. Other times, especially under conditions of fiscal retrenchment, poor coordination may result in too little space for infrastructure (especially when we consider infrastructure's long-term impact on solvency). We next look at the considerable challenge of coordinating infrastructure through decentralized government structures. And, lastly, we look at the challenge of coordination infrastructure in urban areas.

In the final part of this chapter, we reflect on the quality of coordination in four of the region's developing countries—Indonesia, the Philippines, China, and Thailand. These we refer to as the "geese trying to catch up."

The "high-flying geese" theory of infrastructure

The "high-flying geese" explanation of economic development in East Asia essentially says that the flying geese in the lead (that is, the most successful economies) transmit their success to the geese flying just behind them, and so on down the line. The transmission can be accomplished simply through successful geese demanding the exports of other geese, or by making investments in them. Or it can be accomplished through the strategies and institutions of the successful geese inspiring the other geese.

One could argue that the infrastructure strategies of East Asia's developing countries today were inspired, to some degree, by the approach of five of the region's developed economies in a previous era—Hong Kong (China), Japan, Korea, Singapore, and Taiwan (China)—as well as by one of the more successful developing countries, Malaysia. Of course, in each case, that approach has been heavily adapted to country circumstance, and there have been many other influences, but the original inspiration can still be discerned.

In these six economies, political leaders and senior policy makers played a major role in creating the long-term development vision and the sectoral strategies that flowed from that vision.[1] All of these economies had a strong emphasis on export-led growth, high savings and investment levels (sometimes with an FDI focus), and generally balanced social development. Infrastructure strategies were formulated to help achieve those objectives. These strategies usually enjoyed broad consensus amongst the policy-making elites. Policy enjoyed a high degree of predictability.

In each economy, growth was rapid over a period of decades. Sustained periods of high growth helped create the policy consensus behind the infrastructure investment which supported that growth. Infrastructure investment in these economies was high by international norms, with significant increases in infrastructure stocks across sectors (Figure 3.1). The discipline of needing to remain competitive in export markets, and to continue to attract investment, helped inject efficiency into project choice and service delivery.

Sometimes infrastructure investment anticipated demand, but in general it reacted to constraints as they began to emerge. Taiwan (China)'s large infrastructure program, known as the Ten Major Projects, for example, was a response to the transportation bottlenecks that had become apparent by the late 1960s (Reinfeld 1997).

However, the reactions were often rapid and quite strategic. Overall sector strategies tended to adapt as production structures changed, rather than responses being made only in a piecemeal manner. A number of very bold and large single projects were undertaken with success—such as the Kobe-Nagoya Highway and the Tokyo-Osaka Super Express Railway in Japan, and the Seoul-Pusan Highway in Korea—although inevitably some white elephant projects occurred also.

Each country had strong planning agencies to drive infrastructure development at the central or sectoral level—Korea's Economic Planning Bureau, Singapore's Economic Development Board, Malaysia's central planning agency and policy-making body in the Prime Minister's Office,

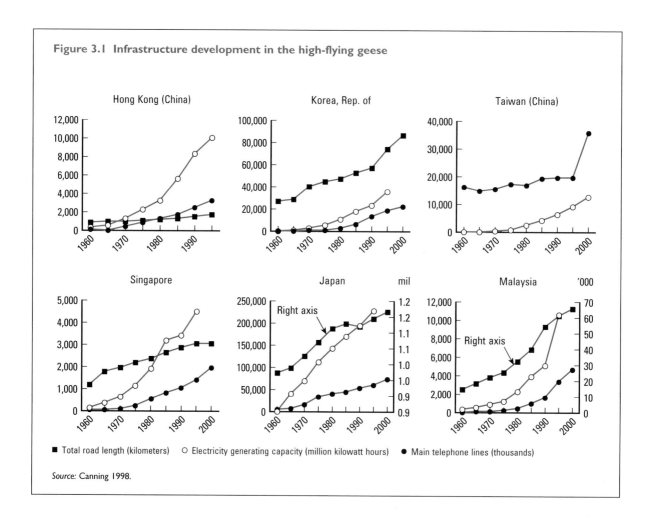

Figure 3.1 Infrastructure development in the high-flying geese

Source: Canning 1998.

and Japan's strong sector ministries and advisory boards. These agencies generally enjoyed considerable political clout. Simultaneously, these agencies were vehicles for political leaders to implement their long-term development vision, major contributors to the creation of that vision, and technocratic restraints on short-term political pressures. The agencies were the focal points for interagency coordination in policy making and implementation.

But much of this did not take place in public view. Individual account-ability tended to be internal to the elite, as long as the broader public were enjoying the fruits of economic growth. In many cases, political life was dominated by one party, which often remained in power for many years.

Infrastructure service delivery in these economies was predominantly the domain of public corporations, often with monopoly status. Oversight by a strong planning agency or more specialized ministries, and a clear incentives framework, appears to have induced better public enterprise performance than seen in most other economies. Cost recovery policies were generally encouraged, and reliance on operational subsidies was limited. For example, Singapore's 1961–64 Development Plan proceeded on the basis that several infrastructure sectors would be self-funding—for example, electricity, water, gas, and certain telecommunications and ports projects (Yuan 1997).

However, service providers were substantial beneficiaries of financing from state-directed domestic financial institutions, which captured high levels of domestic savings. Japan's Fiscal Investment and Loan Program—which mobilized postal savings and social security pensions into infrastructure (and other) investments, and was described as a second national budget—is one of the most prominent of such mechanisms.[2] But similar mechanisms were used extensively across the six economies.

Because these financial mechanisms were often used to lend in line with government sectoral policies, and savings were to some extent locked in by capital controls, infrastructure service providers were effectively in receipt of quasi-fiscal subsidies. The key criteria for success were the degree of risk assessment carried out by financial institutions before lending and the subsequent enforcement of credit discipline.

The model adopted in these six economies delivered impressive infrastructure results, particularly in the relatively early stages of laying the groundwork for sustained economic growth—beginning in the 1950s. However, by the late 1980s and the 1990s, the strains and contradictions in the model were evident. It did not deal well with financial crisis or economic slowdown. Slow growth and tighter financing conditions revealed risks and inefficiencies that were not so apparent until that point. Lending from the financial sector directed by policy makers could become a major public liability, as could a lack of transparency in corporate governance. Strategic approaches could sometimes descend into supply-driven investment, cronyism, and corruption.

The highly top-down approach had restricted the space for civil society participation or decentralized tiers of government. Old models of accountability were increasingly open to question. In the pursuit of growth, environmental considerations had not generally been given strong emphasis (with some exceptions, particularly in Japan), but the public was now demanding a higher quality of life, including a more livable urban environment.

Infrastructure sector restructuring to allow efficiency gains through greater competition or autonomous regulation of monopolies had not been high on the agenda for most economies. Similarly, private participation had usually been confined to greenfield projects, and therefore tended to play a relatively marginal role in improving sector performance (again with some notable exceptions).

As the state's role became more complex, and its objectives more diverse, its ability to squeeze efficiency gains from the existing system of public sector monopolies began to falter. At the same time, continued efficiency gains became all the more important as economies opened up to ever fiercer global competition. In general, greater complexity meant that the state at the center needed to focus more exclusively on the big picture, and delegate more of the details to companies, regulators, local governments, civil society, and the market.

The geese flying behind these economies—particularly China, Indonesia, the Philippines, and Thailand—face the task of adapting the inspiration of the six high-flying geese to how they themselves intend to deal with the future, a future that looks more complex than the past in a number of important ways. We will now consider some of these complexities, before turning to the developing country case studies.

Coordinating infrastructure levels

Infrastructure is important, for reasons we established in Chapters 1 and 2. But infrastructure is only one of many government priorities. And governments face budget constraints. Achieving the right emphasis on infrastructure, for the prevailing conditions, can be difficult. Sometimes, in times of high growth and free fiscal policy, governments may end up spending too much or inefficiently. Other times, in times of fiscal retrenchment, they may spend too little. The first is arguably the case in Vietnam and China. Elements of the latter appear in Thailand, the Philippines, and Indonesia.

One of the reasons that governments may spend too much, or with unacceptably high levels of inefficiency, is because of the separation of investment from financing and difficulties in coordinating policy across these functions. The separation of investment from financing is a common feature of the planning frameworks of many of the countries of the region, with the investment assigned to a ministry of planning and investment, and finance to a finance ministry. Frequently, the institutional separation of planning and financing is given force through a dual budgeting system, with responsibility for investment vested with the planning ministry, and recurrent expenditure assigned to the finance ministry.

The separation of planning and financing functions is not without advantages. Most importantly, it creates space to establish long-term development objectives. It can allow policy makers to think beyond the constraints of a short-term fiscal horizon to consider the big picture.[3]

But as the scope and complexity of East Asia's development challenges have increased, the ability of governments to plan and efficiently resource infrastructure investments has not kept pace. In many countries, this has resulted in unsustainable, delayed, or incomplete projects, and ultimately financial and fiscal stress.

The separation between planning and financing in a dual budgeting system is also a frequent cause of inadequate expenditure on operations and maintenance. This arises both as a result of the bias toward new investment that the system engenders and the division of responsibilities that are better kept together.

In our discussion of China further on in this chapter, we look at how this separation, in particular the financing of local government infrastructure investment, is cause for concern. Box 3.1 takes up this story in the context of Vietnam's roads sector, in which coordination weaknesses within the public finance management system has exposed the government, and the banking and construction sectors, to liabilities that the government now must absorb.

In times of fiscal retrenchment—as is the case in a number of countries in the region following the financial crisis of the late 1990s—a different coordination challenge may arise with respect to the level of infrastructure expenditure.[4] This entails coordination among agencies responsible for fiscal policy and those responsible for infrastructure planning, as well as among those responsible for planning and finance, with sector ministries intent on driving through infrastructure reform.

If—in times of economic downturn—a government is preoccupied with increasing liquidity, it will tend to cut any large spending items it can. This may be justified if the government faces a looming debt crisis, or if it can only meet its expenditure commitments through an

> **Box 3.1 Poorly coordinated planning and finance in the Vietnamese roads sector**
>
> Investment approval and financing often proceed on separate tracks in Vietnam. Frequently, investments are approved without provision for earmarked financing. One of the outcomes of the inefficient resourcing of approved (and sometimes unapproved) investments is that ministries are increasingly borrowing from commercial banks, with the expectation that central government will meet the liabilities they incur.
>
> In the case of the transport sector, this practice has led to considerable government arrears and destabilization of the construction industry. Over 1999 to 2002, about 35 percent of commitments for transport had been approved by the Prime Minister's office, but had not been allocated funding. To meet the shortfall, the Ministry of Transport (MoT) contracted (state-owned) construction companies to undertake work, with the promise of reimbursement at a later time. This has imposed a significant debt burden on contractors, who were in turn forced to take loans from state banks to finance their operations. State banks have subsequently been forced to grant loan rollovers, because in many cases the interest payments due are in excess of enterprise capitalization. Arrears in the MoT to contractors, amount to VND 1,200 billion, and those of the Transport Construction Corporation amount to an additional VND 1,000 billion.
>
> Debts incurred in this way threaten the overall stability of the fiscal framework. Taking into account borrowing for unfunded investment across all sectors, debts totaling approximately VND 11 trillion have been incurred. The government has agreed to absorb VND 5 trillion of debt incurred for projects that were implemented in fulfillment of a master plan. The existence of an additional VND 6 trillion of debt for projects implemented outside of any master plan bears testament to a nontransparent environment.
>
> *Sources: Vietnam Development Report-Governance* 2004; World Bank 2004g.

inflationary printing of money. In such cases, establishing debt sustainability and cutting fiscal deficits are likely to be paramount.

However, what if a liquidity-constrained government cuts out a large infrastructure project with an expected economic rate of return of 30 percent (which is not particularly high for an infrastructure project in a developing country)? It is often infrastructure spending that gets cut in fiscal crisis, because infrastructure spending comes in large lumps of cost today, the benefits of which are usually several years away.

Cutting that project is equivalent to the government borrowing at an interest rate of 30 percent to overcome its liquidity problem. If that happens to be the cheapest way to stave off a crisis, it may well be justified. But if there are cheaper alternatives—such as taking a loan at less than 30 percent—then cutting the project is obviously not a good solution. Indeed, in this case, cutting out the project reduces the government's net worth, and hence worsens its solvency. In other words, across-the-board cuts in infrastructure spending during fiscal crisis are often shortsighted. (If you need a little more convincing, read Box 3.2, which

Box 3.2 Infrastructure and fiscal space—arguments and counterarguments

There are a number of arguments that are made against the view that cutting infrastructure at times of crisis may be shortsighted.

One argument is that the high returns to the infrastructure investment may not accrue directly to the government. But they are likely to accrue indirectly if infrastructure raises economic activity and that activity is taxed. And the tax system can be designed to capture the benefits more directly if that is perceived to be desirable.

A second argument is that infrastructure projects are often white elephants, that is, they don't have high rates of return. But it would be as naïve to believe that all infrastructure spending is for white elephants as it would be to believe that none of it is. The "white elephant" argument doesn't argue for indiscriminate cutting of infrastructure projects during fiscal adjustment (although it obviously does argue for tackling the process of public investment selection).

A third argument is that if the private sector can do it, why should the public sector spend scarce resources? On one level, this argument is misguided: The majority of infrastructure investment in any country is public, and it would take a very long time to make all of it private (if that is even desirable). On another level, a more subtle version of this point can be made: Ministries of Finance can pressure sector agencies toward allowing private participation, where it is indeed possible, by cutting their budgets. More generally, infrastructure reform can often improve solvency through more efficient service provision and reduced fiscal risk, but may only happen if the sector's budget constraint is hard.

In many cases, this "liquidity pressure" approach may be the best way to overcome excessive caution or vested interests on the part of sector agencies, and to hold them accountable for performance. But in other cases, such caution may be well-grounded in terms of the readiness of the sector for private participation or other reforms. And there is a risk that transparent fiscal support will be replaced by nontransparent contingent liabilities, unless the Ministry of Finance has effective control.

And last, but not least, there is a fourth argument that capital markets worry about sovereign liquidity, and therefore governments should worry about it too.

It may be hard to make convincing solvency arguments to capital markets unless the country has an established track record of liquidity. In other words, capital markets may be short term with short-term governments. In such cases, high-return infrastructure projects may well need to be postponed, but this argues for accelerating infrastructure reforms that yield alternative finance in the interim from efficiency gains and greater cost recovery. Of course, it also argues strongly that the economic costs of fiscal crisis—and of short-termism—can be extremely high.

addresses some of the arguments and the counterarguments made against this point.)

And so agencies responsible for fiscal adjustment need to coordinate long-term fiscal policy with those responsible for infrastructure development spending. In most countries, this means the relationship between the finance and planning functions needs to be designed strategically, not merely be allowed to follow the fiscal cycle. That is, infrastructure budgets should get protection where merited during fiscal crisis (but not be allowed to race ahead during fiscal booms). This may sometimes mean that other priority sectors also are protected, and that short-run fiscal deficits are therefore larger than otherwise. In short, less liquidity may be needed to help solvency.

The analysis also suggests that liquidity crises can force infrastructure reform. That means that central agencies (of finance and/or planning) should coordinate with sector agencies to ensure that reform is promoted as much as possible—but not pushed too fast to be sustainable—and ensure that liquidity pressure doesn't just shift state liabilities off-budget. Ultimately, the objective is to ensure that fiscal space—in the broadest sense—provides adequate infrastructure for inclusive development.

Coordinating infrastructure through subnational government

Much of the challenge the governments face in coordinating infrastructure reflects balances that need to be struck among different functions—among planning and financing, infrastructure, and overall fiscal sustainability. When these functions are spread across separate agencies, the challenge becomes all the more difficult. And this is also the case with the challenge of coordinating infrastructure through decentralized government structures.

Decentralization in East Asia is a comparatively recent phenomenon. In the space of less than 20 years, however, previously centralized state structures have been significantly reformed. Subnational government expenditure as a percentage of total expenditure now ranges from 10 percent in Thailand to close on 70 percent in China (World Bank forthcoming a).

If well managed, and accompanied by effective accountability mechanisms, infrastructure decentralization may bring significant benefits—for example, by tailoring service provision to the needs of local constituencies. But it also brings a number of new coordination challenges. Some of these play out horizontally across government structures—managing services whose benefits span jurisdictions (the so-called spillover problem), excessive fragmentation, and destructive competition. Others play out vertically among different levels of government (see UTCE/ALMEC 2004b).

Managing spillovers in service provision

Increased decentralization increases the chances that projects will bring benefits, and incur costs, outside of any one single jurisdiction. Decision making often needs to span municipal boundaries to ensure effective coordination. But frequently, local governments are too small or lack the capacity and incentives to perform such coordinating roles.

Voluntary cooperation among local governments is rare. One prominent exception in voluntary interjurisdictional cooperation in investment planning and project implementation is the construction of a circumferential toll road across Cabanatuan City and the adjacent municipalities of San Leonardo and Santa Rosa in the Philippines.

But more commonly, local governments lack necessary short-run political incentives to cooperate. The CALA (Cavite-Laguna Provinces) peri-urban region in the Philippines, for instance, has paid a particularly high price in terms of loss of competitiveness, arising from the inability of local jurisdictions to jointly fund a common transportation network and solid waste system (Webster 2004).

In Dak Lak, Vietnam, the absence of an intermediate tier of government responsible for integrated water resource management has led to overuse and degradation of natural resources. Local agencies have repeatedly failed to resolve the conflict between upstream and downstream water users in the Ea Tul catchment of the Upper Srepok basin, and Water Users Associations (WUAs) have emerged to take on various coordinating functions (Dupar and Badenoch 2002).

Governments have therefore had to come up with new coordination tools, and a number have done just that. In both Thailand and Vietnam, the provision of fiscal incentives—in the form of matching grants

CONNECTING EAST ASIA: A NEW FRAMEWORK FOR INFRASTRUCTURE

available to projects involving governments that are part of the same extended urban region—have been successful (Webster 2004).

Other mechanisms include the formation of special districts or regions, which comprise several local governments, with the specific mandate of coordinating infrastructure service delivery in extended urban regions. This approach has been successfully implemented in Canada and the United States. The Greater Vancouver Regional District (GVRD) in Canada, for instance, comprises 13 local governments that now cooperate in the planning and provisioning of a variety of services, including regional transportation, solid waste, wastewater, and regional parks.

Excessive fragmentation

Size matters in other ways too. Newly formed municipalities may often be too small to achieve the minimum efficient scale necessary to ensure technical efficiency in service provision—evidence suggests that this may already be the case in Thailand, Indonesia, and the Philippines (see Table 3.1 below for a comparison of average population size by local governments across East Asian countries). This is particularly the case where infrastructure services are local in nature but require large capital investments—water supply, electricity distribution, or public transport.

Where excessive fragmentation is a concern, efficiency gains may be achieved by clustering municipalities to form regional areas of service

Table 3.1 Hierarchy and average population size by local government

		Malaysia	Lao PDR	Cambodia	China	Vietnam	Thailand	Indonesia	Philippines
Area (000 km²)		330	237	181	9,597	330	514	1,919	300
Population (million)		23.8	5.4	12.0	1,270	78.5	61.2	211.7	78.3
State/Province		16	17	24	33	61	75	32	79
Local Governments	Municipality/ Districts	145	142	171	2,457	715	1,133 (795)[a] 6,738	416	1,610
	Communes/ Subdistricts	—	10,868	1,510	45,462	10,594	(7,255, 71,864)[a]	—	41,944
Average Population Size (000)	Municipality/ Districts	184	38	70	517	110	54 (77)	509	49
	Communes/ Subdistricts	—	0.5	7.9	27.9	7.4	0.9	56.3	1.9

Sources: CLAIR 2000, 2004; MRI 2003.
Note: — = not available.
a. Local administrative body with 795 districts; 7,255 subdistricts; 71,864 villages.

provision (albeit at the expenses of local accountability). Often, this requires the creation of an institutional interface at a higher level of government, charged with coordinating the setting of investment priorities and regulating service provision.

Destructive competition

Decentralization may increase efficiency by promoting competition among local governments. But in the absence of coordination at higher tiers of government, excessive competition among municipalities may induce inefficient allocation of resources and overinvestment, with municipalities building or upgrading ports, airports, or other infrastructure facilities in their own areas for reasons of prestige rather than relying on those in adjacent regions.

In Thailand's aviation planning, for instance, the resource allocation process significantly reflected local successes in lobbying for air facilities, resulting in gross oversupply. Most of the local airports managed by the Department of Air Transportation (DAT) have essential facilities, but no commercial service; many are essentially in a state of abandonment. Nevertheless, the pressure to build more regional airports persists (Webster and Theeratham 2004).

So too, in China, amid economic transition and decentralization, municipalities tend to compete with each other to attract outside investment for businesses and for infrastructure projects. The tools of competition primarily comprise preferential policies—tax holidays, free land, and discounted land concessions. Given the absence of other coordination mechanisms, such ad hoc policies tend, in some cases, to unduly distort resource allocation among municipalities as well as among various stakeholders within a given municipality (Liu 2004).

The lesson again is that effective coordination requires effective institutions. Institution building and strengthening are essential, if the allocation of responsibilities across multitiered forms of government is to be successful.

Vertical coordination

Decentralization of infrastructure service delivery to subnational governments changes, but it does not remove the role of central governments. New functional systems need to be developed that allow central ministries to monitor, manage, and coordinate programs in line with policy and regulatory frameworks. The inadequacy of such systems is a frequent cause of suboptimal service delivery and confused authority.

Functional decentralization has frequently not been matched by fiscal decentralization, with local bodies deciding policy and regulatory matters (such as pricing, service standards, and expansion strategies), while central governments often continue to provide the bulk of investment financing and, to some degree, financing for operations and maintenance.

In the absence of adequate coordination of fiscal and regulatory policies, local bodies have little incentive to make sustained progress toward reducing unit costs, recovering those costs, and—where private participation is involved—respecting contractual obligations. This is a story that has played out across most infrastructure sectors in East Asia, as elsewhere, but especially for urban transport, water supply and sanitation, and to some degree rural electrification (see UTCE/ALMEC 2004b).

This situation has been exacerbated by shifts in the composition of central transfers. Revenue-sharing grants and other forms of unconditional transfers frequently constitute an increasing share of central transfers to local authorities, for which there is little if any reporting on uses and costs, and much less accountability in the broader sense of tracking efficiency of expenditure and service delivery performance.

Coordinating urban infrastructure

As we saw in Chapter 1, much of East Asia's infrastructure challenge arises from growth generated by cities. Delivering urban infrastructure and infrastructure services poses arguably the most complex of infrastructure coordination problems, in part, because of the sheer pace of urbanization in East Asia, which frequently outstrips the response capacity of urban managers and, in part, because urban management requires coordination that brings together so many different functions.

Infrastructure has a major role to play in shaping urban space—determining where people work, live, and create wealth; how they travel; and how they sell their goods. Formulating and implementing practical plans with long-term vision is vital. When successful, it can set the stage for long-term growth and prosperity. The development of Thailand's Eastern Seaboard (ESB) area—a peri-urban export-orientated zone developed around state-sponsored infrastructure investment—is among the region's most successful examples (see Box 3.8 in our discussion of Thailand for more details).

But Thailand, as we saw in Chapter 1, is among the least urbanized, and slowest urbanizing countries in the region. In other countries, the pace of population growth has made it difficult for the authorities to keep up. And timing is of the essence. When urbanization precedes the investment necessary to make for livable cities, the costs of improving infrastructure levels tend to escalate because of the costs of land acquisition and resettlement, and infrastructure solutions tend to be suboptimal.

Ideally, land use management—the incentives and restrictions that determine which activities are located in which areas, and of which infrastructure is a large part—is key to managing urban growth. But city managers in many East Asian countries are often hampered in this role in a number of ways, including insufficient legal frameworks, deficient application of existing restrictions, and political intervention.

Coordination among the multiple agencies that are typically involved in urban management and infrastructure delivery is also vital, but is often difficult to achieve. Returning to Thailand, before Bangkok began reforming its urban management, there were at least 27 government departments and state-owned enterprises (SOEs) with responsibilities related to urban transport. Four separate agencies, under three different ministries, had powers to develop mass transit schemes. In one extreme case, two megaprojects were even planned to occupy the same physical space. When competing parties held rival agencies, the incentives for better alignment were even weaker (Carruthers, Bajpai, and Hummels 2003). A similar picture unfolds in the case of Vietnam, despite the country's significantly different political and social context (see Box 3.3).

Coordination across urban boundaries is also a particular challenge. When urbanization spreads beyond administrative boundaries, so do urban activities and urban needs. In water supply, waste management, transport, and other network infrastructure services wider administrative cooperation mechanisms are essential. Frequently, however, they are lacking. In the Philippines, for example, the Metropolitan Manila Development Authority (MMDA) is responsible for coordinating urban development for the entire Metro Manila area, which consists of 17 cities and municipalities. However, its legal authority is not firmly established, and its power is limited to actual coordination and enforcement of land use management and infrastructure development. And with urban growth

Box 3.3 Urban management in Vietnam

In Vietnam, urban management (*quan ly do thi*) is nominally the responsibility of the central Ministry of Construction. However, the Ministry's power is constrained by a web of independent decisions by other government entities responsible for land management, transportation, finance and budget allocation, socioeconomic planning, management of SOEs, and the environment at the national, provincial, city, and district levels.

These actors frequently compete against each other for state financial resources and FDI, with little benefit accruing to individual departments from cooperation. This is further complicated by the traditional vesting of *quan ly* authority with local officials in communes and wards, which often results in the treatment of laws, decrees, and plans as guidance, with ultimate responsibility resting with local officials.

Effective urban planning requires the achievement of objectives in spatial, as well as sectoral, terms. In Vietnam, priority setting in the socioeconomic plans and implementation of physical planning are allocated across two separate planning exercises, and have proved difficult to integrate and coordinate. The plans of the Ministry of Construction, which deal with development in spatial terms, tend to overlook the economic and social dimensions of urban master planning, while the plans of the Ministry of Planning and Investment tend to overlook the spatial and environmental dimensions of investment programs. This frequently results is disconnected and impractical physical plans, weakly related to socioeconomic plans, lacking in implementation mechanisms beyond directing the location of state investment.

Because the spatial plans are unable to produce usable guidelines for challenging urban growth, much growth takes place in unauthorized and unplanned areas, is more unlikely to be inconsistent with overall strategic objectives, and proceeds without adequate provision of required urban services.

Source: World Bank, forthcoming c.

expanding beyond its boundaries, to the adjoining provinces of Cavite and Laguna, its inability to provide infrastructure services is of serious concern (Webster 2001).

The geese catching up: Four snapshots

We are not going to attempt a comprehensive account of strategic vision, planning, and policy coordination for the infrastructure of these four countries. That by itself would be worth a book. Instead, we will tell a brief story about each, illuminating some of the key challenges they face and how they tackle them.

The Philippines[5]

The Philippines' story is that long-term vision and development plans are often undermined by short-term pressures within a fluid and fragmented political system. The fragmentation of the system diminishes accountability and nurtures corruption. Leadership is sporadic, clientilism is strong, and the state has been captured to some degree by special interests. Politicians frequently override technocrats, and policies can be very unpredictable. There have been boom periods of relatively high growth and fiscal stability, but they have alternated with periods of bust. This has substantially impacted Filipino institutions, and their effectiveness in delivering infrastructure services.

The Filipino planning agency is the National Economic and Development Authority (NEDA). In periods of bust, NEDA's long-term development role has tended to be secondary to the goal of fiscal retrenchment (under the leadership of the Department of Budget and Management). In periods of boom, which tend to precede elections, NEDA's role tends to be undermined by multiple pressures to give financial support to highly politicized infrastructure projects. This support is often spread thinly to keep several different constituencies happy (see Box 3.4 for a description of the Philippines' "pork-barrel" funds). Long-term development plans and actual budgets often bear little relation to each other. NEDA's policy-making role—for example on user charges—is frequently preempted by executive authority or eroded by other political influences. And so NEDA's ability to set priorities, and to coordinate policies or projects, is highly constrained. Crisis management tends to be the dominant mode of operation.

Decentralization in the Philippines is a source of further coordination weakness, and it contributes significantly to the government's inability to implement strategic plans. The ports in Manila, for instance, and the roads leading to them, have become highly congested. The government decided to upgrade Batangas port about 100 kilometers from Manila, which could serve factories in the peri-urban areas south of Manila. This required a large investment that would benefit many different local government areas. It could therefore not attract the requisite funds, because each local government preferred to try and freeride on what the others would do. Eventually the port was donor funded, but access to it is restricted by a narrow highway the expansion of which still cannot attract domestic funding.

Box 3.4 "Pork-Barrel" interventions in infrastructure in the Philippines

One of the consequences of the personalization of the Filipino political process is the allocation of budgets to congressmen and senators from which to fund politically or personally motivated "pork-barrel projects," through so-called "augmentation funds."

This results in fragmentation of scarce fiscal resources, weakens accountability, and significantly undermines existing planning and coordination mechanisms.

Table 3.2 gives an indication of the prevalence of this phenomenon.

Between 1997 and 2001, 22.5 percent of the Department of Public Works and Highways' (DPWH) budget—or close to P 50 billion—was allocated to "pork barrel" projects, under various rubrics. And this outweighed the funds allocated to local government units for infrastructure projects by more than 25 percent.

Source: World Bank forthcoming b.

Table 3.2 Augmentation funds for local infrastructure, DPWH budget, 1997–2001 (P billion)

	1997	1998	1999	2000	2001	Total 1997–2001
Total Budget of which—	49.05	38.25	42.65	42.33	48.96	221.24
Augmentation Funds	14.17	3.04	6.83	8.1	17.56	49.7
Various Infrastructure Projects	13.68	2.84	0.32	8.1	17.29	42.23
Project Development Assistance Fund	0	0	0	0	0.27	0.27
Countrywide Development Fund	0.5	0.2	0	0	0	0.7
Rural/Urban Development Infrastructure Fund	0	0	5.36	0	0	5.36
Food Security Program Fund	0	0	1.14	0	0	1.14

Source: Manasan 2004.

The lack of policy coordination has led to generally inadequate fiscal space for infrastructure and low levels of private infrastructure investment. In 2002, total infrastructure investment was only 2.8 percent of GDP.

To cite just one example of weak coordination over fiscal issues: the electricity sector. There is an official policy of minimal and well-targeted subsidies in the sector. In reality, electricity tariff increases are highly politicized—a round of increases was postponed just before the May

2004 presidential election. At the same time, overcontracting by the National Power Corporation (NPC) for independent power producers has resulted in the government taking over service of much of NPC's debt. This has crowded out high-priority expenditures in other sectors (particularly given the Philippines' weak tax collection), and in the power sector itself there are insufficient funds for investment in transmission and distribution capacity. Regulatory autonomy has been undermined. Lack of predictability has deterred further private investment.

In some cases, the state's inability to deliver infrastructure services has led to an ambitious restructuring of the sector—almost in desperation. For example, in telecommunications, before the Philippine Long Distance Telephone Company (PLDT) monopoly was broken up, a typical consumer would have to wait almost a decade for a telephone to be installed, and teledensity was far below that in neighboring countries. Since the introduction of competition in 1995, teledensity has increased dramatically—threefold for fixed lines and by more than 70 percent a year for mobiles (for mobiles, technology is often ahead of the state's ability to control it). Technology and competition have succeeded in the Philippines where the state was failing—and the state facilitated that process.

But even here progress has been undermined by state coordination weaknesses. The telecommunications companies were given lucrative monopoly franchises for certain services (for example, international calls) so that they could cross-subsidize expansion of fixed-line service into unprofitable ("missionary") areas. In essence, competition was restricted because the alternative to the government subsidizing missionary expansion directly had no credibility. Nobody believed the subsidies would flow without disruption, whatever the stated policy. However, to a considerable extent, the franchisees' monopoly power, and hence the ability to cross-subsidize, has been undermined by illegal competition from bypass operators using new technologies (for example, Voice over Internet Protocol [VoIP]), which the state is unable to regulate effectively.

The mainstreaming of poverty reduction and environmental concerns is another area where policy and reality diverge in the Philippines. The formulation of the national development plan is highly consultative, and addresses social and environmental issues as high priorities not just add-ons. However, there is a huge gap between what the plan says, and the projects that receive resources and the policies that are actually implemented. Civil society's main mechanism for affecting decisions with environmental and social implications is not really through partici-pation at the planning stage, but through campaigns and protest at the permitting or implementation stage. The frequency of such protests can be seen as a strength of Filipino democratic culture, reacting to the weakness of the state—it does not represent coordinated environmental and social mainstreaming. Similarly, community and nongovernmental organization (NGO) initiatives for small-scale infrastructure services are vibrant in the Philippines, filling some of the gaps in state provision (Conan 2004).

The effects of weak coordination present themselves across the Philip-pines' infrastructure sectors (see World Bank, forthcoming b). Invest-ment climate assessments show that weaknesses in infrastructure provision—in particular, in electricity supply and transport—have signif-icant adverse affects on investment and competitiveness.[6] The power sector is imposing a financial crisis on the government and cannot fund the needed expansion.[7] Transportation service quality is generally poor and costs are high; the road network is badly interconnected and many roads are in bad condition.[8] Access to improved water appears to be in decline[9] particularly in smaller urban centers across the country, and water quality and service reliability are major issues. Sanitation standards are a major health concern, with only about 4 percent of the population having acceptable on-site treatment and disposal. Telecommunications has seen progress, but performance and access remain behind regional norms.

However, there are positive signs. Filipino political culture undermines long-term strategic vision and the role of the state, but it does allow private and civil society initiative to emerge. Most hope in the Filipino context lies in the ability of technology, competition, community initiative, or small-scale infrastructure to get around the state and make a contribution. In large-scale monopolistic network subsectors, in which a significant state role is inevitable, progress can be expected to be slower.

Indonesia

Indonesia's story is that the pendulum has swung from autocratic technocracy to something considerably more participatory and decentral-ized, but that pendulum has not yet come to rest. Leadership and the center are struggling to find their proper role and define a strategic vision. The old symbiosis between politicians and technocrats has gone, but the new relationship has not yet fully taken shape. The autocratic period was one of generally high growth and macroeconomic stability that ended dramatically in economic crisis; the postcrisis period has seen a painful economic recovery that is now being consolidated. This has been a formative period for Indonesia's economic management institutions.

Under the Suharto regime, policy planning and coordination was centralized in two institutions: Badan Perencanaan Pembangunan Nasional (BAPPENAS), which prepared national five-year development plans and coordinated policy initiatives, and the Coordinating Ministry for the Economy and Industry (EKUIN). In effect, these two institutions operated more or less as one, and had substantial ability to plan strategically and oversee the translation of that vision into reality (see Asanuma 2005; World Bank 2004a). The regime gave considerable technocratic authority to its planning agencies, although, in the regime's declining years, corruption tended to undermine technocracy increasingly.

Under the post-Suharto *reformasi* regimes, the power of the planning agencies has been significantly diffused. The power of the executive as a whole has become circumscribed by the emerging role of the legislature and the judiciary as democratization evolves. Power has been redistributed downwards to local government, under Indonesia's "big-bang" approach to decentralization since 1999. Fiscal crisis, from which Indonesia is only now beginning to recover, shifted influence to the MoF and the central bank and placed a strong emphasis on short-term macroeconomic stability. BAPPENAS is now essentially a planning advisor, without even authority over the state's development budget. EKUIN's successor, the Coordinating Ministry of Economic Affairs, focuses mainly on short-term implementation issues. Strategic vision is in search of a home.

Fiscal space for infrastructure has been limited in the last few years, with infrastructure expenditure as a portion of total expenditure declining significantly. In parallel, private investor interest, which remains significant, has not led to much actual investment (see Figure 3.2). This is in large part because the state abrogated contracts during and after the 1997 crisis, and confidence has not yet been reestablished. Box 3.5 takes up this story in the energy sector.

Severe infrastructure backlogs have emerged. Real spending on road maintenance, for instance, dropped in 2000 to less than 40 percent of its 1985 level. This has resulted in a serious backlog of preservation and upgrading, particularly for the provincial and *kabupaten* (county) road

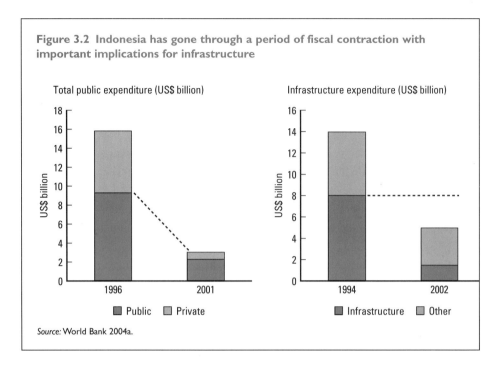

Figure 3.2 Indonesia has gone through a period of fiscal contraction with important implications for infrastructure

Total public expenditure (US$ billion)

Infrastructure expenditure (US$ billion)

■ Public   ■ Private

■ Infrastructure   ■ Other

Source: World Bank 2004a.

networks. And both quality and access have seen little progress—PDAM (Perusahaan Daerah Air Minum; Local Water Supply Enterprise) coverage and electricity access remain extremely low, at 17 and 55 percent, respectively (World Bank 2004a).

The state's ability to pursue growth and poverty reduction objectives through infrastructure provision has thus become very constrained since the crisis. However, the ongoing fiscal recovery may now allow for more public expenditure on infrastructure, although much of the funding burden will need to be born by user charges and tariffs.

Infrastructure investment is now at a crossroads: A rebound in infrastructure expenditure is vital to revamp investment and sustain economic growth. With steady macroeconomic conditions and political stability, Indonesia is well poised to address its infrastructure bottlenecks—provided that it follows through on the policy reforms initiated in a mixture of infrastructure sectors. Failure to seize this window of opportunity may jeopardize growth prospects for decades.

Based on international comparisons, as well as comparisons with levels of government spending before the crisis, it is estimated that an increase in annual total infrastructure investment of US$5 billion above the current trend (amounting to an additional 2 percent of GDP) is

Box 3.5 Indonesia's renegotiated power purchase agreements

Faced by escalating electricity demand, and limited public resources, many East Asian countries had little choice but to invite private, frequently foreign investment in power plants, mostly as Independent Power Producers (IPPs).

In Indonesia, 26 primarily U.S. dollar-denominated power purchase agreements were signed between IPP sponsors and PLN, the state electricity utility, for approximately $18 billion, increasing capacity by roughly 11,000 mW.

Funds for these IPPs were secured from international sources, but were predominantly from unsolicited proposals. Although the government did not issue explicit guarantees, "letters of support" were given to the IPPs though which the MoF or the Ministry of Mines and Energy required PLN to perform its obligations.

As a result of the crisis and devaluation of the rupiah, the government—faced with large and escalating debts—postponed some IPP projects, and directed PLN to reimburse only part of its obligations to the operating IPPs.

Investor response was mixed, depending on whether each took a short- or long-term view of its involvement. In some cases the government was sued and, in one, an international arbitration panel ruled in favor of the IPPs.

The government has now settled or renegotiated all disputes with the IPPs (excluding the case mentioned above).

At the same time, however, it remains exposed to important contingent liabilities associated with its obligations to the IPPs. And future market development will be significantly affected by the set tariffs and dispatchability levels associated with the power purchase agreements.

Source: World Bank 2004a.

required to meet the projected medium-term growth target of 6 percent (World Bank 2004a). Sustained policy reforms would attract sizeable private investment back to Indonesia. However, for the foreseeable future, public sector funding is likely to play an important role in closing the funding gap for infrastructure.

There is little doubt that creating increased fiscal space for economically sound infrastructure projects is vital to build the fundamentals necessary for long-term growth in the country. Further compressing productive public infrastructure expenditure to achieve short-term macroeconomic stability risks engendering a vicious circle, with depressed prospects for growth, user fees, and taxes. The challenge for Indonesia now lies in building the requisite coordinating capacity and accountability mechanisms. This will be needed to strike a careful balance among fiscal prudence and fiscal space, attracting private investment, and implementing infrastructure sector reforms. A more reliable cost-recovery policy, and greater certainty over fiscal space for subsidies, would help attract private investment.

Over the past 10 to 15 years, infrastructure service provision has been increasingly delegated by government to corporatized state enterprises or to the private sector, with some efficiency gains (albeit modest).[10] However, this delegation has not generally been accompanied by sector restructuring to allow competition. Nor has the rule of law yet replaced the rule of a strong leader, so the ability of the judicial system or of capital markets to bring better corporate governance or encourage further private investment is limited.

So for the time being, top-down oversight and regulation remain at a premium to ensure performance and catalyze reform (particularly as vested interests in infrastructure sectors remain strong). But as we have seen, the planning agencies' scope to provide that oversight and regulation is now severely limited, and new institutions have not emerged to fulfill these roles.

In the same way that corporatization and privatization have brought modest performance improvements, Indonesia's radical decentralization to the *kabupaten* (county) and *kota* (municipality) level (with a limited role for provinces) laid the foundation for greater government responsiveness to communities.[11] However, it has also created considerable uncertainty about interjurisdictional responsibilities and has limited fiscal space for central initiatives. The transport sector is a case in point: Conflicting government regulations and sector laws regarding the functions of central and provincial governments have created a coordinating vacuum. As a result, primary infrastructure networks—such as major national and provincial roads—have been neglected. More than 12 percent of the national and provincial road network remains unsealed; in Kalimantan and eastern Indonesia, the percentage rises to 27 percent (World Bank 2004a). Local governments' share of public investment in infrastructure is now almost equal to that of central government (just under 1 percent of GDP a piece in 2002). Interestingly, although this would appear to favor those sectors that are provided locally such as water supply, this does not yet appear to have shown up in enhanced performance.

Since *reformasi* began, civil society has flourished. This has brought with it a new awareness of local environmental and social issues when infrastructure projects are being planned or implemented, which was essentially suppressed under the Suharto regime. As in the Philippines, democratization has also brought forth community initiatives in small-scale infrastructure, where the state has failed to provide. Indonesia's Kecamatan Development Project (KDP) is among the most successful examples of the region's experimentation with community-driven development (CDD) (see Box 3.6). However, the state's ability to take those local initiatives and mainstream them into policies or programs is weak. Indeed, in general, the coordination necessary to mainstream environmental and social considerations has not been strong in Indonesia.[12]

Box 3.6 Coordination from the bottom up in Indonesia: Community-driven development programs

In an effort to provide high-quality and low-cost village infrastructure, many countries in East Asia have adopted CDD approaches, which give more power to local decision making and control mechanisms. When top-down coordination fails to reach the poor, bottom-up coordination can fill the gap.

One of the largest CDD programs in East Asia is the Kecamatan Development Project (KDP) in Indonesia. This project uses a competitive process through which intercommunity forums rank and select proposals based on their own priorities. Particular attention is paid to reducing corruption through public transparency in the allocation and tracking of funds, monitored by local NGOs and independent media. Local communities participate actively in the design, implementation, and maintenance of projects (mainly for village roads, water, and sanitation).

By 2006, KDP will cover some 28,000 villages or almost 40 percent of the villages in Indonesia, including the most impoverished rural areas. The same approach is being used to involve communities in reconstruction decisions following the tsunami in Aceh.

Initial evidence from KDP, and similar programs in Lao PDR and the Philippines, indicates that small-scale local roads using CDD methods can be 25 percent to 40 percent cheaper than similar roads built by local contractors. Some of these savings are due to lower corruption. Although lower initial savings are often evident in water supply projects (mainly because of the need for communities to purchase pipes and so on), there is a growing body of evidence suggesting that community maintenance of systems is far more likely than under the traditional "build it and leave it" approach. While the benefits of CDD projects can be captured by local elites, proper targeting to poorer rural areas, with mechanisms to encourage participation by women and other vulnerable groups, can still have a significant impact on overall poverty levels.

Despite the evident advantages, CDD programs also have their limitations. Experience to date suggests a number of significant challenges to be addressed: First, finding ways for the village-level approach to evolve into mechanisms that allow for the rural poor to affect local government decisions on larger, higher-value types of infrastructure. Second, ensuring the

(Continued on the next page)

Box 3.6 (Continued)

technical quality and environmental soundness of infrastructure works and thus their sustainability. And third, augmenting official financing with larger amounts of domestic resources. (The willingness of governments to fund CDD programs from their own resources, while preserving the hands-off approach to decision making will be one of the ultimate tests of this approach.)

Critics of the CDD approach point out that there is little systematic evidence of the benefits claimed by CDD proponents. For example, Mansuri and Rao (2004) concluded that "there is some evidence that such projects create effective community infrastructure, but not a single study establishes the causal relationship between any outcome and participatory elements of a community-based development project." In response, there is a move to incorporate well-designed monitoring and evaluation systems into CDD projects. This will not only provide more evidence on the pros and cons of this approach, but also suggest ways to improve the design and implementation of future CDD programs.

Source: Burgess 2004.

China[13]

In China, authority has been extensively decentralized to the provincial and municipal levels. Local government projects accounted for 86 percent of fixed asset investment in 2003 (World Bank 2004d). But the center remains substantially in charge and generates the strategic vision that binds the system together.[14] High growth and clear objectives have been a force for institutional cohesion. Politicians and technocrats are not so easily distinguished from each other, given the leadership role of the Communist Party (although obviously the top leaders are distinguishable from the bureaucracy at large).

Accountability is essentially upwards, and civil society's role is limited. Planning has become progressively more strategic and flexible. Market forces play an ever-increasing role in state decision making; the transition has been gradual and adaptive, within a framework of political continuity and authority.

China's principal planning agency is the National Development and Reform Commission (NDRC, formerly the National Planning Commission). Unlike BAPPENAS or NEDA, NDRC has not seen its strategic planning role seriously undermined. China did not face a fiscal crisis after 1997 (indeed it undertook a deliberately countercyclical fiscal expansion), and it has maintained a steady high-growth path. Democratization has not emerged to change the role of leadership or accountability as it has in many other parts of the region, and the executive branch of government remains very strong. NDRC continues to play a major strategic role, in subordination to the Communist Party and the State Council.

The central role of infrastructure in supporting national economic development has been emphasized by the Communist Party of China (CPC) since it took power in 1949. This role has been further emphasized since the CPC made the strategic choice in the 1980s to adopt an export-led economic development strategy and to promote economic growth by attracting FDI. China's infrastructure investment is the highest in the region as a percentage of GDP, and is certainly amongst the very highest in the world.

To a great extent, China benefited as a late comer, learning from its neighboring economies—Japan, Korea, Taiwan (China), Hong Kong (China), and Singapore. The special economic zones (SEZ) and coastal open cities were variants of the tax-free manufacturing zones and industrial parks in neighboring countries. Adaptation and learning have been a hallmark of Chinese planning. The early infrastructure investment was mostly associated with the SEZs. It was concentrated heavily on the port capacity and road transport links in a few selected harbor cities. The significant improvement of economic infrastructure in the coastal urban areas in the 1980s, and the policy to allow rural labor to enter the urban labor market, made these areas highly competitive in attracting manufacturing FDI, setting the precedents for the subsequent waves of infrastructure investment.

As China broadens its infrastructure strategy from a strong growth focus to a more inclusive development model, the shift is very much steered by strategic vision from the top. The Western Regional Development Strategy, for instance, which seeks to narrow income inequality between the richer coast areas and the poorer western regions, has enjoyed high-level party support from its outset. This has helped ensure implementation and, more importantly, administrative commitment in the face of unexpected implementation challenges.

However, the emphasis on strategic direction from the center is not to deny the great significance for infrastructure of decentralization in China, nor the ability of decentralized agencies to undermine some of the intentions of the center. The ability of provinces and cities to borrow from the state-owned financial sector for infrastructure investment with only limited credit assessment has challenged the government's ability to exercise macroeconomic control, as we discuss in Box 3.7. That same

Box 3.7 Coordinating local government infrastructure, macroeconomic stability, and urban land use

In China, the performance of local government officials is measured by a range of criteria that include GDP growth, tax revenue, employment, levels of urbanization, and social stability. This provides strong incentives to local governments to invest in urban infrastructure, attract business, and spur investment. As a result, urban construction has boomed in recent years, increasing from 10 percent of GDP in 2000 to 13 percent in 2003 (or around one-third of total fixed asset investment).

While much of this investment supports economic growth, expenditure of this scale raises a number of concerns. The first of these is the risk of over-investment. As important, however, is the manner in which this expenditure is funded, which in turn reflects the nature of the intergovernmental financial system.

Local governments in China have little taxing powers, limited transfers from higher levels, and no access to borrowing, except from international financial institutions. At the same time, they are responsible for most public services, which account for about 70 percent of government spending. As a result, local governments access resources outside their budgets to finance urban infrastructure. Two of these mechanisms—bank loans and revenue from land transactions—are of particular concern.

A growing share of urban construction is financed by bank loans. According to a People's Bank of China survey conducted in 16 cities, there are three major financing sources for urban construction: fiscal allocations, domestic bank loans, and "self-raised funds." Additional revenues often come from the city maintenance and construction tax, loans secured by land, and land sales.

While the share of fiscal funds has been decreasing, that of bank loans has been increasing—from 28 percent in 2001 to 47 percent in the first half of 2004. Since the Budget Law prohibits borrowing or issuing bonds by local governments, local governments commonly establish urban construction and investment companies that borrow from banks or issue bonds on behalf of the local government.

Local government activity financed by bank loans, land sales, and other forms of extra-budgetary revenues remains largely outside of the central government's purview. Mechanisms to discipline these borrowers to ensure sound repayment capacity and local government fiscal sustainability are absent. The result is large and "hidden" local government liabilities, which are an increasing concern among policy makers.

Revenues raised from land transactions—which may account for between 50 percent and 70 percent of urban construction in some cities—are a second major concern. The cost to local governments of land purchased from farmers is based on its agricultural value. But cities are able to make windfall profits by leasing it out for real estate development. And this acts as an incentive for excessive conversion of peri-urban land into urban land, is a significant source of complaints from affected farmers, and threatens the sustainability of both urban growth and food security.

(Continued on the next page)

Box 3.7 (Continued)

More effective coordination among the needs of urban infrastructure, macroeconomic stability, and efficient land use might entail a number of steps: a revised performance evaluation system for local governments; broadening of the local revenue base; better regulated local access to borrowing; changes to the land-lease system; and appropriate compensation to farmers.

Source: World Bank 2005a.

overheated pace of infrastructure investment has exacerbated environmental degradation and generated social tensions, particularly in the process of land acquisition. At a more microeconomic level, central government is decreasingly able to control the infrastructure investment choices of decentralized governments.

But whatever the difficulties, it is clear that in a country the size of China, rapid infrastructure development would not have been possible without substantial decentralization of responsibilities to local governments and enterprises. And it is interesting to see how China is dealing with the issue of interjurisdictional infrastructure. The Pearl River Delta, the Yangze Delta, and the Beijing-Tianjin region are emerging as highly prosperous and integrated metropolitan areas covering a number of provinces and other jurisdictions. Leaders of localities are beginning to group together in cross-jurisdictional infrastructure initiatives, but with some clear top-down central guidance.

The most ambitious to date is perhaps the initiative for the Pan-Pearl River Delta Regional Cooperation and Development. It involves nine southern provinces, seven ministries, and Hong Kong (China) and Macau, covering almost one-fourth of China's territory. The region includes a few highly-developed coastal urban economic centers and several poor but natural resource-abundant interior provinces. The idea was initiated by the CPC leader of Guangdong Province, a member of the powerful political bureau. The initiative is based on priority investments in highways and railways pledged by the central ministries, and a $2 billion bridge that spans 29 kilometers across the Pearl River Mouth Bay between Hong Kong (China) and Zhuhai.

But China is facing some of the stresses and strains in the system faced by the six geese in front. Complexity is increasing, and objectives are multiplying. Continuing to deliver infrastructure performance will almost certainly require more decentralization and delegation. This will involve an even greater role for market forces (particularly through competition in service provision and increased commercialization of financing), but also will challenge the center to continue to play its crucial strategic role. Savings will need to be transformed into investment more efficiently than in the past, particularly as the population ages. Environmental and equity issues will continue to rise in importance, and will test the coordination abilities of the system.

Thailand[15]

And like China's story, Thailand's is quite close to those of the geese flying in front. Strategic, long-term vision has played a major role, coordination among technocrats has been quite effective on the whole, and growth has been high (with a brief crisis interruption). Participation and decentralization have played a fairly limited role, although civil society is active. However, the relationship between politicians and technocrats has not been a fixed one. At times, technocrats have been the prime generators of vision; at other times, it has been the politicians.

The National Economic and Social Development Board (NESDB) is Thailand's principal planning agency. From late 1992 through 2000, Thailand was governed by coalitions. Different parties controlled different ministries, which substantially weakened coordination and integrated planning at the cabinet level. NESDB effectively filled the gap, through its mandate to produce national development plans and approve all infrastructure projects greater than 1 billion baht in value (about $25 million).

The elections of 2000 brought new direction to infrastructure policy, and reconsideration of the country's coordination mechanisms. With its dominant control over government, the Thai Rack Thai Party initiated a major infrastructure investment program, which included an emphasis on logistics, affordable housing, urban mass transit, and small-settlement water supply. These areas of emphasis derive from an analysis of Thailand's evolving competitiveness needs, as well as from social concerns.[16] The Prime Minister's office took on the role of identifying major new directions in infrastructure. The MoF appeared to rise in importance in the coordination of the new infrastructure strategy, given the crucial role that financing would play in implementation of the new planned megaprojects, and the mandate of the MoF to oversee state enterprises (which account for about 55 percent of infrastructure investment in Thailand).[17] The role of NESDB became uncertain for a while, but it now appears to again be in charge of the coordination of infrastructure planning and megaprojects.

Like many other East Asian countries, Thailand's move toward private participation in infrastructure has been fairly marginal and did not involve much sector restructuring. Competition in infrastructure service provision has been largely avoided, and regulatory institutions enjoy little autonomy. Thailand has strategically managed to preserve its investment climate by remaining broadly predictable in its behavior. Contracts in infrastructure have generally been honored, and its key state enterprises—such as the Electricity Generating Authority of Thailand (EGAT) and the Metropolitan Electricity Authority (MEA) in the electricity sector, and the Provincial Waterworks Authority (PWA) in the water sector—have maintained good creditworthiness and service delivery track records, even through the 1997 crisis and its aftermath.

Decentralization in Thailand has also been quite limited. Indeed, it has progressed little compared with many neighboring countries. After some past perceived failures with decentralization to a low level of government—the *tambon*—the Thai Rack Thai Government has focused decentralization on the 76 provinces. However, the provincial governors—styled "CEO Governors"—are appointed by the government rather than being elected, and their role is more a deconcentration of central authority than a real decentralization. Nonetheless, there has been a marked shift in spending: In 2003, 23 percent of public expenditure was by local governments, up from 8 percent in 1997. Much of this shift has been in infrastructure. As elsewhere in the region, interjurisdictional coordination has been an issue.

Stakeholder participation in infrastructure projects has made significant progress at the local government level. Civic forums in which the expected impacts of proposed projects are debated have become the norm. However, nationally initiated large projects have shown less progress. Environmental impact assessments (EIAs) are prepared for most large projects, but transparency in the EIA process is often lacking, and the EIAs themselves often have little impact on project selection, design, or implementation. EIAs are not generally used to provide frameworks for constructive negotiations among different stakeholders.

Box 3.8 Vision, infrastructure, and spatial planning in Thailand

Spatial development has been an important part of Thailand's infrastructure program since the 1970s—in particular, in the creation of specific economic zones (a development strategy that would be echoed later by the development of China's special economic zones in the 1980s).

The most important of Thailand's zones is the Eastern Seaboard (ESB) area, a peri-urban export-oriented manufacturing zone comprising Chonburi, Chachoengsao, and Rayong provinces. It is home to 3 million people, many of them migrants from northeast Thailand; it is the major industrial production zone in all of southeast Asia; and it is one of the most important automotive clusters in East Asia as a whole.

The ESB development was driven by public policy, co-coordinated by the Spatial Bureau of the NESDB. More than 65 percent of public investment in the ESB was for infrastructure, delivered mainly by state enterprises. The fact that NESDB is responsible for state enterprise investment programming and budgets made this task easier.

ESB achieved notable economic growth from the 1980s to the early 1990s. In the 1990s, in particular, the ESB grew faster than any other region in Thailand, at 12.1 percent per year from 1991–95. Next to the Bangkok metropolitan area, the region established its status as the second largest industrial cluster in Thailand (see Table 3.3). According to an interview survey of 113 firms in the ESB, the most important factors affecting firms' decisions to locate to the region were investment, strong transport infrastructure, and the quality of public utilities (JBIC 2000).

Significant levels of infrastructure have been concentrated in other areas in the country. In the western amenity area, for instance, a causeway has been approved to significantly reduce travel time between Bangkok and Hua Hin / Cha-Am, a prime amenity area known for tourism, spas, retirees, boutique agriculture, and postsecondary education.

Spatial programming also extends to cross-border infrastructure provision. Thailand is active in the Greater Mekong Subregion (GMS) development initiative. Regional cooperation has resulted in development of cross-border links, including bridges across the Mekong river, such as the Friendship bridge linking Nong Khai and Vientiane.

However, explicit spatial infrastructure programming has become somewhat less important in Thailand in recent years. In part, this is due to decentralization, which makes it more difficult to shape the spatial economy and settlement systems to meet strategic goals.

More significantly, as increasing globalization raises the importance of competitiveness, the government has chosen to allow market forces to play a greater role in shaping the spatial distribution of activities directly.

However, Thailand is particularly well-placed to benefit now from its increased participation in the global economy, precisely because of the existence of zones like the ESB.

Source: Webster and Theeratham 2004.

Table 3.3 Real gross regional product per capita in areas of Thailand, 1981–95 (1988 prices)

	Nationwide	Bangkok and vicinities	Eastern (ESB)	Central	Western	Northeastern	Northern	Southern
GDP per Capita								
1981	20,278	63,198	26,212 (35,564)	17,845	18,610	7,860	12,402	15,740
1995	49,514	149,592	80,232 (121,376)	48,558	37,295	16,631	23,681	31,735
GDP per Capita Growth Rate (Annual Average)								
1981–86	3.4%	2.2%	5.8% (7.6%)	2.5%	3.5%	3.7%	3.5%	3.0%
1986–91	9.3%	11.0%	8.4% (8.5%)	9.5%	5.5%	6.2%	5.3%	7.2%
1991–95	7.3%	6.0%	11.5% (12.1%)	11.2%	6.6%	7.0%	5.5%	5.2%
Share of Manufacturing Value Added								
1981	100.0%	72.2%	11.2% (10.6%)	3.3%	3.1%	3.9%	3.5%	2.7%
1995	100.0%	63.2%	15.8% (14.9%)	6.5%	3.6%	5.0%	3.8%	2.1%

Source: JBIC 2000.
Note: ESB = Eastern Seaboard.

Instead they are often just formal attachments to projects, which are already seen by their proponents as a fait accompli (this approach can, of course, lead to conflict and delays).

Thailand's infrastructure planning and coordination have performed fairly well, although some sectors—such as electricity—have performed much better than others—such as wastewater. There have been substantial delays in some key projects—for example, the Suvarnabhumi airport and the Bangkok subway—which are due to very slow and bureaucratic decision making and to the inadequate stakeholder participation process. But, on the whole, the system has been flexible and adaptive; it has dealt well both with crisis and with long-term strategy. In general, the system has evolved effectively as the political context has changed, and strategic vision has usually managed to play a central role.

From coordination to accountability and risk management

We have seen that the strength of infrastructure service delivery in the leading geese—Hong Kong (China), Japan, Korea, Malaysia, Singapore, and Taiwan (China)—was derived from their ability to formulate high-level economic strategy and to translate that into implementation on the ground. They did this principally through top-down planning and coordination, with fairly limited public participation or delegation of service delivery beyond a small number of large monopolies. Accountability was largely vertical.

We saw that this was successful when economic growth was high, and policy makers formed a consensus around relatively simple objectives, centered on sustaining that growth through exports and investment. When those economies began to encounter economic slowdown or crisis, and objectives broadened to include more social and environmental considerations, or monolithic politics started to open to wider participation, the top-down model began to show signs of strain. But underlying those pressures was the region's increasing integration in a rapidly changing global economy, which brought with it exponentially increasing complexity and coordination challenges.

Those challenges that the leading geese began to face in the late 1980s after nearly three decades of high-income growth with the top-down model, the geese flying behind are facing at significantly lower levels of income and economic development. China, Indonesia, the Philippines, Thailand, and other developing countries in the region are increasingly looking for inclusive development and global integration, and are therefore facing increasing complexity. They have been responding to that complexity by delegating: to decentralized tiers of government, to the private sector, to communities, to civil society organizations, to competitive markets, and to arm's length regulators or judicial systems. In general, across the region, public participation has also increased.

The degree of delegation and participation varies considerably among countries. To some extent, the variation is explained simply by the abilities of the center to retain control and continue to provide services in top-down mode. China and Thailand, for example, exhibit a greater role for the center than do Indonesia and the Philippines; this is partly a matter of political objectives and partly of administrative constraints. But, overall, there is a sense that countries throughout the region are struggling to design institutions to reconcile delegation, participation, and effective service delivery.

As we shall see in the next chapter, this will depend critically on the ability of the countries to develop new accountability mechanisms at the sectoral level, and new ways to reward good performance and manage the corresponding risks. We will talk a lot about competition, regulation, subsidies, and risk-sharing. And throughout the discussion will run the themes of change, learning, and trade-offs among increasingly complex priorities.

Spotlight 1. Coordination and a tale of three cities: Mass Rapid Transit in Bangkok, Kuala Lumpur, and Manila

East Asia's congested and polluted cities have often looked to urban rail systems to solve their problems. Urban Mass Rapid Transit (MRT) requires a high degree of vision and coordination of multiple actors to make it work, usually involving several jurisdictions and complex financing arrangements.[18] Paradoxically, when the private sector is involved, the degree of vision and coordination needed ratchets up even higher, because of the precision that private sector procurement brings to the process. We look at the experience of private concessions in MRT in three cities: Bangkok, Kuala Lumpur, and Manila.[19]

Bangkok

Bangkok, now a megacity of 10 million people, started its efforts to put an MRT system in place in 1979. By 1990, no MRT system had yet been built, and Bangkok was notorious for its chronic traffic congestion. The technocratic government that had come to power at this time after public unrest and military intervention, was determined to resolve Bangkok's transport problems. This was a key part of its strategy to restore economic credibility to Thailand after the unrest.

In 1990, the Governor of the Bangkok Metropolitan Administration instructed his officials to search for a private concessionaire to build and operate an MRT project. This initiative and parallel efforts eventually spawned two MRT projects: the BTS Skytrain and the Blue Line. Both had long gestation periods: The Skytrain opened in 1999, and the Blue Line subway opened in July 2004. Both operate under a build-operate-transfer (BOT)-type concession (although the two concession contracts differ in scope).

Kuala Lumpur

The Government of Malaysia is intent on transforming the country into a "developed society" by 2020 (the so-called "Vision 2020"). Infrastructure and the private sector are an integral part of that vision—particularly the Malaysian private sector.

Planning studies for MRT in Kuala Lumpur began in the mid-1980s, and MRT came to be seen as essential to making the fast-growing city livable.[20] Those plans eventually led to three MRT projects: KL STAR, KL PUTRA, and KL Monorail. They opened in 1996, 1998, and 2003 respectively. All operated under BOT arrangements.[21]

Manila

Manila is a rapidly expanding megacity of about 11 million people. Its road network consists of a few major arteries and a little-developed secondary network. Car ownership and congestion are high.

> **Box 3.9 MRT in a nutshell**
>
> "[MRT] rail projects are unique in having a high capital requirement, producing a low return on capital, having a long gestation period and providing considerable construction risk *and* commissioning risk *and* ridership risk. The only redeeming features are that once committed, they are incredibly difficult to stop, once there they are essential—they will never be closed, and once built they are (with maintenance) there for all time."
>
> *Source:* Quote from a financier interviewed for Halcrow Group Ltd. 2004.

Planning for MRT in Manila began in the 1970s under the Marcos regime—see Box 3.9 for a brief description of MRT rail projects. In 1984, Manila's first MRT system opened: MRT1. This was a government-financed project. In the 1990s, the Philippines initiated a wave of private sector infrastructure projects, under the Ramos Government. In urban transport, this resulted in MRT3, a build-lease-transfer concession, which opened in 1999–2000. It also resulted in MRT2, which is government and donor funded, and opened in phases during 2003–04.

What was the performance of MRT concessions in the three cities?

It depends what we mean by MRT "performance." The Bangkok Skytrain has helped to unlock severe congestion, and the Blue Line is now making a further contribution. In Kuala Lumpur, the MRT system has helped toward sustainable development for the city region. In Manila, the evolving MRT system has relieved congestion to some extent, and promises to contribute more now that MRT2 is open.

In terms of project development and implementation, the gestation periods were long: operations typically started 8–12 years from when the MRT was first proposed in each case.[22] There were changes in project concept, reflecting poorly on planning, and decision-making and procurement processes were time consuming. In all three cities, integration has been generally quite poor among each MRT system and the others, and with other forms of transport or with land use planning. In other words, network benefits have been lost, and the economic rates of return correspondingly reduced. The costs of delay and of coordination failures can be very high for MRT systems in congested cities.

In financial terms, most projects could be deemed a failure in some sense. The projects have not made the expected financial rate of return, some private investors and financial institutions have lost money, and the state has decided to step in to salvage some of the systems. However, this appearance of financial "failure" is rather misleading. No MRT system in the world gets by without subsidies,[23] yet the private concessions in these three cities were optimistically conceived without subsidies.[24] In short, the "failure" is only by reference to unrealistic financial expectations (albeit somewhat understandable given that the three cities were among the pioneers in private concessions for MRT).[25] The economic rates of return could still be high enough to justify the projects.

The case for MRT subsidies is straightforward—at least in principle. MRT systems can generate large external benefits for vehicle owners and users, and for those who benefit indirectly from reduced congestion and pollution. Users of the MRT system cannot be expected to pay for those external benefits, and the external beneficiaries can only be made to pay through some form of taxation or road pricing channeled back to the MRT network through subsidies.

Of course, that doesn't mean that subsidized MRT will always be the best way to provide public transport, but it sometimes will be in East Asia's wealthier, highly-congested, and polluted megacities. Choosing between subsidizing MRT or something else is essentially a strategic vision and coordination challenge.

What have we learned about government's role in private MRT concessions?

Halcrow Group Ltd. (2004) found that in these three cities the involvement of the private sector made projects happen that otherwise would not have happened, or made them happen sooner, and brought greater efficiency to operations than would otherwise have been the case. But this is perhaps not the major lesson of the tale of these three cities.

MRT systems represent a long network of expensive infrastructure cutting through densely packed urban corridors, and shaping the future geography of their cities. As such, governments need to be intimately involved. There are many tasks that the private sector cannot or should not carry out in planning and implementing an MRT project.

Principal among these government functions are defining how a particular MRT project is intended to fit within the city's overall transport and land use plans (which will almost inevitably be fragmented and fall under multiple jurisdictions), how to acquire the land, how the project will be designed and procured, how to integrate different transport systems, what the government's financial contribution will be, how risk-sharing will be negotiated, and how performance will be regulated. The demands placed by an MRT concession on government's strategic planning and coordination capabilities are heavy, and time is of the essence. MRT won't make its contribution without vision and a strong drive to implement that vision.

4

Accountability and Risk Management

What are accountability and risk management, and how are
they connected?

Accountability is a set of institutional tools that reward organizations that con-
sistently perform well for their stakeholders (and penalize those that perform
badly).

   Risk management is a set of institutional tools that endeavor to make
risks and rewards commensurate with each other to drive good performance.

   In infrastructure services, multiple actors interact. How they hold each
other accountable—what we call the "push and pull" of accountability—is
intimately related to how they share rewards and risk with each other.

In Chapter 3, we looked at how strategic vision is formulated, and
traced some of the paths through which vision is translated, through
service delivery, into outcomes. In this chapter, our perspective is different. We leave strategic vision behind, and try to understand what happens
at the level at which services are delivered and outcomes achieved.

Service delivery and outcomes reflect vision (or the lack of it). But
services are delivered by people, groups, and institutions with incentives
and objectives to other people and groups with incentives and objectives
of their own. How do we make sense of the interactions among these
actors, and what is it about these interactions that lead to good or bad
infrastructure outcomes?

In this chapter, we look at this question in terms of two interlinked
concepts: accountability and risk management.[1] Think of the multiple

actors to which we referred—governments, communities, investors, service providers, and NGOs—engaged with each other in dynamic tension, each with their own goals, each with their own expectations of the other actors, each trying to hold the others accountable for delivery against those expectations. This is what we call the "push and pull of accountability."

And as each actor pushes or pulls, they seek to maximize their rewards and minimize their risks, subject to the constraint that everyone else is doing the same thing. This is what we mean by "risk management." In this chapter, we look at the institutions that help balance competing claims to try and make risks commensurate with rewards. Accountability lubricates that balancing process and helps make development inclusive; lack of accountability means sharp imbalances among stakeholders, and brings unpredictability and instability.

As in previous chapters, we will look at our theme from a number of angles. We begin by considering three available mechanisms through which service provision can be made accountable to both consumers and taxpayers. The first is through community participation. The second is through competition. And the third is through regulation. In the second part of this chapter, we turn our attention to the risk and accountability issues that arise specifically when governments provide support to service providers—through subsidies and other forms of fiscal support—and how the relationship between them can be managed.

But before addressing these issues, consider what happens when accountability relationships and risk management do not do what they're meant to do.

When accountability and risk management fail

Accountability and risk management are often most recognizable when they are absent. In its most dramatic form, the outcome of poorly functioning accountability and risk management frameworks takes the form of financial collapse, as one or other stakeholder is shouldered with obligations that they cannot bear.

Poorly structured infrastructure concessions are part of the story of Asia's financial instability in the late 1990s (see, for example, Box 3.5 on Indonesia in Chapter 3). And they continue to be a source of important macro, fiscal, and financial fragility in a number of countries (see the Vietnamese and Chinese case studies in Chapter 3, Boxes 3.1 and 3.7).

But the most pervasive outcome of poorly functioning accountability systems is corruption. And while the sources of corruption are many and various, there are a number of peculiarities in the infrastructure sectors that make them a frequent target.

In Chapter 2, we saw that infrastructure tends to be capital intensive, that it is often lumpy, long lasting, and space-specific, and that it may run most efficiently on a large scale. As a result, it is often provided by monopolies and can generate large rents. We saw too that infrastructure provides vital services, which people and firms prize highly, and to which politicians assign strategic importance.

And so, infrastructure often involves political protection and intervention. Financial discipline can be weak because of a lack of competition in the market or the knowledge that politicians will guarantee service provision without disruption. If monopoly profits are earned, this can attract rent-seekers; if the services are underpriced through heavy regulation of monopoly power, then rents can be earned from allocating the scarce services. The close association of politics and infrastructure can cement those arrangements in place.

The absence of financial discipline may provide cover for the kinds of practices through which corruption thrives. For example, many utilities in East Asia tend to be overstaffed and employees paid more than the going rate in the market. Inefficiency, patronage, and corruption are not the same thing, but the lines between them may be fine and often crossed. In the Philippines, for example, rural electric cooperatives employ on average twice as many staff per customer as comparable privately owned firms. Elected cooperative board members are frequently accused of dispensing jobs to favored groups or individuals.

With a lumpy, long-term infrastructure asset it is often not easy to discern the relationship between the level of capital investment and flow of infrastructure services. For instance, the thickness of a road will ultimately affect the level of required maintenance, but in the short run will make little difference to the throughput capacity of a road project. This means that, without strong controls, infrastructure providers can inflate the levels of capital spending needed and hide the effects of actual underinvestment. Competition for the market can help hold the provider accountable, but those making the procurement decision need to be accountable as well.

And last but not least, the large size of many types of infrastructure creates opportunities for large kickbacks associated with its procurement. The added fact that infrastructure's benefits are complex means they are hard to measure: It is easy to claim the virtue of new investments. New assets can be favored over better management of those already in place. Corruption can thrive in that environment (see Box 4.1).

Box 4.1 Corruption in infrastructure in the Philippines

Detailed information on corruption in infrastructure—as in any activity—is difficult to obtain and likely to be anecdotal, given its intrinsically covert nature. But a number of studies in the Philippines provide some scope of the problem.

One study on governance issues in public service delivery estimated that the misuse of resources in public works was between 20 percent and 40 percent (Azfar and others 2000). The study noted that on certain procurement and infrastructure projects, regional directors of central agencies are said to receive a 10 percent commission and Department of Budget and Management officers receive 15 percent.

A more recent study lends support to this view, finding that infrastructure projects selected by local development councils, but actually built by the Department of Public Works and Highways or other central agencies, triggered multiple bribes and unofficial payments at each layer of government involvement

Source: World Bank, forthcoming a.

Box 4.2 Public spending in Indonesia and the search for accountability

It is hard to judge whether corruption in Indonesia has worsened or improved since the fall of the New Order Regime and decentralization reforms. But corruption still features high among popular and investor concerns, and poses considerable obstacles to future infrastructure programs in Indonesia.

Opportunity for corruption arises at most stages of Indonesia's infrastructure project cycle—project identification, contract award, and negotiation, as well as financing and implementation—while weaknesses in public finance management, as a whole, blur accountability across government.

In project identification, public sector corruption has been most common in the design of projects that entail SOE and government procurement of highly specialized products, usually from abroad. Here, collusion takes place

(Continued on the next page)

Box 4.2 (Continued)

between local agents and suppliers, with deals struck at marked-up prices, and narrow bid specifications precluding competition.

There are some indications, however, that this practice is waning, with increased exposure to competition, through privatization or capital market discipline, and as the MoF implements SOE performance audits.

In the private sector, unsolicited bids are the most important source of corruption. During the Suharto era, the political connections of a local partner, or financial pay-offs, would often ensure quick project approval, without due attention to the merits of projects. And many formal review processes, where they existed, were ignored.

Public procurement is an additional considerable source of corruption, with estimates of up to 30 percent of the approximately $7 billion in annually procured goods and services that are lost to corruption.

Most corruption in procurement is related to the design of bid specifications, bid invitation, selection, and negotiation. Commonly employed practices include providing restrictive bid specifications to tailor bids to particular manufacturers' products, restricting eligible bidders, and fixing the evaluation process.

Most recent public procurement regulations, set out in 2003, are an improvement on previous decrees. These regulations establish an Institution for Development of Public Procurement Policy, require procurement certification for bid committees, remove prequalification for contracts below $6 million, and introduce "integrity pacts" for suppliers and contractors.

But they remain weak in several respects. The government still needs to work out many unresolved details to ensure proper implementation and enforcement. And additional regulations are needed to promote the transparent selection of private partners for private infrastructure projects.

Finally, corruption in implementation is also common, and usually involves undersupplying on quantity and quality. While such practices should be detected in supervision, in practice they are not, because of frequent collusion among project managers, contractors, and supervisors.

But the problem is not only procurement itself. At a general level, poor budget formulation gives rise to risk of duplication of spending, and diversion of funds to unintended purposes. Budgets are systematically underfunded, budget procedures are unpredictable, financial controls weak, and auditing is ineffective. In this environment, government agencies are implicitly expected to find other means of meeting their needs, blurring the line between public and private expenditures and encouraging rent-seeking behavior.

In this respect, the new State Finance Law creates an opening for reforms. Accountability can be improved by strengthening parliamentary oversight, equipping the Supreme Audit Agency to do its job properly, and holding State Treasurers responsible for handling public money. An additional key medium-term reform will be a complete overhaul of public spending over a five-year period, providing adequate funding for all key activities, and eliminating off-budget sources of funds.

Sources: World Bank 2003a, 2004a.

Mechanisms to strengthen accountability

So how do mechanisms of accountability help prevent these kinds of outcomes and ensure that risks are equitably allocated? In the next part of this chapter, we focus on three important aspects of this question: the role of communities, of competition, and of regulation.

Communities for accountability

We saw in Chapter 2 how infrastructure can reach out to communities, particularly to the poor, and help them manage the risk in their lives. Local roads, irrigation, and safe and reliable drinking water can make an enormous difference to the development prospects of communities. Accessing markets, raising crop yields, and avoiding waterborne disease can both raise and stabilize the incomes of the vulnerable and poor. This is infrastructure for "protective security," one of Amartya Sen's "five freedoms."[2]

But how do you ensure that infrastructure provision answers the real needs of communities? For some types of infrastructure service, the best way to ensure this accountability is to empower the communities to manage their own infrastructure. Indonesia's KDP (highlighted in Chapter 3, Box 3.6) is among the largest and best known in East Asia. But community participation in infrastructure is now increasingly common across the region—from China to Lao PDR, the Philippines to Cambodia.

For many governments, and most of the international development community, it has been a long hard road to arrive at this realization: Local people often know more than enough about their priorities and possible solutions, but they may just need resources and external catalysts to unlock their energies. Local people have more incentive to maintain assets that they choose and maybe even build themselves, and more reason to watch out for corruption.

Sometimes NGOs can be more effective as external catalysts of local energies than governments, or large donors, can. More traditional, top-down approaches to infrastructure service provision have often been unresponsive to needs at the community level.

An NGO perception survey undertaken for this study suggests that greater provision of information to communities, greater involvement of local government and community-based organizations, and more public participation in decision making are key concerns in an otherwise broadly optimistic outlook (see Box 4.3).

Clearly community empowerment works best when infrastructure is small and can be within the control of a single community. Small town water supply systems are often ideal candidates for local community management, as one survey from Vietnam suggests (van den Berg 2002). But in the case of large infrastructure, complexity and sheer scale can make direct community management and self-accountability infeasible.

Box 4.3 Infrastructure, accountability, and NGO perceptions: Survey results

In fall 2004, 132 representatives from NGOs in six East Asian countries participated in a survey to measure their perceptions of infrastructure development in East Asia. The data show that NGOs in these countries are quite optimistic, overall, about the direction of infrastructure development (72 percent of the sample said they were optimistic), but those surveyed believe that more should be done to engender better infrastructure development on the ground.

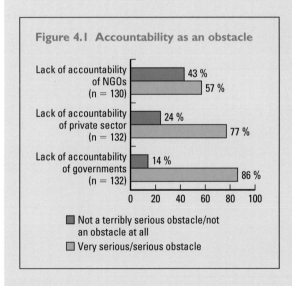

Figure 4.1 Accountability as an obstacle

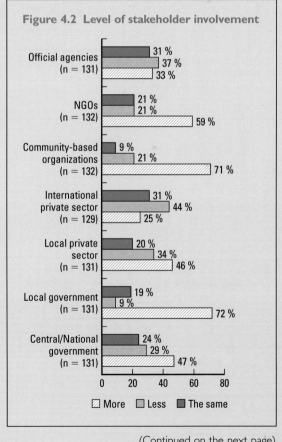

Figure 4.2 Level of stakeholder involvement

(Continued on the next page)

Box 4.3 (Continued)

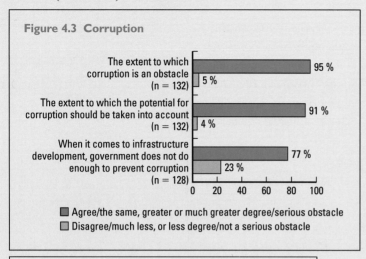

Figure 4.3 Corruption

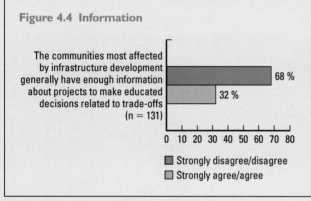

Figure 4.4 Information

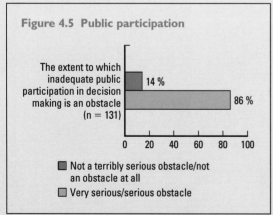

Figure 4.5 Public participation

Source: Civil Society Perception 2004.
Note: Survey conducted in China, Indonesia, Japan, Philippines, Thailand, and Vietnam. Respondents were randomly chosen from lists provided by a number of sources including the Australian Council for International Development, ADB, Bank Information Centre, JBIC, and the World Bank.

Box 4.4 Community action in rolling back environmental externalities in postwar Japan

In the years immediately following World War II, Japan embarked on a period of extremely rapid industrial growth, which, while highly successful in conventional economic terms, brought with it major environmental externalities. The consequences of air and water pollution were exemplified in the 1960s by the well-documented cases of Yokkaichi Asthma and Minamata Disease.

The Japanese response to such environmental problems originated at the municipal and local levels, where citizens exerted pressure on elected officials to take measures against offending industrial enterprises. A series of voluntary agreements were made between industrial enterprises and local governments, which in many cases did not have any explicit environmental jurisdiction or responsibility. National legislation tended to follow later, and national standards for air and water quality invariably remain lower than those contained in the approximately 40,000 voluntary agreements now in place in Japan.

As far as domestic air and water quality is concerned, there is universal agreement that Japan has been an exemplary case, and a number of factors are widely cited as reasons for this. These include a free press that publicized environmental issues; universal literacy, with a strong emphasis on technical education, which enabled citizens to understand the impact of environmental degradation on their own health and well-being; and a democratic system in which local officials were compelled to take citizens' complaints seriously, yet were powerful and efficient enough to address complex technical issues and take measures to address pollution.

Source: Aoyama 1994.

This does not preclude community participation in aspects of infrastructure that directly affect their lives. The role that communities played in Japan in responding to environmental externalities is indicative of the circumstances under which community participation can bring about change (see Box 4.4).

The experience and the literature on stakeholder participation in infrastructure projects is vast, but there are some very consistent themes that emerge. Providing as much information as possible to communities is essential. Communities need to know particularly about technological and location options to be able to decide how those projects could benefit them most, and how the negative impacts and the risks could be best mitigated. Giving stakeholders a genuine chance to be heard, and to make a difference, requires involving them very early in the project planning process.[3] When those with relatively little negotiating power come late to

> **Box 4.5 Making a deal with the community: Water supply and accountability in Indonesia**
>
> Most drinking water in Indonesia is supplied by local government-owned water companies (PDAMs).
>
> Audits of a number of PDAMs have found serious problems, including low coverage levels, high levels of unaccounted-for-water, non-potable water, and severe financial difficulties because of low tariffs and mismanagement. While the local councils demand increased coverage and improved service, they often do not provide the PDAMs with sufficient resources to be able to achieve these objectives.
>
> A U.S. Agency for International Development (USAID) project assisted PDAMs to break the vicious cycle by developing corporate plans focused on using excess capacity, reducing water losses, increasing productivity, reducing staffing ratios, and enabling tariff increases.
>
> Emphasis on customer service is an important part of the plans. By communicating the PDAM's plan for improving service and focusing on customer service, the PDAMs gained the support of the community, which in turn enabled the local councils to grant the much-needed tariff increases.
>
> For example, PDAM Banjar in South Kalimantan was in poor condition, with revenues barely covering out-of-pocket costs, water losses reaching 40 percent, and water provided only 12 hours a day.
>
> A plan was developed to enable the PDAM to improve services. But the success of the plan depended on increased revenue from tariffs, and the local council would not approve the tariff increases. The PDAM therefore took the plan to the community, explaining the objectives and why the tariff revenues were needed. To cement its promises, the PDAM entered into a contract with the community, a contract which required real improvement in customer service.
>
> By gaining the support of the community, the PDAM was able to obtain the tariff increase from the local council and has been able to decrease water losses, increase supply, improve water quality, and redesign their billing and collection system to virtually eliminate long lines and waiting periods.
>
> *Source:* Parton 2003.

the process, their voices are likely to be drowned out and the participation process becomes tokenism.

And once the infrastructure is built, stakeholder participation need not end there. Participation can help ensure service provision remains appropriate to the community's needs. Box 4.5 illustrates the innovative role that community participation has played in water supply in Indonesia.

Community participation may be vital in one more respect. Some kinds of infrastructure frequently bring significant costs to communities that do not enjoy many of the benefits. Power generators, sewage treatment plants, and dams often have to be built in somebody's backyard. Provision for adequate compensation to affected communities is a generally endorsed principle for all infrastructure projects of this nature. But ensuring that all costs are compensated, and risks mitigated, is difficult even when strong accountability mechanisms are in place. In countries in which the governance environment is poor, it is even harder.

Community consultation should always be at the center of such processes. But official lenders and donors may also have an important role to play. The risk mitigation mechanisms established around the Nam Theun 2 dam project in Lao PDR are examples of how official lenders and donors have attempted to do this (see Box 4.6).

But outside of this special case, for large-scale network infrastructure, participation is generally beyond the scope of individual communities, except for the "last kilometer" of the network that comes to them: the situating of an electricity substation, the routing of a feeder road, the choice of community standpipe versus in-house connection, and choosing whether to connect to the network at all. At the sector level, the pull of accountability needs to be more institutionalized through markets, regulators, and governments. Lets start with markets.

Box 4.6 Putting accountability mechanisms into large infrastructure projects: The Nam Theun 2 dam project

Nam Theun 2 (NT2) is a major hydropower project currently under consideration in the Lao PDR. The project would entail an investment of $1.2 billion, to be undertaken by the private sector, on the Nam Theun River, which is 250 km east of the Lao PDR capital, Vientiane. Its goal is to generate more than 1,000 mW of electricity, almost all of which would be exported to neighboring Thailand.

By any scale, the project is large. In Lao terms it is enormous—nearly equal to the country's current annual GDP. The returns of the project to the country are significant. And Lao PDR has few development alternatives.

But the project comes with a number of important risks, arising from the structure of the investment, and Lao PDR's accountability environment.

The first of these risks—common to major enclave investments in developing countries—is the highly unequal allocation of cost and benefits. In the case of NT2, the major benefits of the project take the form of payments to the government, arising from its 25 percent shareholding in the project, in the form of dividends, royalties, and taxes. The main costs, however, are carried by communities and the environment in the project area, arising from the construction of the dam, the flooding of the Nakai Plateau, and downstream effects associated with the interbasin transfer of water from the Nam Theun to the Xe Bang Fai River.

(Continued on the next page)

Box 4.6 (Continued)

This raises issues both of equity and incentives. Because the government carries limited costs, and enjoys most benefits, its incentives to intervene in the case of those that do carry costs are limited. When those who are most likely to suffer negative impacts are poor and marginalized, and when mechanisms of accountability and participation are highly constrained, this becomes all the more so.

The second feature of the project is the major risk that the substantial benefits accruing to the government will not be effectively translated into benefits for the country. While NT2 inflows to the government are likely to account for only 5 percent of government revenue, their impact on expenditures has the potential to be highly significant if effectively targeted. Projected NT2 revenues to the government in 2011, adjusted to today's prices, are equivalent to approximately half of domestically financed expenditure on education and health.

However, widespread weaknesses in governance constrain the ability of Lao PDR to significantly address its poor development outcomes. As Figure 4.6 shows, Lao PDR's governance performances rate poorly against averages for both low-income regions and the region as a whole, particularly on voice and accountability, and on control of corruption. The government's capacity to

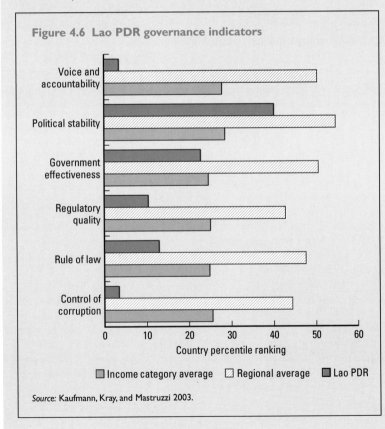

Figure 4.6 Lao PDR governance indicators

Source: Kaufmann, Kray, and Mastruzzi 2003.

channel resources into poverty reduction is also constrained by one of the least effective service delivery mechanisms in the region. Public expenditure management remains both weak, and highly untransparent. The government has only recently resumed publication of the state budget, and the public finance management system fails to meet any of the Highly Indebted Poor Country (HIPC) Initiative benchmarks.

The design of NT2 attempts to address these issues in a number of overlapping ways: first, in assigning joint responsibility to the concessionaire and the government—through provisions written into the concession agreement—to finance and implement measures to compensate for impacts and costs suffered in the project area; second, in making changes to the project design to mitigate the risk of negative externalities, where feasible; third, by bringing international financial institutions into the financing of the project, effectively making continued donor support conditional on the government's commitment to fulfilling its responsibilities in terms of the concession; and fourth, through the establishment of mechanisms to earmark project revenues for poverty reduction, while improving the public finance management system through which they—and all expenditures—must be delivered.

Active participation of the international community has helped encourage local public consultation and disclosure to ensure that affected people are fully informed of the project and that their views are taken into account. More than 200 consultations and workshops were conducted in project-affected areas to ensure that affected people would participate in the measures to protect them from the impact of the project. A total of $89 million has been designated as capital and operating expenditures for environmental and social mitigation and compensation.[a] These obligations are defined, and costed in the concession agreement, which has been signed by the government and the private sector concessionaires.

Mechanisms have also been developed to address weak accountability arrangements in the public finance management system, in particular, to facilitate more effective and transparent targeting of NT2 revenues toward poverty reduction goals.

Proposed revenue and expenditure management arrangements will focus on the development of the government's core public expenditure management system and will avoid building parallel systems through which to channel NT2 revenues. Under this approach, NT2 revenues will be channeled through the central treasury account to finance expenditures on eligible poverty reduction and conservation programs. These programs will be required to meet management and reporting standards. Expenditures and program impact will be monitored through a program of expenditure reviews and expenditure tracking surveys. In this way, the implementation of NT2 revenue and expenditure management arrangements will support broader public expenditure management reforms.

Source: World Bank staff.
Note: a. See ADB (2004a), and http://www.namtheun2.com for a detailed discussion of these proposed mechanisms.

Competition for accountability

Competitive infrastructure service providers can be held accountable by consumers. If an airline, a jeepney, or a mobile phone company provides an unreliable or expensive service, you go elsewhere.[4] These kinds of markets reward those who are efficient. This is the short route to accountability.

Most infrastructure networks cannot feasibly be provided competitively—the economies of scale are too great—but many infrastructure services provided through those networks can be competitive. The potential for such competition varies by sector for a combination of technological, economic, and political reasons. The "standard model" for harnessing such competition is to unbundle utilities, both horizontally and vertically, and to introduce private sector participation under conditions of competition where possible. This can take the form of full divestiture of certain assets, but may equally take the form of management contracts, where—for instance—market size is insufficient to allow for unbundling.

In the case of water distribution, for instance, markets tend to be localized and hence small, because the costs of transmitting water over long distances is prohibitive—bulk water costs can increase by up to 50 percent per 100 km transported, compared with 5 percent for electricity and 2.5 percent for gas.[5] This limits scope for competition in the market, and it's further limited by the technical challenges of ensuring water quality and safety if different suppliers access the same network (as well as being limited by availability of a variety of bulk freshwater sources in a given area). There has been experimentation with third-party access in some developed countries (as is the case with "inset" appointments in England and Wales[6]), but so far water supply competition is rare—although there can still of course be competition *for* the market through the tendering of concession rights (which is fairly common in East Asia).[7]

However, in telecommunications, electricity, gas, and most transport services, competition to supply services over networks is technically much more feasible than in water supply. The last two decades have seen an enormous increase in the prevalence of competition in those sectors worldwide (see Box 4.7 for a discussion of telecoms in particular). But East Asia has not been in the forefront of introducing infrastructure service competition. Even in telecommunications, in which the technological

Box 4.7 Technology, competition, and regulation: The push and pull of accountability in the telecoms sector

The interaction among technology, markets, and sound regulation is at the heart of the recent transformation of the telecoms industry across the world.

This is the push and pull of accountability at its best, as regulators ensure that the levers of technology and market forces are exploited by private operators to the benefit of consumers and that markets, in turn, allow consumers to join with regulators in holding private operators accountable.

Technology has been the catalyzing force. As technology has lowered barriers to entry, previously unprofitable sectors have been transformed, new markets have opened, both in turn increasing competition and spurring the development of yet more innovative business solutions and service.

Market forces have helped hold service providers accountable—competition has forced carriers to tailor services to the needs of the users, inducing operators, for example, to offer bundled free voice calls and value-added services. In China and Thailand, it has driven the trend toward bundling of fixed and wireless services, and it is likely to promote industry convergence, as new business models replace old.

Among the most important implications are the new possibilities for universal services. Cellular mobile penetration in rural areas has forced policy makers to broaden the concept of universal access, originally conceived for fixed-line telephony, to include substitute products.

The interplay between market-based mechanisms and technology innovation has proved to be more successful in connecting new users than the traditional business model, which was based on an incumbent monopoly service provider. With the introduction of prepaid technology, the mobile operators in Cambodia, China, Thailand, and the Philippines are now competing for business in rural villages previously uneconomic to serve.

Regulation has a crucial role to play at the interface between technology and market forces. Its role is to facilitate market liberalization and technology diffusion, and provide a level playing field for incumbent service providers and new entrants. This means technology neutrality, that is, allowing the development of new technologies, like VoIP, and resisting pressures to protect incumbent business models based on outmoded technology. Ensuring that subsidies can be funded in a competition-neutral manner is equally important. Imposing uniform pricing on universal service providers on equity grounds (regardless of cost differentials) has proved an obstacle to market liberalization, because the most profitable segments of the market are competed away by new entrants, leaving universal service providers with the loss-making sections of the customer base.

Source: Ure 2004.

basis of competition is comparatively straightforward, competition in East Asia is still limited by international standards (see Map 4.1).

In electricity, competition is also quite restricted. Indeed, the example of the way that IPPs have been introduced in most East Asian electricity

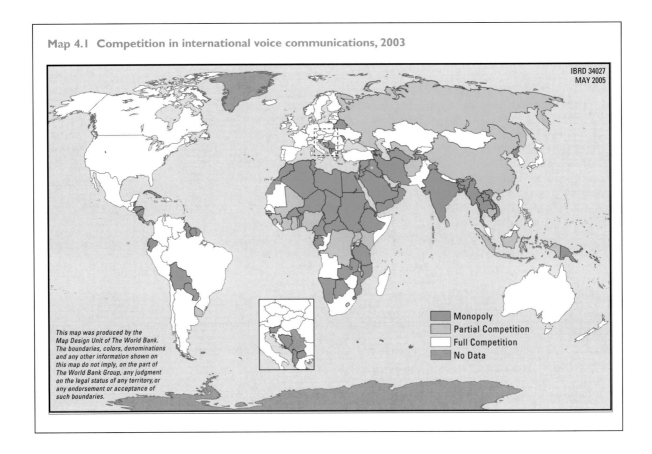

Map 4.1 **Competition in international voice communications, 2003**

IBRD 34027
MAY 2005

This map was produced by the
Map Design Unit of The World Bank.
The boundaries, colors, denominations
and any other information shown on
this map do not imply, on the part of
The World Bank Group, any judgment
on the legal status of any territory, or
any endorsement or acceptance of
such boundaries.

Monopoly
Partial Competition
Full Competition
No Data

sectors is illustrative of some of the factors that can limit competition in the region's infrastructure services more broadly (see Box 4.8).

IPPs have brought private participation to East Asian electricity sectors, but they don't generally sell power in a competitive market. Instead they usually sell to a state-owned single buyer (often a transmission company), which then sells the power (as a monopolist) directly to large final customers or to unbundled distribution companies.[8] Typically, the IPP sells power under a long-term power purchase agreement (PPA), with at least a portion of the payment guaranteed at a predetermined price regardless of actual demand (so-called "take-or-pay" provisions).[9]

Why have East Asian countries chosen to impose a single buyer (which is simultaneously a single seller) between the IPP generators and the customers? One common reason is that the single buyer can facilitate the introduction of private finance for generation quickly when capacity shortages are looming.[10] This was the principal reason for using the

Box 4.8 Choice of power sector structure in East Asia

The variety of market structures emerging from reforms to power sectors can be categorized according to increasing degree of competition, as set out in Table 4.1 (after the classification of Hunt and Shuttleworth 1996). Under Models 1 and 2, generation companies (which may be part of the national utility, a state-owned company, or an IPP) sell power to a state-owned single buyer. In the developing world, few countries—mainly in Latin America—have advanced power sector reforms far beyond the single-buyer model. To date, countries in East Asia have strongly opted for Model 1.

Source: Besant-Jones 2004.

Table 4.1 Distribution of developing and transition countries by structure of power supply (mid-2004)

Model 1 A national utility and/or regional vertically integrated utilities		Model 2 Regional discos, a national or regional genco/transco	Model 3 Regional discos, many gencos, a national transco	Model 4 A wholesale power market, many gencos and discos, national/regional transco(s)
Albania	Nigeria	Armenia	Bulgaria	Argentina
Algeria	**Malaysia**	Czech Rep.	Ecuador	Bolivia
Azerbaijan	Mexico	Estonia	Georgia	Brazil
Belarus	Nepal	India[a]	Hungary	Chile
Cambodia	Paraguay	Kenya	India (Orissa)	Colombia
China	Serbia	Latvia	**Philippines**	El Salvador
Croatia	South Africa	Lithuania	Poland	Panama
Egypt, Arab Rep. of	Sri Lanka	Kazakhstan	Romania	Peru
Ethiopia	Tanzania	Moldova	Russian Fed.	Spain
India[a]	Turkmenistan	**Mongolia**	Ukraine	Turkey
Indonesia	Uruguay	Pakistan		
Jordan	Uzbekistan	Slovak Republic		
Tanzania	**Vietnam**	**Thailand**		
Korea, Rep. of	Zambia	Uganda		
Lao PDR	Zimbabwe	Venezuela		
Montenegro				

Sources: APEC 2002; World Energy Council 2001; World Bank staff.
Note: disco = distribution company; genco = generation company; transco = transmission company.
a. Many states.

single-buyer/IPP model in the Philippines, Indonesia, Thailand, and elsewhere in the region. Private financing may be wanted to bring efficiency in design, construction, or operation—or simply to relieve the immediate burden on the public purse (and sometimes just to hide the burden on the public purse). Another objective for keeping single buyers has been to extract monopoly rent for political or personal gain. An additional reason has been a feeling that national control over strategic infrastructure assets can be politically important (particularly when there is foreign investment involved in generation).

Yet another—and very powerful—objective is that a single buyer can easily cross-subsidize. In Indonesia, for example, the state electricity utility (PLN) maintains explicit subsidies between large and small consumers. At one end of the range, a small residential consumer with a 450 volt-amp (VA) connection and consumption of 50 kWh per month currently pays 3.5 cents per kWh, while a large residential consumer with a connected capacity of 16,500 VA and monthly consumption of 2,000 kWh per month pays approximately 10.1 cents per kWh (World Bank 2004a).

Cross-subsidies can be important for social and political reasons (as we shall discuss in more detail later). Single buyers can retain creditworthy customers, who might be lured away by private generators if competition were possible. Competition therefore makes it difficult for less-creditworthy customers to be cross-subsidized, or indeed for the state utility to cross-subsidize its own excessive costs.

A perhaps more benign way of making the cross-subsidies point is that a single buyer can shield private generators from taking on the less-creditworthy customers directly, with the attendant commercial or regulatory risks. Usually, single buyers are either creditworthy or can be assumed to have sovereign creditworthiness standing behind them. A single buyer therefore represents a lower risk to the generator than would direct sales to customers with poor creditworthiness. Whether a particular single buyer actually mitigates the generator's risk overall depends on the preponderance of bad customers over good and on the reliability of the single buyer as a customer.[11] This is clearly very country-specific.[12]

However, one thing is universal about the single-buyer model: it loses much of the accountability for performance that comes from competition. This is relevant well beyond the electricity sector. Competition has been limited in other infrastructure sectors for some of the same reasons that it has in the IPP case, namely, cross-subsidies for sociopolitical objectives, monopoly rent-seeking, the protection of incumbent state enterprises, risk mitigation for the private sector, and the political control of strategic assets. In essence, the policy coordination challenge is how to achieve accountability when competition competes with these other objectives.

Box 4.9 Manila water: The challenges of structuring competition for the market

Few instances of private sector participation in infrastructure in East Asia have attracted as much attention as Manila's twin water concessions. There are many ways in which the story has been told. Most prominently feature the impact of the Asian financial crisis on the sustainability of the contracts. But the story runs far deeper than that, into the challenges of structuring private and public sector relations, and harnessing competition.

In 1997, the Metropolitan Water Supply and Sewerage System (MWSS), the public water supply and sewerage company for Metro Manila, was privatized. At the time, this was the largest privatization in Asia, totaling a promised investment of $5.7 billion.

MWSS is one of the oldest water systems in Asia, covering more than 14 cities and municipalities, with a population of around 11 million people and a land area of 2,000 km^2. By 1994, when privatization plans were first conceptualized, the prevailing view was that MWSS had largely failed in its mission to provide water and sewerage to its coverage population. MWSS had a nonrevenue water (NRW) ratio of around 60 percent and was supplying water for at least 16 hours per day to only two-thirds of the population in its coverage area. Only 10 percent of the customers were connected to the sewerage system.

Private participation in MWSS took the form of two concession contracts with private operators: one for the east zone (Manila Water Company, MWCI) and one for the west zone (Manila Water Services, MWSI). The concessions were granted on the basis of the lowest initial tariff (this would be important for garnering political support) and made provision for concession fees equal to the debt service payments on MWSS's preexisting debts, denominated mostly in dollars. Ninety percent (later 80 percent) of the fees were assigned to the western concession, MWSI.

Tariff adjustments were provided for in a number of ways. First, there would be a rebasing every five years (initially, the concession allowed for the first rebasing in only the tenth year of operation, at the option of the regulatory office). In addition, the concession agreement provided for automatic annual inflation adjustments, and extraordinary price adjustment and cost recovery for events outside their direct control (such as large changes in the exchange rates) at any time during the intervening period.

The winning bids for the concessions entailed significant reductions in tariffs—to less than one-third of the prevailing levels in the case of the east zone. Did this mean that competition for the market brought greater efficiency, that risks would be better managed? Not on its own. Because infrastructure, and infrastructure concessions, are a long-term business. What the Manila concessions highlight is the difficulty of sustaining efficient outcomes as circumstances change, and participants respond to different incentives.

The most serious challenge to the concessions was the impact of the Asian financial crisis on debt inherited from MWSS—in particular for MWSI. Provision for automatic inflation adjustments proved to be insufficient to protect MWSI from the peso depreciation, because currency depreciation

(Continued on the next page)

Box 4.9 (Continued)

outstripped inflation. And an inbuilt extraordinary price adjustment (EPA) mechanism was insufficient to make up the difference—partly because the EPA required cost increases to be amortized over the life of the contract, and also because the basis for computing changes in unit cost arising from the depreciation of the peso was MWSI's own overly optimistic projections of the reduction in NRW (which resulted in overly optimistic projections of future growth in sales volume). In 2003, MWSI gave notice to terminate its concession and has been in dispute with the government ever since.

This outcome highlights the difficulty of developing long-term contractual mechanisms that are rigid enough to reduce parties' exposure to risk, while remaining flexible enough to adjust to circumstances covering 20- to 30-year periods. But this is linked also to how the contracts were awarded and the incentives that bidders faced in the bidding process.

One of the risks of a concession contract of the kind used in Manila is the risk that bidders submit unrealistically low bids in the expectation of recovering losses through higher tariffs when the tariffs are rebased, structuring their financing accordingly. When this happens, initially low tariffs are a kind of loan to water consumers who "pay back" their initial savings in subsequent concession periods, and sometimes at a high interest rate.

This was partly the case with Manila water. Between 1997 and 2003, tariffs for both east and west concessions have more than tripled in peso terms. In dollar terms, they have more than doubled. It is clear that tariffs increased not only to cover the effects of peso depreciation but also to make adjustments for the fact that the financial and technical models that were used by the concessionaires to generate their bid tariffs were too optimistic. For instance, NRW reduction targets promised in the winning bids, from 45 percent to 16 percent in the east, and from 64 percent to 31 percent in the west, proved to be highly overoptimistic. NRW levels in both east and west zones have in fact hovered in the region of 57 percent.

This was partly a fault of the concession design. The concession had not specified penalties for NRW reduction shortfalls, because the designers thought that failure to achieve NRW targets by itself would be a sufficient penalty (on the assumption that concessionaires would have to bring more equity to the concessions, particularly if lenders refused to finance the shortfall resulting from insufficient NRW outcomes).

Did the concessions bring about value for money? In terms of new connections, improvement of water pressure, and the number of households enjoying at least 16 hours of water supply per day, both concessions have performed much better than MWSS did before privatization. Coverage, for instance, increased to 75 percent by 2002, from 61 percent in 1996. But these outcomes do not match the high expectations raised by private participation. And those who have to pay more for water may protest more loudly than those with new connections or improved service may praise the concessionaires.

Sources: Castalia 2004c; Medalla 2004; JBIC 2003.

Regulators for accountability

Where the invisible hand of competition does not reach, regulation will generally be needed to bring accountability to infrastructure service providers. There is a rich literature on infrastructure regulation, but our purpose in this section is specific: to clarify for what regulators are trying to hold service providers accountable, how regulators themselves can be held accountable, and how all this fits into the East Asian political context.

It is sometimes said that, while making service providers accountable, the regulator needs to protect their interests in parallel with those of consumers to minimize regulatory risk for investors. But this is rather misleading. As we saw in Chapter 1, infrastructure is ultimately paid for by consumers or taxpayers. Regulators can certainly affect the risks of investing in infrastructure service provision; however, if they increase the risk, the cost of capital increases, and it's the consumers or taxpayers who pay for it. So the regulator's role is really to serve the interests of consumers and taxpayers and to hold service providers accountable for providing the service that consumers and taxpayers want.[13] Minimizing regulatory risk is just one way to fulfill that role.[14]

But how is the regulator itself held accountable? Well, there are a number of classic measures that can help.[15] Some relate to process and participation, including writing statutes that clearly specify the rights and responsibilities of the regulator, and explain how to prioritize when there are multiple objectives; allowing judicial review or effective arbitration of regulatory decisions; requiring the production of annual reports and subjecting the performance of the regulator to independent audit or parliamentary review; ensuring meritocratic appointment and removal of regulators; and allowing stakeholder submissions on issues under review.

Other measures relate to transparency: requiring regulators to publish decisions (and the reasoning behind the decisions), as well as licenses and benchmarked performance of regulated service providers. The Indonesian Water Supply Association (PERPAMSI), for instance, benchmarks and reports on 29 indicators, with information made available to the public on its Web site (see Box 4.10 for how this plays out in East Asia as a whole). Mechanisms are also needed to allow the voices of consumers and potential consumers to be heard in policy and regulatory decisions. And so in the Philippines, for instance, tariff hearings are public, and customers are allowed to speak and ask questions (Castalia 2004c). These

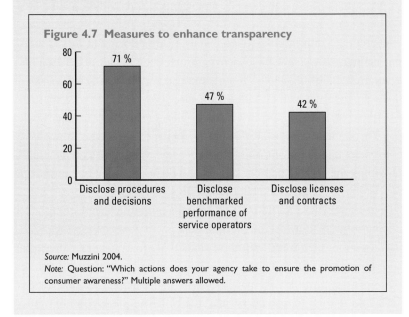

Box 4.10 Holding regulators accountable through transparency

The results of the recent survey of East Asian regulators suggests that around two-thirds of the surveyed regulators in the East Asian region disclose procedures and decisions, while half of the regulators also release to the public performance indicators of regulated service providers. However, licenses and contracts with private service providers are still kept confidential by the majority of the regulating entities.

Source: Muzzini 2004.

Figure 4.7 Measures to enhance transparency

Source: Muzzini 2004.
Note: Question: "Which actions does your agency take to ensure the promotion of consumer awareness?" Multiple answers allowed.

issues are addressed in Spotlight 2 of this chapter, which discusses consumer participation in regulation.

But infrastructure is intensely political, and the accountability of the regulator therefore cannot be divorced from broader institutions of political accountability. Nor can the ability of the regulator to hold service providers accountable be separated from the political context. To some readers, these will seem like radical statements. In the last two decades, much energy had been expended in the industrial and developing worlds in pursuit of independence for regulators. This has been based on a view that infrastructure regulation should be depoliticized.

There is much value in this argument, and, in the pursuit of independence, political intervention in infrastructure can often be damaging, particularly if it is short term. But independence is a relative concept.

Many countries find their sovereign independence to be evolutionary rather than absolute, and many countries struggle to create a separation of powers in their basic political institutions. So it's not too surprising that independence for infrastructure regulators would take time.

And it is indeed taking time. According to one recent paper, "Most new regulators in developing countries, when asked whether they have the independence provided for in law, will either say 'no' or avert their glance and change the subject" (Bakovic, Tenenbaum, and Woolf 2003). According to another, "The label 'independent' is somewhat exaggerated when applied to new regulators in developing and transition economies" (Kessides 2004).

East Asia is certainly no exception, which is unsurprising given its tradition of strong central control. "Independence" is obviously hard to measure in a comparable manner; however, in the survey of East Asian regulators discussed in Spotlight 2 of this chapter, less than 40 percent described themselves as even nominally independent.

So how can the design of regulatory institutions accommodate the evolutionary nature of independence? One basic method is to ensure that the degree of discretion allowed to the regulator does not exceed what the political culture can absorb. This implies that fledgling regulators should have relatively limited discretionary powers and that discretion should build over time. A key example is that regulators could start out with multiyear tariff-setting systems in which tariffs are set by specific formulae in the first few years, and according to more general principles in later years.

Another example is that regulation for specific service providers could be established by concession contract negotiated between the investors and the government (according to principles and parameters laid down in generally applicable legislation). The day-to-day application of the contract would be delegated to the regulator. Yet another example is that key aspects of regulation could initially be contracted out to third-party experts, enhancing the credibility of regulatory decisions, until such time as greater discretion can be allowed (see Box 4.11).

We saw in Chapter 1 that the infrastructure investor perceptions survey conducted for this study showed that investor interest in the region was strong, but heavily contingent on reducing policy-based risk. That survey found that predictability of regulation was a major cause for concern in the region and a significant determinant of actual investment. Respondents rarely talked about a need for regulators to be independent,

Box 4.11 Contracting out regulatory functions

Contracting out regulatory functions is a well-established practice in infrastructure sectors of developing and industrial countries. Regulators can outsource technical tasks, specific regulatory decisions, or the whole regulatory process. Contracting out arrangements can be built into the institutional framework, as it is often the case when contracted-out recommendations are binding or pursued on an ad hoc basis. The external contracted agency may consist of individual consultants, government agencies (at the national or regional level), or NGOs.

The rationale for seeking external advice or contracting out regulatory decisions varies, to a significant extent, according to the local context and the stage of the life of the regulatory agency. Experienced regulators tend to outsource specific regulatory functions (albeit retaining decision-making responsibilities) to reduce costs and bridge the information asymmetry between the regulator and service providers. For example, the energy regulator in the United Kingdom, Ofgem, employs contractors to conduct independent audits of regulated companies and monitor their compliance with quality targets. Nascent regulators may decide to contract out binding regulatory functions to leverage the international expertise required to gain regulatory credibility relative to private operators. For example, in 1998, the newly established Bucharest Agency for Water and Sewerage Regulation (ARBAC) appointed a panel of experts to conduct the tariff review; in 1996, the Palestinian Water Authority relied on a third-party technical and financial audit to review, on an annual basis, the performance-based management fee for the first water utility management contract in Gaza. The practice of contracting out is more widespread in the water sector, in which most regulators are set up at the local level and have limited regulatory capacity, and in the telecommunication sector, in which regulators need to be kept abreast of a rapidly evolving environment.

The practice of contracting out regulatory decision making to regional institutions can yield significant benefits for very small countries, where scarcity of technical skills may make it efficient to limit the number of regulatory agencies. In such a context, a regional regulatory agency might be in a better position than small national regulatory bodies to build the critical mass of regulatory capacity required to ensure legitimacy of regulatory decisions. For example, the Eastern Caribbean Telecommunication Authority (ECTEL) serves the member countries of the Organization of the Eastern Caribbean States as a shared regulatory body. ECTEL's mandate is to coordinate regional telecommunication policies in addition to providing advice and support to national regulatory agencies.

Similarly, there is merit in adopting a regional regulatory approach when infrastructure regulation affects inter- and intraregional trade, resulting in additional transaction costs for operators. For example, national transportation safety regulations may conflict with each other and, hence, limit or distort opportunities for trade. In such a context, there is a clear economic argument for national regulators to relinquish partially their regulatory jurisdiction to super-national entities better placed to promote standard harmonization.

(Continued on the next page)

Box 4.11 (Continued)

There may be, for example, a rationale for setting up a regional transport regulator in the Pacific Islands, which are part of the same trade area. A number of Pacific island countries have been moving in this direction by exploring the possibility of establishing a regional aviation safety authority, the Pacific Aviation Safety Office (PASO). This organization would be responsible for setting and ensuring compliance with standards of safety and security in the aviation and airport sector across member countries.

However, several challenges arise when regulatory decision making is contracted out. Contracting out regulatory decisions can weaken the accountability of the regulator relative to the local consumer constituency. To avoid loss of accountability, national regulators need to maintain sufficient in-house regulatory capacity to monitor the contract performance and ensure the transparency of the contracting out process. Contracting out core regulatory decisions is often a politically sensitive decision, because governments may be reluctant to surrender their sovereign regulatory authority on contentious issues (such as tariff reviews). For example, ECTEL is not authorized to impinge on member countries' authority to issue licenses to operators, although disputes can be referred to ECTEL for mediation.

Overall, contracting out regulatory functions to third-party agencies appears to be an effective instrument to strengthen the legitimacy and capacity of nascent regulators as well as to promote standard harmonization and regional coordination among national regulatory bodies, provided that it is accompanied by transparency and accountability mechanisms and there is enough political commitment to move forward with infrastructure reforms.

Sources: Environmental Resource Management, Ltd. 2004; Castalia 2004b.

and they often argued that predictable regulation required explicit agreements with political authorities in the East Asia region (and showed a corresponding lack of faith in independent regulation or judicial review). In essence, respondents acknowledged the coordination role of the East Asian state discussed in Chapter 3. Indeed, respondents showed a marked preference for investing in countries that have strong strategic vision about infrastructure.

This survey response can be interpreted in various ways, but one key theme emerges: Investors want predictability, and predictability in East Asia may not require initially high levels of independence for regulators. Indeed, an evolutionary approach to the discretionary power of independent regulators seems appropriate. If discretion exceeds political absorption capacities at any point in time, a political backlash is likely (for example, the head of state overturns a regulator's tariff increase). Conversely, if regulators' discretion does not grow as the ability of

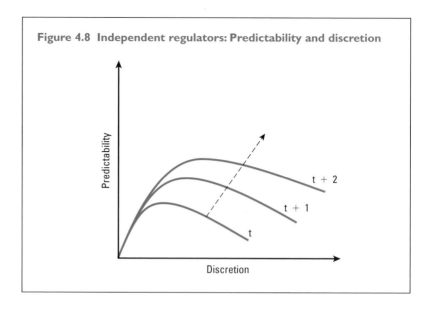

Figure 4.8 Independent regulators: Predictability and discretion

governments to exercise top-down control declines, a regulatory vacuum could emerge. Discretion that grows over time, and liberates itself progressively from political pressures, could enhance predictability (see Figure 4.8 for an illustration).

Risk-sharing, accountability, and managing government support

We have discussed the various ways in which accountability can be brought into the provision of infrastructure services, and how risk can be managed. We looked at the roles of communities, regulators, and competition in respect to the relationship between service providers and consumers. In the last part of this chapter, we look at the role of government and, in particular, at how accountability can be shaped so that it shares risks with infrastructure providers in the delivery of services.

When governments delegate service provision, they typically do it under some kind of risk-sharing arrangement. Often this involves government support and, most frequently, it's in the form of subsidies or guarantees. By providing this support, the government effectively reduces the risk exposure of service providers (or their financiers) by some corresponding amount, because higher tariffs would have entailed greater political or market risk.

Risk-sharing arrangements of this kind are often crucial to delegation of service provision, but it raises important accountability challenges. Subsidizing the provision of services weakens the accountability relationships that bind providers and governments (and, through them, to the consumers and taxpayers) by diminishing the incentive to provide services in the most efficient manner possible. In the remainder of this chapter, we highlight these issues and set out what governments can do about it.

Subsidies, accountability, and risk management

Infrastructure is riddled with subsidies. Some subsidies are obvious, some are hidden. Some protect the poor, some benefit the well-off. Some damage the environment, and some improve it. Some were created by policy, and others are there by accident. There are perhaps only two things we can say with any certainty about infrastructure subsidies: they are often necessary and they are always risky.

Subsidies can be needed for a variety of reasons. Perhaps the least controversial of reasons are the objectives of environmental protection and poverty reduction. Sometimes people are unable to pay for services. Other times, they're unwilling to pay. People typically won't pay the full social value of sanitation services, because they can easily take a free ride on the environmental health benefits. Individuals' risks of ill-health are more affected by other people's behavior regarding sanitation than by their own. MRT passengers often won't pay the full value of the service, because the benefits of reduced traffic congestion and pollution are diffuse. When renewable energy is more expensive than fossil fuels, as is often the case, most consumers won't voluntarily pay more, even if they worry about the risk of climate change. A case can be made for subsidies on the grounds of environmental protection.

The best subsidy scheme for poverty reduction would not target infrastructure specifically, but would raise the incomes of the poor so that they could afford the basic goods and services they choose to consume. The reality, however, is that general social safety nets are often not feasible, at least in the near term, and targeted subsidies are then the best available option. When infrastructure is a high priority for poverty reduction, it can be a high priority for subsidies. Water, sanitation, and rural roads are oft-quoted examples. One important criterion for granting subsidies is not just whether the subsidy raises the disposable income of the poor, but also whether it reduces the volatility of their disposable

Box 4.12 Franchising in Fiji

In Fiji, the main island routes are open to competition and, in 1997, a franchising scheme was introduced for outer islands shipping where competition is limited. Under this scheme, the government defines a minimum service level for shipping to inadequately served areas and specifies maximum freight rates in the franchise tender documents. Operators submit tenders on the basis of the subsidy they would require to operate these services. The service provider requiring the least subsidy gets the contract.

Source: Castalia 2004b.

income. In other words, does the subsidy provide protective security and reduce the risk of the poor becoming even poorer?

And so to a controversial reason for subsidies: politics. Nobody has done a comprehensive global calculation, but it is almost certain that the majority of subsidies go to the relatively well-off not to the poor, for the obvious reason that the well-off have more political influence. But should policy makers always strive to remove subsidies to the well-off to free up resources for the poor?

What if a water sector reform in a particular country would increase access for the poor, but the urban middle classes might resist the reform if their subsidies were removed? A strong government might forge ahead and remove the subsidies anyway. A more risk-averse government might consider it preferable to maintain the subsidies at least for a while, particularly if the reform will eventually bring benefits to that middle class (for example, more reliable water supply after investments have been made). Transitional subsidies for political reasons can be justified sometimes. And it's probably desirable to be transparent about the justification.

But subsidies are risky for a well-known reason: They can be addictive. The more you get, the more you ask for. They blur accountability, because they undermine the financial discipline of the service provider through which they are channeled. It is very hard to maintain effective performance in the presence of subsidies, and therefore hard to achieve the very objectives of those subsidies. So how do we reinject accountability into subsidies?

One area to focus on is the origin of the problem—that is, higher costs than we think people can afford or want to pay. Can we use regulated service standards and technology to bring costs down? This is evident, for example, in Manila's Bayan Tubig water-delivery program, where appropriate technology standards have helped to reduce water costs by up to 25 percent in densely populated slum areas (World Bank 2003d).

Can we use competition in the market or for the subsidies (for example, bidders for an infrastructure concession being evaluated according to who asks for the lowest subsidy)? This is commonly the case in transport services.

And perhaps most difficult of all, can public enterprise reform help reduce financial losses, as in the case of the Phnom Penh Water Supply Authority, where the successful top-down turnaround of the company helped boost revenues to cost-recovery levels (see Box 4.13)?

If we've worked on the cost side, what can we do to minimize the subsidies directly? Can we make them transparent so that they are more likely to be subject to overall budget prioritization? This is the approach China is taking in establishing water and wastewater tariff adjustment programs over specified timeframes (Castalia 2004c).

Can we make subsidies performance-based so that they are disbursed only if certain specific targets are reached? In Cambodia, for example, the government is piloting performance-based subsidies for water connection, making the bulk of the subsidy to the private operator contingent on the number of connections of poor households to water supply (Yogita 2004). Can we make one-time payments to minimize the risk that the subsidy tap remains open?[16] Or can we adjust taxes or subsidies on competing services to cut the subsidy requirement (for example, reduce fuel subsidies/increase fuel taxation to increase MRT ridership)?

Another option for injecting accountability into subsidies might be to design cross-subsidies rather than direct ones. Sometimes, there are enough consumers who are able and willing to pay above the price that covers average costs and, in doing so, subsidize those who are charged less than cost. The accountability of the bottom line can thereby be preserved.

One advantage cross-subsidies can have over direct subsidies is they minimize subsidy risk, that is, the risk that investments will be made contingent on an expected subsidy flow that actually is interrupted. If there is a significant risk that subsidy policy will be poorly coordinated with policy on service delivery, it might be preferable for the two policies to be made by one agency—the service provider (or a regulator).[17]

Cross-subsidies can also minimize another risk—namely, that givers of direct subsidies (for example, MoFs) and regulators of tariffs may find it difficult to coordinate policies. A regulator may prefer to tacitly encourage higher subsidies rather than approve higher tariffs; tariffs make the

Box 4.13 Top-down turnaround: The Phnom Penh Water Supply Authority

The Phnom Penh Water Supply Authority, the public water company that serves Cambodia's capital city, has undergone a remarkable transformation into an autonomous, commercially oriented and financially self-sufficient water company. In 1993, the company was highly subsidized, inefficient, and served only 20 percent of the city. Under new leadership supported by strong government and external assistance, the company embarked on a process to change the culture within the organization. Today, virtually the whole city (excluding suburbs and peri-urban areas) now has access to water 24 hours a day with a quality that meets international standards, and the company is no longer dependent on government financial support.

The key steps that the company has undertaken to enable this change included the following:

- *Organizational restructuring.* New management was brought in, staffing was streamlined, and incentives for good performance were introduced.

- *Water metering and stopping illegal connections.* Today, all water connections are metered and there are heavy penalties assessed on those using illegal connections.

- *Improved customer management.* A customer survey was carried out and an automated billing system installed.

- *Public education.* Consumers (including high-level politicians) were educated about paying their bills.

Water tariffs were also increased during this time. To avoid a huge tariff increase, the company proposed a three-step tariff increase over a period of seven years. The first increase was in 1997 and the second in 2001. The company did not push for the third increase because its revenue already covered its cost, because of a higher collection ratio and reductions in NRW.

Source: Castalia 2004c.

Table 4.2 Comparison of performance, 1993 and 2003

	1993	2003
Customers	26,881	105,771
Billing ratio (%)	28	83
Collection ratio (%)	50	101.10
Nonrevenue water (NRW) (%)	72	17
Total revenue	0.7 billion riels	38.6 billion riels
Total operating expenses	1.4 billion riels	10.1 billion riels

Sources: Castalia 2004c; World Bank staff.

regulator unpopular, while another agency is accountable for subsidies. For the subsidy giver, the incentives are reversed. Coordination could be difficult and it could perhaps be more difficult if the regulator is independent. Box 4.1 provides an interesting example from the Philippines, where poor coordination passed on the cost of electricity provision from consumers to taxpayers.

However, cross-subsidies come at a cost. They can overtax certain consumers (for example, high electricity tariffs charged to industry, which in effect taxes employment), they are often not transparent (and may sometimes encounter resistance to pay if they are), and they escape budgetary prioritization. And, as we saw above for IPPs, they can make it difficult to introduce competition. So we might gain one accountability instrument only at the expense of another (probably better) one. Indeed, it might be preferable to institute competition, and compensate with direct subsidies those who lose the benefit of cross-subsidies. Overall, accountability could be substantially increased.

Contingent liabilities, accountability, and risk management

In addition to subsidies, there are other forms of fiscal support that share risk but are less direct—for example, power-purchase obligations in the Philippines, or Thai government backing for borrowing of the state railways. Table 4.3 summarizes some of the most common forms of fiscal support in East Asia. This kind of fiscal support perhaps raises even more difficult accountability issues, particularly given the probabilistic (or contingent) nature of the claims, that many of them occur off-budget, and that responsibilities are not always well-defined (that is, claims are implicit).

The ability of a government to manage its share of the risk in an infrastructure asset, and to be held accountable for that management, depends critically on its fiscal institutions. At a general level, this requires that the government is appropriately reconciling solvency and liquidity as discussed in the previous chapter. This, in turn, depends on the quality of fiscal information and the degree of disclosure (for example, use of accrual accounting and risk annotation of financial statements to ensure good disclosure of risk exposure).

Of critical importance is the actual use of this information about fiscal risk during the budget process (including at the subnational level where infrastructure can create considerable fiscal risk). Ideally, governments

Table 4.3 Common types of central government fiscal support for infrastructure

	Direct (Obligation in any event)	Contingent (Obligation if a particular event occurs)
Explicit (Government liability created by a law or contract)	Sovereign debt (or long-term purchase agreements) contracted by central government for infrastructure investments (e.g., China's infrastructure bonds)	State guarantees of long-term purchase contracts of state-owned utilities (e.g., the Philippines' guarantees of NPC's power-purchase obligations) State guarantees of debt, revenue, exchange rates, and construction costs in private infrastructure projects (e.g., minimum-revenue and exchange-rate guarantees in Korean toll roads)
	Central government subsidies	State guarantees for borrowing of public infrastructure companies (e.g., of Thai state railways) State guarantees of financial institutions involved in infrastructure financing
	Tax expenditures, such as exemptions, that reduce future government revenue	State guarantees for borrowing of local governments related to infrastructure
Implicit (A political obligation of government that reflects public and interest-group pressures)	The future cost of any non-contractual but politically unavoidable budget subsidies	Noncontractual claims arising from private investment in infrastructure (e.g., various claims in Indonesia)
	Future recurrent costs of public investment infrastructure projects	Claims by state-owned infrastructure enterprises to help cover their losses, arrears, deferred maintenance, and debt (e.g., debt and arrears of energy generators in Mongolia) Claims by local governments to help cover their nonguaranteed debt, their own guarantees, arrears, and other obligations related to infrastructure (e.g., municipal bonds to finance infrastructure in Vietnam) Claims by failing financial institutions whose portfolios have been weakened by financing infrastructure (e.g., China)

Source: Brixi and Irwin 2004.
Note: NPC = National Power Corporation.

would decide on overall ceilings for fiscal risk, issue guidelines on risk assumption to sector agencies and local governments, monitor centrally how much risk is being assumed, and generally require central approval of the assumption of risk. The outcomes should be subject to audit to facilitate accountability for risk-taking.[18] Publication of any licenses and contracts that give rise to fiscal risk would also facilitate accountability.

The criterion of fiscal solvency is central to sound management of infrastructure risk. Governments in the region have often resorted to risk-sharing transactions with the private sector rather than undertaking straightforward public investment simply to get an expenditure "off the books." In other words, liquidity improves because a direct claim has been transformed into a contingent one that is within an accounting framework that does not fully account for contingent claims (as in the vast majority of countries). But, in general, solvency will have improved

Box 4.14 Coordination failure: Regulators and subsidies in the Philippine electricity sector

The Small Power Utilities Group (SPUG) is in charge of electricity generation in off-grid areas for the National Power Corporation (NPC) in the Philippines. SPUG has two sources of revenues: tariffs charged to local distribution utilities, and cross-subsidies paid out of a regulator-approved levy charged to all electricity users.

In 2003, SPUG estimated that its total revenue requirement was around $0.30/kWh, while its average tariff was around $0.08/kWh. SPUG applied to the regulator for a levy that would cover the $0.22 kWh revenue gap.

But arguing that SPUG's costs were too high, the regulator approved a levy that was below SPUG's request, and gave SPUG only part of the cross-subsidy it requested.

Rather than reducing its total costs to meet the expected cross-subsidy and tariff revenues, SPUG financed the revenue shortfall with bridge loans. These loans are ultimately absorbed by NPC, and eventually the government and taxpayers, in effect transforming them into a direct subsidy.

In short, lack of coordination caused the taxpayer to pick up the bill instead of the consumer. Given the lack of coordination between the regulator and the fiscal authorities, SPUG's financial accountability may decline, and taxpayers' bills might be larger than the consumers' bills would have been. But should the regulator be held accountable?

Source: Castalia 2004a.

only if the transfer of risk to the private sector has brought efficiency gains, which depends on the accountability framework in place for the service provider.[19]

And we have seen that competition is very important to service provision accountability. Indeed, we have also seen that competition is intimately linked to the degree of risk that can be transferred to the private sector. When the state restricts competition by imposing a monopoly between the private supplier and the final customer (as in the IPP/single-buyer case described above), it prevents the private supplier from competing for the more-creditworthy customers in the market. The state's consequent assumption of risk may be seen as compensating the private sector for this exclusion.

This points to a critical coordination issue: a MoF who wants to minimize fiscal risk might strongly desire competition in infrastructure sectors, while sector agencies might have strong incentives to preserve monopoly power. And other ministries (for example, social affairs, industry, and environment) might want the efficiency gains that could come from competition.

Balancing those interests is never easy, particularly when private sector objectives are involved also. In some cases, the private sector might see competitive markets as an opportunity, but in others its efforts to mitigate overall risk might preclude competition. In many cases, overall investment climates present considerable risk, and infrastructure investments present extra risk for all the regulatory and other reasons discussed in earlier chapters. Against a highly risky background, private investors often seek government guarantees and commitments to protect the rewards from the risks (for example, fixed-price, long-term PPAs, and minimum revenue guarantees for toll roads, under which risks become fiscal, as we saw in Table 4.3). Once the rewards are protected and the government is carrying the risk, there's little to compete for. In short, if a government minimized infrastructure investment risk it would often minimize fiscal risk and facilitate infrastructure service competition as well. This could create a very virtuous loop.

But we shouldn't talk as if it is easy to determine how risks are really being shared in a particular arrangement, or how those arrangements compare with potential alternatives. In Chapter 3, for example, we saw in the three cities the MRT story that the private sector appeared to bear most of the risks, but when that proved excessive, much of it ended up de facto with the state (presumably because the projects couldn't be allowed to fail).

Another prominent example is the treatment of currency depreciation risk under various institutional arrangements in the power sector. In this example, risk is hidden under certain arrangements, and is more open under others (particularly those involving private or foreign capital). There are many different ways for currency depreciation to impose costs on utility consumers or taxpayers. Some are transparent and some are hidden, but the economic costs may not differ much (see Box 4.15).

The involvement of foreign owners makes the economic costs of currency depreciation more transparent, which raises the political stakes. But the foreign owners may well have brought substantial efficiency gains, which were masked by the effect of the currency depreciation, but that could benefit consumers and taxpayers in the long run. The dilemma for policy makers is whether to strive for efficiency or for a quiet political life. Or, put another way, should policy makers strive for a quiet life in the long run, because of efficiency, or in the short run, because of populism? The answer depends on accountability.

Box 4.15 "Now you see it, now you don't": The case of currency risk

In the 1997 crisis in East Asia, rapid currency depreciation led to ruptures in relationships between some governments and foreign infrastructure investors. Contracts implied sharp tariff increases in a time of severe economic crisis and political unrest. The use of foreign capital, and the governments that attracted it, were often blamed. But was it so simple? Let's look at the following hypothetical cases to examine what was going on.

Case 1: A utility is privatized to foreign owners. The owners insist that tariff regulation includes tariff adjustment in case of currency depreciation to protect the return on their capital. The currency depreciates sharply, tariffs rise substantially, and consumers take a large loss. Popular sentiment asks why the foreigners were invited in. People say, "We could have avoided this if we had used our own capital."

Case 2: A utility is state owned. Tariff regulation does not include tariff adjustment in case of currency depreciation. Foreign equity or loan financing for the utility is not possible as a result. A state-owned bank finances the utility in domestic currency. The currency depreciates, tariffs do not rise, and the utility is unaffected. But the state-owned bank could instead have acquired foreign currency assets (for example, U.S. Treasury Bills) instead of financing the utility. The state-owned bank has therefore missed a huge capital gain, and taxpayers have taken a large loss (although they may not know).

Case 3: A utility is state owned, and tariff regulation does not include tariff adjustment in case of currency depreciation. Domestic banks finance the utility in domestic currency. However, interest rates are high because of currency depreciation risk, and the banks require tariffs to reflect those interest rates. When the currency actually depreciates, tariffs do not need to rise, but consumers have taken a large loss already. (An alternative to this case is one in which loans are made at variable interest rates and interest rates rise once the currency deprecation occurs. In this case, either tariffs are allowed to rise or there would need to have been a government guarantee to protect the banks, and the guarantee now gets called up. So consumers or taxpayers take a large loss.)

Case 4: A utility is state owned. Tariff regulation does not include tariff adjustment in case of currency depreciation. Foreign loan financing for the utility is therefore possible only with government guarantees. The currency depreciates, and tariffs do not rise. But the utility cannot service the loan, and the government guarantee is called up. Taxpayers have therefore taken a large loss.

Case 5: A utility is state owned, and tariff regulation does not include tariff adjustment in case of currency depreciation. The government budget finances the utility in domestic currency. The currency depreciates, tariffs do not rise, and the utility is unaffected. But if the government had not financed the utility, it would have run a surplus, which the central bank would have held as foreign assets on which it now would have made a huge capital gain. Taxpayers have therefore taken a large loss (although they may not know).

Case 6: A utility is privatized to domestic owners. Would they ask for the same tariff protection of the return on capital as the foreigners did? Probably, yes, if their capital were mobile—unless they were compensated in some other way (that is, the currency risk was hidden).

More generally, a significant proportion of infrastructure concession contracts are formally renegotiated during the contract lifetime, and risks then are redistributed.[20] Nothing can chill an investment climate like contract renegotiations forced by governments. Sometimes renegotiation reflects a shift in bargaining power in favor of government once the concessionaire has sunk costs, which is often combined with an inability by concessionaires to enforce contracts through the court system. Sometimes renegotiation reflects a shock or crisis that neither party anticipated at the time of concluding the contract, such as in Indonesia in the aftermath of the Asian crisis. And it can also reflect a legitimate learning process. Public-private risk-sharing in infrastructure is a relatively new science, the technology needs to be adapted for each sector and each country, and some experimentation is needed (see Spotlight 2 for an example of that learning process in Partnerships Victoria).

Indeed, one lesson to be learned from crises is that they do recur and perhaps can be anticipated in a renegotiated contract. For example, many concession contracts did not anticipate the currency crisis of 1997, yet the probability of a sharp currency depreciation during the 15- to 30-year typical period of such contracts is high in almost every country in the world, and all the more so in developing countries. Contracts could conceivably include provisions for tariff increases to be phased if they result from currency depreciations in excess of a specified rate, with an agreement about how transitional liquidity is to be injected. This would avoid renegotiation during crisis when political constraints are at their highest, and the country's investment climate and creditworthiness at its most vulnerable.

Ownership, accountability, and beyond

And so to the eternal ownership issue. Are privately owned infrastructure service providers more or less accountable for performance than publicly owned providers? We can't really measure accountability directly, but we can measure performance. And we saw in Chapter 2 that the empirical evidence shows that private providers perform better, on average, when the incentive environment gives them a good reason to do so. When faced with competition or with well-designed regulation that rewards efficiency gains, private ownership seems to yield greater accountability; private ownership by itself doesn't seem to make much difference.[21]

But when ownership is public, and markets are not competitive (whether for policy or for natural monopoly reasons), the accountability challenge is great. Experience suggests that independent regulation is effective even less often with public monopoly providers than with private ones.

East Asian solutions to public enterprise accountability seem to lie in strong oversight by planning agencies, finance ministries, or sector ministries; meritocratic public services; and a political commitment to effective service delivery. In Chapter 3, we examined the success story of the leading geese. Public monopoly service providers did great things, for a while. In Box 4.13, we saw that even in the chaos of postconflict Cambodia, strong commitment created a near-miracle turnaround in performance in the Phnom Penh state-owned water supply company. The top-down solution can clearly bring accountability in certain circumstances, but long-term sustainability will often be in question.

Concluding remarks

In this chapter, we came down from the strategic vision at the top of the accountability hierarchy and looked from a sectoral and a community level at how accountability mechanisms can work. We saw that, when the traditional East Asian top-down model shows signs of strain, there are ways of delegating service provision, while maintaining accountability for performance.

This chapter outlined several accountability mechanisms. First, we looked at how communities can manage small-scale infrastructure themselves, how they can participate in the "last kilometer" of larger network infrastructure, how community consultation on large projects could be more than just tokens, and how consumers have a role in regulation. Community accountability is a powerful force in parts of the region and, over time, could be even greater.

We next discussed the role of competition as a great force for accountability and saw that technological change and institutional innovation have considerably expanded the potential for competition in infrastructure service provision in recent decades. And yet competition in East Asian infrastructure still plays a relatively marginal role. The top is reluctant to let go.

We talked about economic regulation as an accountability mechanism in which competition is limited, and we saw that regulation remains quite highly politicized in the region. Cost recovery is not yet on solid ground.

In this context, we saw the importance of subsidies and the politicization of those subsidies, and suggested ways to make regulators and subsidy givers more accountable. But much remains to be done.

We saw that risk-sharing arrangements were crucial to delegation of service provision and that risk-sharing raises substantial accountability and coordination challenges. Most importantly, we talked about risk-sharing as a learning process. Mistakes are made, experiences teaches, and new information comes in—all this can contribute to sharing risk in a manner more commensurate with each party's ability to bear the risk and manage it. Since the 1997 crisis, some East Asian economies have been hesitant to participate in this learning process—once bitten, twice shy—but others, like Korea, are now forging ahead.

And last but not least, we saw that ownership does not matter by itself. We have seen plenty of disappointments in private provision in East Asia. What does matter is that private provision tends, on average, to respond better to competition and well-crafted regulation than does public provision. If infrastructure provision and efficiency are to keep pace with East Asia's needs, this means that the more the system outgrows the top-down model and needs to delegate, the more it will need to attract the private sector. But this time around, private participation should come with competition and good regulation.

Throughout the report we have seen a centralized system that is showing some ability to adapt, endeavoring to overcome the strains by decentralizing some accountability through local government autonomy, private provision, competition, arm's length regulation, and community initiative. The challenge going forward is to be less tentative and hesitant in that adaptation, and to have the confidence to deepen the process. And East Asia has plenty of reasons for confidence.

Spotlight 2. Learning how to share risk: The case of Partnerships Victoria[22]

The State of Victoria, in Australia, is one of a number of authorities across the world with programs to facilitate private sector participation in the provision of a range of infrastructure (and other) services through so-called Public Private Partnerships (PPP).

The state's current "Partnerships Victoria" policy sets out principles and procedures for PPPs undertaken by agencies within the state. The policy is overseen by a dedicated unit within the Department of Treasury and Finance. The framework builds on more than 15 years of PPP experience, which has included many significant successes as well as a number of mistakes. But lessons have been drawn from both to create a PPP framework that maximizes value for money, based on the careful calculation and assignment of optimal—as opposed to maximum—risk to the private sector.

PPPs use the private sector to deliver traditionally public sector infrastructure services through a process that focuses on services and outputs, rather than short-term inputs. Under a typical PPP arrangement, one private party (usually a consortium) is engaged to design, construct, finance, maintain, and at times operate an infrastructure facility. Payments are usually made only after the facility passes commissioning tests, over the term of the contract, based on service delivery meeting key performance indicators specified in the concession contract.

This contrasts with typical government infrastructure procurement, in which an architect would be engaged to design the facility, based on specified input requirements; a contractor would be engaged to construct the facility; government would operate the facility; and progress payments would be made to architects and contractors before commissioning.

Victoria's experimentation with infrastructure PPPs began in the late 1980s, and early 1990s, and included the Victorian Accelerated Infrastructure Program, as well as train and locomotive leases. During this time, the use of PPPs largely reflected a desire to finance infrastructure off balance sheet, rather than a concern for increased efficiency and value for money. The financing arrangements that resulted had little impact on the nature of service delivery arrangements, and entailed minimal risk transfer, with the government often providing indemnities and guarantees to private parties. Some of the PPPs of the time were unwound later at significant cost to taxpayers.

The PPPs undertaken between 1994 and 1999 were governed by the Infrastructure Investment Policy for Victoria, which cast the role of the private sector in terms of increased efficiency and growth. Examples of infrastructure PPPs of that period include the Melbourne CityLink, various water and wastewater treatment plants, and public transport franchises. During this period, the role of the private sector was expanded to also include operation and service delivery, with payment made only on commencement of services, as well as significantly higher levels of risk transfer, including the removal of government guarantees on returns.

While the assessment of PPP projects of the time is largely positive, the excessive concern with risk transfer led to unsustainable financing arrangements in some cases. Other shortcomings included insufficient attention to social and regional impact, limited benchmarking of performance, and insufficient attention to economic evaluation in some cases.

Since 2000, PPPs have been delivered through the state's new Partnerships Victoria policy framework. The approach is becoming an increasingly important tool for infrastructure delivery as a whole. Already, 12 projects have been signed with a capital value of more than AU$2.5 billion, covering a range of infrastructure sectors, including water, information and communications technology, and transport, in addition to health and justice. The largest project so far is the Mitcham Frankston Freeway Project signed in October 2004 with a capital value of AU$2.5 billion. Three projects valued at almost AU$1 billion are currently in the market and a number of projects are under development.

PPPs in Victoria currently account for approximately 10 percent of total capital investment in infrastructure. The public sector continues to deliver the majority of Victoria's infrastructure needs, with PPPs most frequently used in large, complex, or innovative infrastructure projects, in which the private sector is best able to add value.

The new framework draws on lessons of the past in a number of important ways: Value for money—rather than scarcity of capital, or any preference for off-balance-sheet financing—is the key rationale for whether PPP or traditional procurement arrangements are used to deliver infrastructure services. Emphasis is placed on whole-of-life costing, as well as on optimal risk transfer to the private sector. PPP projects are allocated funding as if they were to be built and owned by government. The funding is then available to be converted into a recurrent stream in the event of a Partnerships Victoria contract being executed.

The essence of the Partnerships Victoria approach is that government does not purchase an asset, but rather a service, or set of services, at an agreed quality, quantity, cost, and timeliness—with payment withheld if services are not provided to specified levels. The government only enters into a PPP contract if private sector delivery mechanisms can pass a test demonstrating superior value for money, in comparison with the most efficient and likely method of providing the required output through public sector ownership and operation. The approach provides for a range of partnership models, depending on different private and public sector roles, and commercial scenarios.[23] It sets out a rigorous procurement process to be followed by all agencies in the development of Partnerships Victoria projects. It also includes a formal public interest test, in which all projects are assessed in terms of their effectiveness, accountability, transparency, impact on individuals and communities, equity, consumer rights, public access, security, and privacy.

Estimation of whether the private sector can deliver superior value for money takes into account qualitative and quantitative factors. Quantitative evaluation criteria include the construction of a public sector comparator (PSC), which is defined in the framework as an estimate of the "hypothetical risk-adjusted cost if a project were to be financed, owned, and implemented by government" (Partnerships Victoria 2001). This PSC is compared with the cost of providing a service through a PPP, and the service delivery option that offers the better value for money is selected. Quantitative evaluation may also include a calculation of the impact of private sector participation on the delivery of those core services that would remain under direct government provision, if the government retains direct delivery of such services. Factors that cannot be quantified include the track record of bidders, differences in risk transfer, and any intangible difference in service delivery.

The PSC against which the PPP bids are compared includes four components. Fairly straightforwardly, it takes into account retained risk (risks that the government would bear itself under a PPP), as well as the so-called "raw" PSC. The latter includes all capital and operating costs associated with government construction (but with all contingencies removed). It then takes into account a competitive neutrality adjustment, which removes the net competitive advantages that accrue to a government, such as exemption from land tax. Finally, and often most importantly, it takes into account transferable risk—the risk that the government would bear under traditional procurement, but is likely to transfer to the private sector under a PPP. Costing, and taking into account this risk, often makes the difference between whether private or public sector provision is preferable.

Figure 4.9 shows how the PSC typically is compared with the costs associated with provision through a PPP in the Partnerships Victoria framework.

Service delivery through PPPs tends to be feasible under a number of specific circumstances. Projects more suited to private sector delivery are usually large (infrequently less than AU$50 million to AU$100 million) to offset the transaction and ongoing management costs associated with

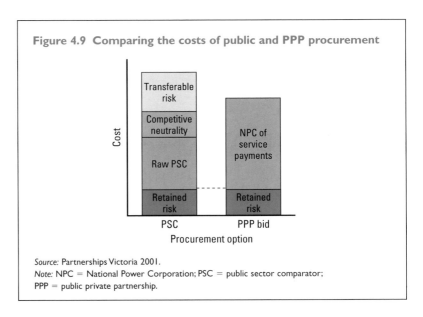

Figure 4.9 Comparing the costs of public and PPP procurement

Source: Partnerships Victoria 2001.
Note: NPC = National Power Corporation; PSC = public sector comparator;
PPP = public private partnership.

the Partnerships Victoria approach. These projects require that government need can be defined in measurable output terms, that there is opportunity for efficient risk transfer to the private sector, and that there is scope for the private sector to demonstrate particular skills and/or capacity for innovation. They also tend to be favored in cases when opportunity exists for revenue from third-party asset utilization (thereby decreasing the net cost to government) and when projects are able to generate competitive market interest.

Spotlight 3. Consumer participation, regulators, and accountability

The mandate for infrastructure regulators is to shape the regulatory contract between consumers and service providers with monopoly power. Regulators are a countervailing power exercised on behalf of consumers. However, consumers are composed of diffuse interest groups, who may not be used to voicing their concerns effectively. Regulators need to actively engage consumers to hold service providers accountable for the delivery of the regulatory contract. Moreover, consumer participation provides the checks and balances required to ensure that the regulator does not stray from its mandate as protector of consumer rights. This Spotlight discusses the status of consumer participation in infrastructure regulation in East Asia, drawing on the results of a survey questionnaire conducted among infrastructure regulators.[24]

Regulatory functions

The following regulatory functions are considered essential to involve consumers in the regulatory process:

Informing and educating consumers

Informing and educating consumers is necessary to hold service providers and regulators accountable to the consumer constituency. An effective strategy to redress information asymmetries between the parties hinges on a transparent regulatory process and effective information campaigns.

The degree of transparency of a regulatory regime largely depends on the disclosure policy of the regulating bodies. Almost two-thirds of the surveyed regulators in the region disclose procedures and decisions, while half of them also release to the public the benchmarked performance of regulated service providers. However, licenses and contracts with private service providers are still kept confidential by the majority of the regulating entities.

The regulator is also responsible for raising consumer awareness of their rights and obligations under the regulatory contract. The media is the most common channel of communication employed by the surveyed regulators; in addition, more than half of the surveyed regulators draw on two-way vehicles of communications (either workshops or one-on-one meetings), which have the advantage of leading to a deeper form of consumer engagement. Most of the regulators rely on government and service providers as intermediaries to raise consumer awareness. Regulators also tend to leverage the expertise of sector-specific intermediaries (such as NGOs in the water sector and community leaders in the energy sector) to reach consumers. Consumer associations do not appear to play a significant role in raising consumer awareness.

Handling consumer complaints

An effective complaint-handling mechanism should be established under any regulatory regime to hold regulated service providers accountable to consumers for the delivery of the regulatory contract. Two-thirds of the surveyed regulatory bodies have in place formal consumer redress mechanisms. While almost half of the regulators (42 percent) represent the first port of call for handling consumer complaints; for an equal number of cases, consumer complaints are directed in the first instance to service providers. Consumer associations do not appear to play a significant role in the redress process.[25] Even when regulators do not represent the first port of call for handling consumer complaints, they retain important regulatory functions throughout the redress process; around half (53 percent) of the surveyed regulators are responsible for monitoring the responsiveness of service providers in handling consumer complaints; half (47 percent) maintain the right to step in should the complaint not be solved. However, only five regulatory agencies have in place financial incentives to reward or penalize service providers on the basis of their performance in addressing consumer complaints.

Soliciting consumer input

In nonmonopolistic markets, consumers can reveal their preference and/or voice their dissatisfaction by exercising the option of switching to substitute products. This system of checks and balances ensures that service providers do value consumer information to enhance their competitiveness against rival firms. No similar mechanism is in place in monopolistic industries, in which customers are generally locked in to the incumbent service provider. The onus is therefore on the regulator to solicit consumer input throughout the regulatory process to ensure that provision of infrastructure services is aligned with consumer expectations.

In line with regulatory best practice, the two inputs most often solicited by East Asian regulators to inform decision making are quality of service and consumer satisfaction. The survey findings indicate that the majority of the regulators have in place well-structured mechanisms to consult with consumers throughout the regulatory process. Informal consultations with consumer representatives appear to be the most common mechanism in place to solicit information from consumers, being adopted by two-thirds of the regulators. In addition, 64 percent of the surveyed regulators have in place at least one formal consultation mechanism (that is, public hearings and/or formal consultations with advisory bodies), with more than half of the surveyed regulators (56 percent) drawing on formal and informal consultation processes.

Options for consumer representation

Being a diffuse stakeholder group, consumers need to rely on a representative body that is able to engage in the regulatory process on their behalf. Among the entities that could be tasked with the role of representing consumer rights are the following:

In-house consumer affairs bureaus

Regulators can establish in-house consumer departments as a basic form of institutional representation of consumer interests. Economies of scope can often be achieved by entrusting the same entity with consumer representation and regulatory functions. For example, an in-house consumer department would benefit from direct access to consumer-related information that could be used to inform the representation function. The findings of the survey questionnaire indicate that in-house consumer affairs bureaus are the most common institutional option for consumer representation in East Asia, being adopted by 42 percent of the surveyed regulators.

Consumer representation in the decision-making body

Another option is to institutionalize consumer representation in the regulatory board, the decision-making body of the regulating entity. This model is currently adopted in several African countries (such as Burundi, Ghana, and Senegal), but in only a few regulatory regimes in East Asia (20 percent).[26] In theory, this form of consumer representation can lead to the highest levels of consumer engagement in the regulatory process by establishing a direct channel for feeding consumer input into decision making. In practice, the potential benefits derived from consumer representation in the regulatory board are often outweighed by its costs. Board representation may have the downside effect of trapping consumer representatives in a conflict-of-interest situation by making them accountable to both the regulatory body and consumers. Aside from the risk of regulatory capture, having consumers represented in the regulatory board may bring the regulatory process to a standstill, because it empowers consumer representatives to exercise a right of veto to halt the decision-making process. In addition, the top-down appointment of consumer representatives to the regulatory board may undermine their legitimacy and accountability to the consumer constituency.

External consumer bodies

Consumer representation could also be delegated to external independent entities, such as noninstitutionalized consumer associations or statutory consumer councils. Being independent from the regulator itself, external consumer bodies are better positioned than in-house consumer departments to take a stance against regulatory decisions perceived as unfair to consumers. As a downside, independent consumer bodies risk being captured by specific interest groups at the expenses of the marginalized segments of the customer base. This risk is particularly high in developing countries, where independent consumer associations may be taken over by middle-class consumer groups whose interests are not necessarily aligned (and in fact are often conflicting) with those of the poorest customers.[27] Delegation of consumer representation to an external body (such as consumer associations) is adopted by one-third of the surveyed regulators. Moreover, 30 percent of the regulators rely on more than one option for consumer representation—the most common arrangement being the combination of an in-house consumer affairs bureau with an external advisory body.

Overall, most of the infrastructure regimes in the region appear to have reached the rung of consultation in the ladder of consumer engagement in infrastructure regulation, and most of the regulatory regimes have in place well-structured processes to interact with consumers through the regulatory process. The findings of the survey questionnaire suggest that, while the onus is on the regulator to ensure effective consumer participation in the regulatory process, most of the regulators in the region rely on governments and service providers, as well as a number of sector-specific intermediaries, to interact with consumers.

5

The Way Forward

S O WHAT DOES THIS FRAMEWORK MEAN FOR ACTION IN EAST ASIAN infrastructure? How does this framework point to challenges in the road ahead and give guidance toward solutions?

The framework set out in this study is analytical. It suggests a way of approaching problems, but is not a "tool kit" for implementing particular policies. Nonetheless, the framework has important policy implications. Here we trace 12 of them. They reflect key concerns articulated in the consultations undertaken in preparing this report, with the region's policy makers, policy implementers, infrastructure service providers, civil society organizations, and other stakeholders.

The 12 policy messages constitute an approach to strengthening infrastructure's contribution to inclusive development, as set out in Chapter 2. They promote the role of infrastructure in underpinning growth and poverty reduction. Infrastructure does not lead to inclusive development on its own—it requires actions that support the delivery of services to the poor who need them, and that underpin the growth dynamics on which improvements in welfare depend (Box 5.1). What do we need to think about to achieve this?

The discussion of coordination in Chapter 3 provides the basis for three of the policy messages arising from the framework. In Chapter 3, we saw how strategic vision has proved crucial for ensuring the effectiveness of infrastructure interventions. We also looked at a number of the challenges that arise in formulating and implementing this vision—coordination across financing and planning institutions, coordination across infrastructure and fiscal institutions, and coordination across

> **Box 5.1 Managing the contribution of infrastructure to inclusive development**
>
> While infrastructure is important, on its own it is not enough. Infrastructure has to work with other policies and interventions that also have an impact on inclusive development—on investment, innovation, or policy stability that affect growth; on those factors that affect people's ability to access services.
>
> The impact of infrastructure on inclusive development also depends on a range of choices that countries have to make, and balances that they have to strike. Sharing of the benefits of infrastructure is not automatic. Broad-based impacts on poverty may be positive, but the local impacts can sometimes be negative, unless deliberately mitigated. There are genuine choices to be made between investments that will have a greater impact on poverty and those that will have a greater impact on growth—on rural roads, for instance, as opposed to port logistics. There are trade-offs to be made between the interests of the poor and the nonpoor.
>
> How infrastructure contributes to inclusive development will vary by the nature of each country's growth and poverty challenges. In Lao PDR, it may be through greater links with the region. In Thailand, it may be through the creation of high-transaction business environments with easy accessibility. We know that infrastructure does have an impact on poverty, but precisely what investments are needed depends on whether a country faces mass poverty, or whether poverty is location specific; whether isolation is a root cause of poverty, or whether other factors such as caste, race, or a history of discrimination are more important.

decentralized government. The analysis set out in Chapter 3 gives us the following three policy messages:

1. The center matters—infrastructure demands strong planning and coordination functions

Infrastructure provides basic services on which survival and livelihoods depend; infrastructure is the backbone of economies and societies; infrastructure has major environmental impacts; infrastructure can bring powerful monopolies and foreign participation into areas of great sensitivity. As such, infrastructure is intensely political.

But infrastructure is also economically and technically complex, and has long-term implications. So the technocrats, too, have a critical role to play as they complement the role of politicians. This extraordinary blend of technocracy and politics places a premium on high-level, central institutions, which can articulate strategies that are politically sustainable and economically effective.

Institutions that can formulate those long-term strategies, and can coordinate the policies of different agencies to implement them, are essential to effective infrastructure service provision. Objectives that move beyond the purely economic, to mainstream environmental and social considerations, demand higher levels of coordinating capacity than hitherto. Sector ministries and local governments cannot work in policy-making isolation.

Old top-down models of detailed economic planning should be eschewed, but new models of strategic planning and central coordination need to evolve. This should underpin tendencies toward democratization, decentralization, independent regulation, private participation, and the commercialization of service providers.

2. Decentralization is important, but raises a host of coordination challenges

There has been substantial decentralization of government in East Asia, and this has often increased the responsiveness of infrastructure service provision to local needs. Decentralization has undoubtedly played an essential political role.

However, decentralization poses a number of coordination challenges, both vertically (between central and local governments) and horizontally (among various subnational institutions).

Decentralized governments have sometimes been isolated within their own jurisdiction. This is problematic because most network infrastructure has interjurisdictional backbones. Isolation can mean secondary or tertiary infrastructure lacks connections to primary infrastructure—in a sense, it goes nowhere. Some municipalities may be too small to achieve the scale necessary to deliver infrastructure efficiently. In competing with each other, municipalities may duplicate expensive infrastructure facilities, when such facilities, in fact, could have been shared. Avoiding these pitfalls depends critically on interjurisdictional cooperation—on filling in the missing middle.

Higher tiers of government need to encourage lower tiers to collaborate where primary infrastructure requires such collaboration. Matching grants to induce decentralized governments to participate in such investments, and institutional mechanisms to encourage cooperation in infrastructure planning will play a major role.

Central governments also have to ensure that they maintain sufficient capacity to monitor, manage, and coordinate in a manner that is in line with policy and regulatory frameworks. The inadequacy of such systems is a frequent cause of suboptimal service delivery and confused authority.

3. Fiscal space for infrastructure is critical

Ultimately, all infrastructure is paid for by users through tariffs or taxpayers through subsidies. Covering costs through user charges is a critical long-term objective. In the short term, user charges might be legitimately constrained by a variety of factors (see below under "subsidies") or large investment needs might require upfront financing to be recovered gradually from user charges.

Sometimes those financial shortfalls can be filled by the private sector, but sometimes private financing will be insufficient, unavailable, or unacceptably expensive. Even where the private sector comes in, it often requires risk-sharing with the public sector. In cases in which the private sector cannot or will not provide all the financing or bear all the risk, investments with adequate economic rates of return should be allocated fiscal space.[1]

Adequacy will depend in part on competing claims from noninfrastructure expenditures and from the need to keep fiscal deficits low. It will also depend on the veracity of the claim that user charges or private financing cannot fill the gap; sometimes it requires fiscal tightening to induce sector agencies to make reforms and seek other sources of funds.

In some East Asian countries, expenditure on infrastructure appears to have been less than optimal in recent years. Cambodia, Indonesia, Lao PDR, the Philippines, and Thailand could be candidates for this list of countries. This may have undermined economic growth and poverty reduction, and even long-run fiscal solvency.

This does not mean that more fiscal space for infrastructure should be the first step in those countries. In several cases, fiscal tightening for macroeconomic stability and debt sustainability would take higher priority. In most cases, the possibility exists for stronger promotion of private financing in infrastructure and for higher user charges. And there can be opportunities for cost reductions, or better management and maintenance of existing assets. In some cases, strengthening public expenditure management should come before more public expenditure. If adequate institutions and controls are not in place, countries can easily veer from underspending to overspending.

But if and when those difficult preconditions are met, governments should allocate fiscal space based on long-run growth objectives and in pursuit of fiscal solvency. Infrastructure spending on worthwhile projects can create a virtuous circle: more growth, more fiscal revenue, more fiscal space. The challenge is to select the right projects—and put in place the policy and institutional frameworks that actually make them worthwhile.

***

Our discussion of accountability and risk management in Chapter 4 provides the basis for five additional policy messages. In this chapter, we looked at a number of mechanisms through which accountability in infrastructure service provision can be strengthened—through the community, through regulation, and through competition—and how accountability and risk management arrangements can play out when governments provide support to infrastructure providers. The analysis set out in this chapter supports the following five policy messages:

4. "Subsidy" is not a dirty word—subsidies can be important, but are always risky, and should be handled with care

Infrastructure subsidies can be justified on a number of grounds, including environmental protection and poverty reduction. Although they would enjoy the environmental benefits, people often won't pay the full cost of sanitation, mass rapid transit, or renewable energy. In cases in which those benefits are external to consumers, subsidies may be needed to realize the benefits. Clean water or rural roads may have an important impact on poverty, but they may not be affordable by the poor. Such projects may require subsidies. And reform programs that help the poor or the environment may not be politically sustainable without subsidies for those with the power to derail the reforms. Similarly, transitional subsidies sometimes may be worth considering during short periods of economic crisis.

But subsidies can become open-ended and addictive, their fiscal impact can explode, they can undermine financial discipline and blur accountability, and they can postpone much-needed reform. Subsidies need to be employed with great care.

Subsidies should be a last resort after costs have been minimized through competition, regulation, appropriate technology and service standards, or public enterprise reform. Subsidies can be minimized through transparency, making them contingent on performance, or through subsidy bidding processes.

5. Competition is hard to achieve in infrastructure, but it's the best way to bring accountability

Infrastructure is quite often a natural monopoly, but institutional and technological innovation are expanding the potential for competition. It is now feasible to provide most infrastructure services (if not always the infrastructure itself) competitively. The most direct, and hence most effective, way of holding service providers accountable is through competition.

East Asia has been cautious about the introduction of infrastructure service competition; it has often preferred to "throw" more infrastructure at a problem rather than provide incentives for more efficient infrastructure services or address the political economy obstacles to competition.

This approach may have been effective when the basic infrastructure was being built, when economic objectives were relatively simple, and when top-down command solutions prevailed. But, as complexity increases, those approaches can be expected to work less well, and the role of competition will need to increase.

6. Regulatory independence matters more in the long run than in the short run

When competition is not yet firmly in place, regulation of monopolies will be needed. Regulatory independence from politics is an important long-term goal to ensure that service providers can cover costs and earn an adequate return on investments. However, regulators can establish their credibility with consumers, politicians, and investors only gradually. If regulators exercise more discretion than the political culture can absorb, a backlash can occur, creating unpredictability and instability.

Regulatory independence is a relative concept, and independence should grow step-by-step. New regulators should rely more on transparent rules than on discretionary power, and some responsibilities should be delegated to outside experts until in-house capacity can be built. Credibility, and hence independence, can be enhanced by transparency: Hearings should be public, as should contracts and licenses whenever possible. Accountability for regulators is key to their independence.

7. Civil society has a key role to play in ensuring accountability in service provision

Local communities within civil society can often manage local projects. They can participate in decision making about the large infrastructure networks that touch their community, or those aspects of large projects that affect them directly. They may need special protection, as long as the larger needs of society don't get lost.

Civil society can play an important role in accountability of infrastructure institutions through parliaments or through consumer participation in regulation. Civil society organizations and NGOs can provide small-scale infrastructure services, act as watchdogs against corruption and vested interest, and play an advocacy role for more sustainable infrastructure policies and services.

Advocacy NGOs face difficult choices between representing the interests of specific groups or issues and representing the interests of society at large. How effectively and accountably they make those choices can have a significant impact on development outcomes.

8. Infrastructure has to clean up its act—addressing corruption is a priority

Infrastructure is often provided by monopolies, and can generate large rents. It often provides vital services, which are highly prized and highly political. As a result, financial discipline can be weak, political intervention intense, and rent-seeking prevalent. And the benefits of infrastructure can be easy to claim and hard to verify.

This combination of circumstances can create fertile ground for corruption. But that corruption discredits the very infrastructure on which it preys. This can undermine the political sustainability of infrastructure development, and deter those investors and financiers concerned about reputational risk and other costs of corruption.

Combating corruption is a long, hard struggle requiring strong top-down political commitment. Major reforms of the judiciary and civil service lie at the heart of any anticorruption effort. While these longer-term reforms are being put in place, significant progress can be made by removing rent-seeking opportunities and exposing transactions to public scrutiny.

***

Four additional policy messages derive from analysis developed across this study, although they all take their departure from what we described as the "funding story" in Chapter 1. Here we saw that infrastructure can only be *funded* from two sources: the resources of consumers, and the resources of taxpayers. But infrastructure can be *financed* by two other actors: the private sector (which may also include service providers), and official lenders and donors. The policy messages are as follows:

9. The private sector will come back—if the right policies evolve

Private investment in East Asian infrastructure peaked in 1997 and declined dramatically thereafter. It is now showing modest signs of recovery, but it still has not come close to matching the levels initially expected in the mid-1990s.

A perceptions survey was carried out for this study among 50 private companies active or interested in East Asian infrastructure investment. One survey response stood out above all others: A majority of investors said they were keen to invest, and would do so if policies were more predictable.

The private sector certainly has not disappeared from East Asian infrastructure; however, it is not actually making large investments. More predictable policies would bring it back. Moreover, if it came back, better regulation or more competitive market structures would help ensure efficiency gains from its return.

10. Public sector reform matters, but be realistic

In some places, the private sector won't come in sufficient scale, or will only do so on terms that are politically unacceptable (at least to specific groups with strong voice). This is likely to be particularly relevant in countries with small markets (population or purchasing power), those which are emerging from conflict, those where ideological opposition to private or foreign investment is particularly strong, or those where adjustment of large state-owned infrastructure is politically difficult because of employment effects. In some sectors, natural monopoly remains strong, so competition to induce the efficiency gains from private participation is not yet possible.

In sectoral terms, water and sanitation, large-scale hydropower and electricity transmission, some types of transport, and rural or cross-border infrastructure seem to have the hardest time attracting private investment, or using it to promote efficiency (although there are notable exceptions). In those situations, reform of the public sector may sometimes be the most feasible option for efficiency gains, at least in the near term.

But public sector reform is difficult to achieve, and even harder to sustain, so expectations should be modest. If the private sector can't be attracted because the state is unpredictable and lacks vision, or because tariffs and subsidies are below costs, then public sector performance is likely to be disappointing as well. Even if costs are covered, public resources may be better used in sectors other than infrastructure. The alternative of more thorough reform in the medium term to attract private investment should always be considered.

11. Local capital markets matter, but are not a panacea

East Asia's success is built, in part, on channeling high savings into domestic investment in infrastructure. The 1997 crisis underlined that domestic savings tend to be less footloose than foreign savings, and that domestic currency financing is less exposed to foreign currency risk. As domestic savings become more scarce, their efficient allocation becomes more necessary. As government functions become more complex, the delegation of resource allocation and risk assessment becomes more important. For these reasons, the contribution of the domestic financial sector to infrastructure development needs to grow.

Government will play an important role in regulating the domestic financial sector and encouraging financial innovation, as well as in promoting regional capital market initiatives. In countries where the policy—or quasi-fiscal role—of the financial sector has led to high levels of nonperforming loans to infrastructure, commercialization of the sector will be a priority in the near term. This will restore health to the financial sector and financial discipline to the infrastructure sector.

But to promote the financial sector's contribution most effectively over the long term, policies to improve the investment climate for infrastructure should take the highest priority. Trying to make a poorly designed infrastructure project work through financial engineering can have only limited effect; making it into a viable project through reform beyond the financial sector will usually have a greater impact.

12. Infrastructure needs reliable and responsive development partners

The development community is now reasserting its role in infrastructure in East Asia. But infrastructure is a long-term asset, and development partners need to stay for the long haul. Reliable partnerships—with quick response and harmonized procedures—are critical. Moreover, the nature of this partnership (financing, guarantees, policy advice, capacity building, and so on) will have to be tailored to country conditions. The needs of East Asia's large, middle-income countries are different from the smaller and poorer countries in the region.

Official development assistance (ODA) accounts for approximately 1 percent of gross investment in low- and middle-income countries of East Asia. However, aid financing plays a more significant role in the poorer countries of the region, accounting for more than half of gross investment in Mongolia and Cambodia. Aid flows also play a significant role in most Pacific island countries, Timor-Leste, Papua New Guinea, and Lao PDR. The level of aid, and how it is allocated (including the share for infrastructure), plays a big role in the public spending and investment priorities of these countries.

The case for official financing depends on how well it can be used, the availability of other sources of financing, and the overall debt position of the government. The level of aid usually declines, and the blend of loans and grants usually becomes harder, as income levels rise in recipient countries. However, even higher-income countries may see benefits in tapping official financing to ease the debt burden on their budget and to catalyze private sources of funds. The technical assistance embedded in aid-financed projects—for project preparation, environmental and social assessments, and procurement practices—can be beneficial for shaping the government's overall policies and procedures.

During the 1990s, some key development partners in East Asia focused their efforts away from infrastructure, at least from infrastructure on a large scale. These partners felt that poverty reduction should be more targeted or that the private sector should step in to finance infrastructure projects. This tendency was intensified by the 1997 financial crisis, as the creditworthiness of affected countries and many infrastructure service providers declined. Aid financing in crisis-affected countries shifted to program support, as budgets were cut and new investments in infrastructure were sharply curtailed.

The role of official financing for infrastructure is now being reappraised. It is acknowledged that growth is crucial to poverty reduction, that targeting complements growth, and that infrastructure is essential for both. The private sector did step in, then partly stepped out, and may now step in again. But even at its peak, the private sector was a relatively minor player in financing terms, especially in the poorer countries of the region, and official financing could be helpful to catalyze private investment. Some countries are now emerging from fiscal compression and need official financing to catalyze the private sector and provide more fiscal space for infrastructure spending. Support for more complex projects and new approaches can be particularly valuable.

As official financing for infrastructure increases again, it's important that it is used in a way that maximizes development impact. In the past, infrastructure projects have not always been well linked to a country's overall development and poverty reduction strategy. Aid must be used to support (rather than undermine) good policies. In some cases, this may mean funding sectoral programs, including recurrent spending for operations and maintenance and even subsidies. The broader impact of large-scale projects on government revenues must also be taken into account (as seen in the case of the Nam Theun 2 dam project, Chapter 4, Box 4.6).

Some official lenders and donors can provide instruments to back up government commitments to the private sector at a time when credibility with the private sector is still being established (for example, guarantees, insurance, official lending to the private sector). The overall case for the use of those instruments depends on a number of factors: first, the economic justification for the project; second, the proper allocation of risks among stakeholders and the ability to structure the guarantee to strengthen rather than dilute operators' incentives to deliver; and third, a robust budget framework for managing any contingent liabilities arising from government commitments.

However, in no case should such instruments be substitutes for good policies. Sound policies can reduce risks and demonstrate the government's commitment to reform. They are therefore more valuable to investors than official agency support per se.

Finally, official lenders and donors can provide important knowledge about what works and what doesn't in different countries and sectors. Some of this knowledge comes from higher-income countries that have been there before and learned from their mistakes and successes. It's therefore important that countries like Singapore and Korea stay engaged with the broader development community.

The type of knowledge needed will also vary by country—from basic institution and capacity building in poorer countries to more sophisticated market instruments in middle-income countries. For the latter, innovative ways are needed to combine private and public financing to extend maturities for long gestation projects. New approaches to developing financing mechanisms at subsovereign levels also need special attention.

Spotlight 4. The way forward in Indonesia and the Philippines

Indonesia

Indonesia is emerging from a period of fiscal consolidation and political turmoil with a renewed commitment to addressing a number of delayed development priorities. Infrastructure has been identified as one of these priorities. The framework developed in this report provides important insights into the nature of Indonesia's infrastructure challenge.

Poor infrastructure outcomes are undermining inclusive development both through poor service delivery and growth impacts. Infrastructure in Indonesia has been neglected in the aftermath of the 1997 crisis and the impact on economic growth and people's well-being is apparent. Indonesia's current GDP growth—which levels off at around 4 percent—is limited by insufficient infrastructure investments. Several business climate surveys identify poor infrastructure as a key bottleneck.

Examples of direct negative impacts on poverty abound: Poor, or non-existent sewerage systems and solid waste facilities, for instance, have caused widespread contamination of surface and groundwater and lies behind the fact that Indonesia has the highest incidence of typhoid in East Asia.

Increased participation and rapid decentralization have given rise to a host of coordination challenges. Coordination between central and local authorities has suffered, as decision-making authority has been delegated but financial resources have not. Instruments to ensure that national priorities are reflected at the local level—such as matching grants for example—remain to be developed. Additionally, the provincial level of government remains underdeveloped, and as a result, local jurisdictions have often failed to coordinate, to take externalities into account, or take advantage of economies of scales.

Insufficient accountability is arguably the most critical problem affecting infrastructure in Indonesia. Transparency International Corruption Perceptions Index 2004[2] has ranked Indonesia 133rd out of 145 countries and perceptions of corruption remain pervasive in infrastructure

(Transparency International 2004). Opportunities for corruption arise at all stages of the infrastructure project cycle and a significant amount of public funds are being lost through corrupt practices.

New regulations on public procurement represent a clear improvement over previous policies, but serious weaknesses remain: for example, regulations leave room for excessive discretion in the selection of bidders; they fail to establish clear procedures to handle complaints from aggrieved bidders; and they do not apply mandatory sanctions to guilty parties.

Risk-sharing arrangements are at the heart of the government's infrastructure policy. Measures are urgently needed on several fronts. At present, the cost of infrastructure is being borne to a large extent by taxpayers. For instance, various fuel subsidies account for nearly 2 percent of GDP, and over two-thirds of water utilities operate with losses, because of inefficient operations as well as low tariffs. This distorts consumption and investment, and imposes fiscal strains, as consumers do not face the real costs of the infrastructure services they consume.

Risk allocation between public and private actors is also cause for concern. As the government seeks to restore private infrastructure investments, it is coming under pressure to offer guarantees to private investors in virtually all infrastructure sectors. A robust framework is urgently needed to help the authorities decide when public support should be provided and when it should not.

Within 100 days of coming to power, the new government held a successful "Infrastructure Summit" to develop a consensus between public and private actors on how to meet the challenges set out above. The Jakarta Declaration, issued at the end of the Summit, affirms the government's confidence that the challenges can be met, and outlines an agenda very much in keeping with the operational priorities laid out in the present chapter.

The summit highlighted the importance of infrastructure for growth and poverty alleviation. Increasing infrastructure spending while maintaining macroeconomic stability is identified as a priority. Indonesia is fortunate that the budget adjustment implemented by the government over the past five years has restored fiscal discipline and opened the possibility of additional public spending on infrastructure.

However, fiscal policy needs to remain prudent, which puts a premium on improving revenue mobilization over the medium term. And prudent fiscal policy will need to be matched with prudent financial policy—which allows sound projects to be financed but does not lead to pressure for state banks to lend indiscriminately in the name of infrastructure.

The difficult coordination issues raised by the decentralization process need to be tackled. Greater clarity in the responsibilities and resources of different levels of government; financial instruments that would strengthen local authorities' incentives to take national priorities into account; a stronger provincial role to ensure better coordination among local jurisdictions; and effective capacity building at the local level would go a long way to improving the institutional framework for infrastructure development.

Increasing accountability has been identified as a central objective. One of the ways in which government is pursuing this is through regulatory reform. The government is committed to turning the embryonic telecommunications agency into a competent entity, and to implement recently adopted laws that call for the creation of regulatory agencies in the electricity and in the oil and natural gas sectors. In addition, regulations are being prepared to ensure the transparent and competitive selection of private partners for infrastructure projects. Additional measures on information disclosure and the imposition of tough sanctions on those convicted of corruption would further strengthen the framework for accountability.

The allocation of risks between taxpayers and users, and between public and private actors needs to be reviewed. Gradual tariff increases (accompanied by measures to increase operational efficiency) are required, especially in the water sector. Subsidies, such as those on gasoline and on automotive diesel oil, will need to be progressively eliminated in order to convey more precise price signals to users.

The government has started to review the framework for public support to private infrastructure projects. Its objective is to put in place the tools and processes required to better identify the projects warranting public support, to design such support in a way that strengthens operators' incentives to deliver, and to adequately evaluate and manage the liabilities that the government incurs in providing such support.

Finally, development agencies have been invited to help. The government has signaled that it would welcome investments geared at eliminating key infrastructure bottlenecks, as well as support in improving the conditions for private participation in infrastructure. An international workshop was held in 2004 to sound investors on their assessment of opportunities in the power sector, and work has started on evaluating what needs to be done to clarify when and how public support will be extended to private infrastructure projects. In terms of instruments, the government would welcome financial and technical support in the implementation of sector-wide reforms, development interventions targeted at provincial and local authorities, and uses of development agencies' funds in ways that maximize catalytic impact with private investors.

The Philippines

While the Philippines performs better than Indonesia on key infrastructure access indicators (see Table 1.4), the impact of infrastructure on poverty, through growth and service access is still problematic. Levels of expenditure on infrastructure are low, at 2.8 percent of GDP—well below the estimate of 3.8 percent[3] of GDP required for middle-income developing countries to meet infrastructure needs (see Figure 1.10).

Strains are clearly showing. Performance in some areas, such as access to clean water, has deteriorated in recent years. There is also evidence to suggest that insufficient investments in infrastructure is partly responsible for relatively weak GDP growth: preliminary studies indicate a causal relationship from infrastructure to GDP in the Philippines, and that growth of the infrastructure capital stock has a positive and long-term impact on the level of GDP (World Bank, forthcoming b).

Challenges of coordination are one important part of this outcome. As we saw in Chapter 3, centralized infrastructure planning in the Philippines has been significantly weakened in recent years. Public infrastructure spending has been largely reactive, with short periods of high spending followed by longer periods of insufficient investments.

Infrastructure delivered at the subnational level has been neglected in the wake of decentralization, both because subnational plans have few champions at the central level, and because revenues do not match devolved responsibilities at the provincial level. This has resulted in underinvestment in particular in facilities such as solid and toxic waste disposal, in transport, and wastewater and watershed management. Local government units too have failed to rise to the challenge of local infrastructure provision as technical capacity and financial resource constraints have been pervasive.

Accountability presents similar challenges in the Philippines as in Indonesia, with a Transparency International Corruption Perceptions

Index ranking of 103 out of 145 countries (Transparency International 2004). Insufficient competition and regulation prone to capture by special interests create significant opportunities for graft. And, as set out in Box 3.4, discretionary "pork barrel" funds allocated to individual legislators are spent with little oversight and are major contributors to inefficiency.

Risk-sharing between taxpayers and users is affected, as in Indonesia, by the fact that tariffs, across infrastructure sectors, are insufficient to cover costs. The situation is particularly difficult in the water and sanitation sector, where tariffs are barely sufficient to cover operation and maintenance costs and certainly do not provide for rehabilitation or extension work.

Allocation of risks between public and private parties in infrastructure projects has also tended to be suboptimal. In the power sector, for instance, the government offered attractive power purchase agreements to private developers to try and eliminate severe power shortages in the early 1990s. As a result, excessive private investments in generation have burdened the sector with substantial stranded costs.

As in Indonesia, measures are needed on each one of these four fronts. Allocation of resources to infrastructure is an urgent priority. But the Philippine fiscal position differs markedly from that of Indonesia, with significant constraints on any further public investment. Under these circumstances, the country has little choice but to take gradual steps in increasing user charges. Meaningful tariff increases have already been implemented in the power sector.

Actions on tariffs need to be coupled with measures aimed at cutting costs and increasing efficiency. Here, the most promising course of action for the Philippines is to progressively open the provision of infrastructure services to competition. An ambitious liberalization program is in preparation in the power sector. A pro-competition strategy has also been at least partially implemented already in the telecommunications sector.

Improvement of coordination capacity requires strengthening of the central agencies with responsibility for infrastructure. Support of inter-jurisdictional cooperation arises as a further priority. Central agencies can help by strengthening linkages among national, regional, provincial and municipal planning. Finally, an adequate incentive framework needs to be developed to reward local government performance. This needs to be combined with the provision of assistance to local governments, both with respect to strategic planning and with respect to project selection, preparation, and implementation.

Measures to address poor accountability have already been undertaken. The establishment of the Office of the Ombudsman, passage of the Government Procurement Reform Act of 2003, and involvement of civil society organizations as observers in bidding processes are encouraging developments. In addition, successful experiences with community-driven development have increased the transparency of infrastructure service provisions in specific cases.

But these efforts need to be sustained. This requires, for instance, vigorous implementation of the Government Procurement Reform Act, complemented by financial management reforms, and strengthening of the monitoring and enforcement capabilities of key anticorruption oversight agencies, such as the Office of the Ombudsman. Enhancing competition, and more effective regulation, will equally help foster accountability.

As far as risk sharing is concerned, the prescriptions for the Philippines are similar to those applicable to Indonesia. Tariff increases need to be implemented in a progressive manner, particularly in the water and sanitation sector, and the framework for provision of public support to private infrastructure projects needs to be strengthened. As in Indonesia, the government is well aware of such priorities and work is starting on a review of the framework for providing guarantees and other forms of public support to infrastructure.

The government has invited development partners to support its efforts on three broad fronts. At the national level, priority has been placed on helping to strengthen governance mechanisms and sector reforms through budget support and sector-wide approaches. At the local level, the focus will be on local government capacity building and inter-jurisdictional coordination. Finally, the government has set the goal of fostering private sector involvement in infrastructure through a combination of loans to public and private entities, investments in private projects, and guarantees.

Appendix A

Statistical Annex: Infrastructure Indicators

Introduction

This statistical annex provides an overview of the state of economic infrastructure in the main developing countries of East Asia. It contains information for selected years on stock, access, affordability, efficiency, the state of reform, and financial performance of the energy, water supply and sanitation (WSS), telecom, and transport sectors. In addition, the annex also presents figures on urban issues and rough estimates of infrastructure investment. The annex comprises 7 tables and 165 infrastructure indicators.

Data collection

The annex attempts to present the most relevant data needed to assess infrastructure. Because the official lenders' and donors' primary business is to provide lending and advice to low- and middle-income countries, the annex focuses on the main client countries in the region. Most of the data are on the national level, the exception being WSS indicators, some of which are at the city, urban, and rural levels. Virtually all of the data were collected using publicly available sources, including publications and Internet Web sites from development institutions, sector-specific international agencies, and national statistical offices. In some cases, data were also collected through conversations with national government agencies or World Bank sector specialists and reports. This dataset was collected in Washington, DC, and in World Bank field offices.

Reliability and comparability

Data collected from publicly available, country-specific sources are always subject to reliability and comparability issues. These inconsistencies arise from a number of factors, including differences in classifications, definitions, and coverage across countries. Given these inevitable challenges, although all efforts were made to verify the data in this annex and note any definitional peculiarities by local World Bank staff and consultants, care must be taken when analyzing these indicators. It is impossible to guarantee the validity of the data presented, although the figures are current best estimates of the indicators presented. In some instances, available data deemed to be too unreliable were excluded from the annex. A complete list of indicator definitions, along with any definitional discrepancies or notes needed to correctly interpret the data by country, is available in the technical notes section. Readers are strongly encouraged to consult the technical notes when interpreting the figures presented in this annex. More detailed information, including the dataset for all available years along with sources for each figure, can be found on the East Asia and Pacific (EAP) Infrastructure Flagship Web site located at: http://www.worldbank.org/eapinfrastructure.

Key

Units are provided in the tables next to the indicator name. In addition, a number of notations that are present in the tables require further explanation, including the following:

— Not available
0.0 = Less than half the unit shown
Y = yes; N = no
* See notes on the figure(s) in the technical annex

Figures in italics indicate data that are for years or periods other than those specified, or data that include figures from years other than those specified (for example, the sum of data from other years).

Technical notes

Energy

E1: Household with an Electricity Connection—Electricity access at the household level. It comprises commercially sold electricity, both on-grid and off-grid. It also includes self-generated electricity for those countries where access to electricity has been assessed through surveys by government or government agencies. The data do not capture unauthorized connections.

- Country Notes
  i. China—Areas covered by the State Grid Corporation

E2: Households Using Solid Fuels—The percentage of households using solid fuels, which include wood, straw, dung, coal, and charcoal.

- Country Notes
  i. China—Figure is for urban households only; 95 percent of rural households use solid fuels.

E3: Spending on Energy Services—The average share of total household expenditure spent of energy services.

- Country Notes
  i. Cambodia—Urban areas only; figure ranges from 12 to 30 percent

    ii. Lao People's Democratic Republic (Lao PDR)—1.4 percent for urban areas; 0.6 percent for rural areas

    iii. Mongolia—All utilities, not just energy

    iv. Thailand—Electricity only

E4: Hours of Power Outages from Public Grid—The number of hours of service interruptions in a year.

- Country Notes
  - i. Lao PDR—Vientiane area only

E5: Average Residential Electricity Tariff—The national average residential electricity tariff.

- Country Notes
  - i. Cambodia—Phnom Penh only
  - ii. China—There is no available weighted average for the country. It has not changed much in the last five years, although it increased slightly in 2003.
  - iii. Philippines—Manila area only
  - iv. Vietnam—1998 figure includes tax; 2003 figure does not include tax

E6: Average Industrial Electricity Tariff—The national average industrial electricity tariff.

- Country Notes
  - i. Cambodia—Phnom Penh only
  - ii. China—There is no available weighted average for the country. The figure is for the general industry. It is much lower for heavy industry.
  - iii. Philippines—Manila area only
  - iv. Vietnam—1998 figure includes tax; 2003 figure does not include tax

E7: Transmission and Distribution Losses—Technical and nontechnical losses. Includes electricity losses because of operation of the system and the delivery of electricity as well as those caused by unmetered supply. This includes all losses due to transport and distribution of electrical energy and heat.

- Country Notes
  - i. Cambodia—Phnom Penh only

    ii. China—This is the average for the State Grid. It does not include losses in some counties that own their own distribution companies.

    iii. Lao PDR—1998 figure for Region 1 only; 2003 figure for the entire country

E8, E14, E20, E26, E32: Power, Oil, or Gas: Has the utility (state-owned enterprise) been commercialized and corporatized? This first step of reform involves (1) the removal of the utility from the direct control that results from being a part of a ministry, and (2) the creation of an independent legal corporation with the goal of behaving like a commercial company (for example, maximizing profits).

E9, E15, E21, E27, E33: Power, Oil, or Gas: Has an Energy Law been completely passed by parliament (a law that permits the creation of a sector that could be unbundled and/or privatized in part or whole)? This second step is crucial to allowing the sale of a state utility to the private sector. It should be noted that the question specifically asks whether the law is completely passed, because many countries have started the process of drafting and validating a new law but have not enacted it, despite the passage of a considerable period of time.

- Country Notes
    i. Indonesia—Yes, for power sector, but the law was annulled by the Constitution Court

E10, E16, E22, E28, E34: Power, Oil, or Gas: Has a regulatory body that is separate from the utility and ministry started work? Note that the question focuses only on those cases in which the regulatory body is actually in place.

- Country Notes
    i. Indonesia—Yes, for power sector, but the law was annulled by the Constitution Court

E11, E17, E23, E29, E35: Power, Oil, or Gas: Has there been any private sector investment on greenfield sites in operation or under construction? A greenfield site refers to the construction of an entirely new plant, rather than the change in ownership of an existing plant or extension of capacity at an existing plant.

E12, E18, E24, E30, E36: Power, Oil, or Gas: Has the core state-owned utility been restructured/separated? Restructuring/separation results in separate generation, transmission, and distribution entities.

- Country Notes
    i. Indonesia—Upstream oil and gas sector currently undergoing restructuring

E13, E19, E25, E31, E37: Power, Oil, or Gas: Have any of the existing state-owned enterprises been privatized (including outright sale, voucher privatization, or joint ventures)? This question asks whether there is *some* privatization, not whether the sector has been completely privatized. To this extent, it treats as equal those cases in which the state has sold a minority of shares in a company to private shareholders, and cases in which the whole of a generating plant or regional distribution network has been sold outright to a single owner. Hence, the answer must been seen as measuring whether the country has proved itself willing to permit private ownership of previously state-owned assets, rather than measuring the extent of private ownership.

Water supply and sanitation

W1: Access to Improved Water Services—"Improved" water supply technologies include household connection, public standpipe, borehole, protected dug well, protected spring, and rainwater collection. Availability of at least 20 liters per person per day from a source within 1 kilometer of the user's dwelling. "Not improved" technologies include unprotected well, unprotected spring, vendor-provided water, bottled water (based on concerns about the quantity of supplied water, not concerns over the water quality), and tanker-truck-provided water.

W2: Urban Access to Improved Water Services—See W1 above; limited to urban population only.

W3: Rural Access to Improved Water Services—See W1 above; limited to rural population only.

W4: Access to Improved Sanitation Services—"Improved" sanitation technologies are connection to a public sewer, connection to septic system, pour-flush latrine, simple pit latrine, ventilated improved pit

Table 1 Energy

		Cambodia		China		Indonesia		Lao PDR		Mongolia		Philippines		Thailand		Vietnam	
	Indicator	Unit	1998	2003	1998	2003	1998	2003	1998	2003	1998	2003	1998	2003	1998	2003	1998	2003
E1	Households with an Electricity Connection	Percent	13	17	97*	99*	—	55	30	41	67	90	72	79	82	84	63	81
E2	Households Using Solid Fuels	Percent	100	100	62*	51*	—	—	—	—	72	72	—	—	—	40	88	—
E3	Spending on Energy Services (% household expenditure)	Percent of Household Expenditure	20*	24*	7.0	7.6	—	9.0	0.8*	—	4.9*	2.5*	2.7	3.3	2.5*	2.6*	—	2.9
E4	Hours of Power Outages from Public Grid	Hours (unless otherwise specified)	10.4	0.9	—	—	—	—		1,097 outages*	66 outages	16 outages	—	—	27	21	—	—
E5	Average Residential Electricity Tariff	Nominal US$/kWh	0.09-0.15*	0.09-0.15*	0.05-0.07*	0.05-0.08*	—	0.02-0.07	0.01	0.04	0.04	0.05	0.10*	0.11*	0.06	0.06	0.04*	0.05*
E6	Average Industrial Electricity Tariff	Nominal US$/kWh	0.21*	0.12-0.15*	0.05-0.09*	0.05-0.09*	—	0.02-0.05	0.01	0.05	0.04	0.05	0.09*	0.10*	0.05	0.06	0.05*	0.05*
E7	Transmission and Distribution Losses	Percent	20.6*	12.7*	8.1*	7.7*	12.2	11.7	22.6*	21.2*	—	22.0	14.1	12.4	8.7	7.3	15.6	13.4
E8	Power: Has the utility (state-owned enterprise) been commercialized and corporatized?	Yes/No	Y	Y	Y	Y	—	Y	Y	Y	N	Y	N	Y	N	N	N	N
E9	Power: Has an "Energy Law" been completely passed by Parliament (a law that permits the creation of a sector that could be unbundled and/or privatized in part or whole)?	Yes/No	N	N	N	N	—	Y*	Y	Y	N	Y	N	Y	N	N	N	N
E10	Power: Has a regulatory body that is separate from the utility and ministry started work?	Yes/No	N	Y	N	Y	—	Y*	N	N	N	Y	N	Y	N	N	N	N

(Continued on the next page)

Table 1 (Continued)

Indicator	Unit	Cambodia 1998	Cambodia 2003	China 1998	China 2003	Indonesia 1998	Indonesia 2003	Lao PDR 1998	Lao PDR 2003	Mongolia 1998	Mongolia 2003	Philippines 1998	Philippines 2003	Thailand 1998	Thailand 2003	Vietnam 1998	Vietnam 2003
E11 Power: Is there any private sector investment on greenfield sites in operation or under construction?	Yes/No	Y	Y	Y	Y	—	Y	Y	Y	N	N	Y	Y	Y	Y	N	Y
E12 Power: Has the core state-owned utility been restructured/separated?	Yes/No	N	N	N	Y	—	Y	Y	Y	N	Y	N	Y	N	N	N	N
E13 Power: Have any of the existing state-owned enterprises been privatized (including outright sale, voucher privatization, or joint ventures)?	Yes/No	Y	Y	Y	Y	—	N	N	N	N	Y	Y	Y	Y	Y	N	N
E14 Upstream Oil and Gas: Has the utility (state-owned enterprise) been commercialized and corporatized?	Yes/No	N	N	Y	Y	—	Y	Sector does not exist	Sector does not exist	N	N	N	N	N	N	N	N
E15 Upstream Oil and Gas: Has an "Energy Law" been completely passed by Parliament (a law that permits the creation of a sector that could be unbundled and/or privatized in part or whole)?	Yes/No	N	N	N	N	—	Y	Sector does not exist	Sector does not exist	Y	Y	N	N	N	N	N	N
E16 Upstream Oil and Gas: Has a regulatory body that is separate from the utility and ministry started work?	Yes/No	N	N	N	N	—	Y	Sector does not exist	Sector does not exist	N	N	N	N	N	N	N	N
E17 Upstream Oil and Gas: Is there any private sector investment on greenfield sites in operation or under construction?	Yes/No	N	Y	Y	Y	—	Y	Sector does not exist	Sector does not exist	Y	Y	N	N	Y	Y	N	N

E18	Upstream Oil and Gas: Has the core state-owned utility been restructured/separated?	Yes/No	N	N	N	N	N	N	N	—	N*	Sector does not exist	Sector does not exist	N	N	N	N	N	N	N	N	N
E19	Upstream Oil and Gas: Have any of the existing state-owned enterprises been privatized (including outright sale, voucher privatization, or joint ventures)?	Yes/No	N	N	N	Y	Y	Y	N	—	N	Sector does not exist	Sector does not exist	N	N	N	N	N	N	Y	N	N
E20	Downstream Gas: Has the utility (state-owned enterprise) been commercialized and corporatized?	Yes/No	N	N	N	Y	Y	Y	Y	—	Y	Sector does not exist	Sector does not exist	Y	N	Y	N	N	N	N	N	N
E21	Downstream Gas: Has an "Energy Law" been completely passed by Parliament (a law that permits the creation of a sector that could be unbundled and/or privatized in part or whole)?	Yes/No	N	N	N	N	N	N	N	—	Y	Sector does not exist	Sector does not exist	N	N	N	N	N	N	N	N	N
E22	Downstream Gas: Has a regulatory body that is separate from the utility and ministry started work?	Yes/No	N	N	N	N	N	N	N	—	Y	Sector does not exist	Sector does not exist	Y	N	N	N	N	N	N	N	N
E23	Downstream Gas: Is there any private sector investment on greenfield sites in operation or under construction?	Yes/No	N	N	N	Y	Y	Y	Y	—	Y	Sector does not exist	Sector does not exist	Y	Y	Y	Y	Y	Y	—	N	N
E24	Downstream Gas: Has the core state-owned utility been restructured/separated?	Yes/No	N	N	N	Y	Y	Y	Y	—	Y	Sector does not exist	Sector does not exist	Y	Y	N	N	N	N	N	N	N
E25	Downstream Gas: Have any of the existing state-owned enterprises been privatized (including outright sale, voucher privatization, or joint ventures)?	Yes/No	N	N	N	Y	Y	Y	Y	—	Y	Sector does not exist	Sector does not exist	N	N	Y	N	N	N	Y	N	N

(Continued on the next page)

Table 1 (Continued)

		Cambodia		China		Indonesia		Lao PDR		Mongolia		Philippines		Thailand		Vietnam	
Indicator	Unit	1998	2003	1998	2003	1998	2003	1998	2003	1998	2003	1998	2003	1998	2003	1998	2003
E26 Downstream Oil Refining: Has the utility (state-owned enterprise) been commercialized and corporatized?	Yes/No	N	N	Y	Y	—	Y	Sector does not exist	Sector does not exist	N	N	Y	Y	N	N	N	N
E27 Downstream Oil Refining: Has an "Energy Law" been completely passed by Parliament (a law that permits the creation of a sector that could be unbundled and/or privatized in part or whole)?	Yes/No	N	N	N	N	—	Y	Sector does not exist	Sector does not exist	N	N	Y	Y	N	N	N	N
E28 Downstream Oil Refining: Has a regulatory body that is separate from the utility and ministry started work?	Yes/No	N	N	N	N	—	Y	Sector does not exist	Sector does not exist	N	N	N	N	N	N	N	N
E29 Downstream Oil Refining: Is there any private sector investment on greenfield sites in operation or under construction?	Yes/No	N	N	Y	Y	—	Y	Sector does not exist	Sector does not exist	N	N	N	N	Y	Y	N	N
E30 Downstream Oil Refining: Has the core state-owned utility been restructured/separated?	Yes/No	N	N	Y	Y	—	Y	Sector does not exist	Sector does not exist	N	N	Y	Y	N	N	N	N
E31 Downstream Oil Refining: Have any of the existing state-owned enterprises been privatized (including outright sale, voucher privatization, or joint ventures)?	Yes/No	N	N	Y	Y	—	N	Sector does not exist	Sector does not exist	N	N	Y	Y	Y	Y	N	N
E32 Downstream Oil Wholesale and Retail: Has the utility (state-owned enterprise) been commercialized and corporatized?	Yes/No	N	N	Y	Y	—	Y	N	N	Y	Y	Y	Y	N	N	N	N

E33	Downstream Oil Wholesale and Retail: Has an "Energy Law" been completely passed by Parliament (a law that permits the creation of a sector that could be unbundled and/or privatized in part or whole)?	Yes/No	N	N	N	N	—	Y	N	N	N	N	N	N	N	Y	N	N	N	N
E34	Downstream Oil Wholesale and Retail: Has a regulatory body that is separate from the utility and ministry started work?	Yes/No	N	N	N	N	—	Y	N	N	N	N	N	N	N	N	N	N	N	N
E35	Downstream Oil Wholesale and Retail: Is there any private sector investment on greenfield sites in operation or under construction?	Yes/No	N	Y	Y	Y	—	Y	Y	Y	Y	Y	Y	Y	Y	Y	Y	—	Y	N
E36	Downstream Oil Wholesale and Retail: Has the core state-owned utility been restructured/separated?	Yes/No	N	N	N	Y	—	Y	N	N	N	Y	Y	Y	Y	N	N	N	N	N
E37	Downstream Oil Wholesale and Retail: Have any of the existing state-owned enterprises been privatized (including outright sale, voucher privatization, or joint ventures)?	Yes/No	N	N	Y	Y	—	N	N	N	N	N	N	Y	Y	Y	Y	Y	N	N

latrine. The excreta disposal system is considered adequate if it is private or shared (but not public) and if it hygienically separates human excreta from human contact. "Not improved" technologies include service or bucket latrines (where excreta are manually removed), public latrines, and latrines with an open pit.

W5: Urban Access to Improved Sanitation Services—See W4 above; limited to urban population only.

W6: Rural Access to Improved Sanitation Services—See W4 above; limited to urban population only.

W7: Spending on Water Services—Average share of total household expenditure spent of water services.
- Country Notes
    - i. Cambodia—Urban residents only
    - ii. Indonesia—Perusahaan Daerah Air Minum (Local Water Supply Enterprise) (PDAM) customers in Jakarta and Bandung pay between 1 and 2 percent of average annual income on water; in areas not served by PDAMs, surveys have found that some of the poorest households pay between 16 and 33 percent.
    - iii. Lao PDR—Public utility connection only; households without a connection spend 1.4 percent
    - iv. Mongolia—All utilities, not just WSS

W8: Average Volume of Water Used—Volume of water used from all sources.
- Country Notes
    - i. Indonesia—Low-income PDAM customers use about 3.8 meters cubed per week (m^3/week); the same figure for high-income customers is 9.6 m^3/week

W9: Average Water Tariff from Water Utility—The average water tariff of water sold from main utility in the specified city.
- Country Notes
    - i. Manila—The two main providers are Manila Water Company (MWCI) and Maynilad Water Services (MWSI)

W10–W11: Average Water Tariff from Alternative Sources 2 and 3—The average water tariff of water sold from alternative sources in the specified city.

- Country Notes
  - i. Manila—Source 2 is water vendors reselling MWSI water
  - ii. Phnom Penh—Source 2 is private networks pumping untreated water from rivers; Source 3 is further treated Phnom Penh Water Supply Authority (PPWSA) water sold as bottled water
  - iii. Ho Chi Minh—Source 2 is tankers; Source 3 is bottled water
  - iv. Jakarta—Source 2 is private tankers; Source 3 is bottled water from refilling stations
  - v. Ulaanbaatar—Source 2 is bottle water
  - vi. Vientiane, Savannakhet—Source 2 is 20 liter bottles; Source 3 is 1L drinking water bottles

W12: Average Sanitation Tariff—The average sanitation tariff from main utility in the specified city.

W13: Percentage of Utility Service Area with 24-Hour Supply—Percentage of the population served by main utility in the specified city with a 24-hour supply.

W14: Working Ratio—Operating cost divided by operating revenue for main utility in the specified city.

W15: Staff Ratio—Number of staff divided by thousands of connections for main utility in the specified city.

- Country Notes
  - i. Mongolian cities—Connections in Mongolia are bulk connections

W16: Collection Rate—Collections divided by billings for main utility in the specified city.

W17: Average Revenue per m^3 Produced—Total revenue divided by total water production for main utility in the specified city.

W18: Type of Sewerage Treatment—Type of treatment process for wastewater in the specified city.

W19: Type of Water Supply Treatment—Type of treatment process for water supply in the specified city.

W20: Water Volume Billed per Connection—Total volume of water billed divided by the total number of connections for the main utility in the specified city.

- Country Notes
    i. Beijing—Each connection serves approximately 35 people
    ii. Ulaanbaatar, Darkhan—Each connection serves approximately 260 and 113 people, respectively

Telecoms

T1: Cellular Subscribers per 100 Inhabitants—Calculated by dividing the number of cellular mobile subscribers by the population and multiplying by 100.

T2: Main Lines per 100 Inhabitants—Calculated by dividing the number of main lines by the population and multiplying by 100.

T3: Total Telephone Subscribers per 100 Inhabitants—Calculated by summing cellular subscribers per 100 inhabitants and main lines per 100 inhabitants.

T4: Internet Users per 100 Inhabitants—Calculated by dividing the number of Internet users by the population and multiplying by 100.

T5: Telephone Faults per 100 Main Lines—This is calculated by dividing the total number of reported faults for the year by the total number of main lines in operation and multiplying by 100. The definition of fault can vary. Some countries include faulty customer equipment. Others distinguish between reported and actual found faults. Sometimes there is a distinction between residential and business lines. Another consideration is the time period because some countries report this indicator on a monthly basis; in these cases, data are converted to yearly estimates.

T6: Price of Analog Cellular Three-Minute Call—Cellular cost of three-minute local peak call.

T7: Analog Cellular Monthly Subscription Charge—Cellular monthly subscription refers to the recurring charge for a cellular subscriber. The charge should cover the rental of the line but not the rental of the terminal (for example, telephone set) when the terminal equipment market is liberalized. In some cases, the rental charge includes an allowance for free or reduced rate call units. If there are different charges for different exchange areas, the largest urban area is used.

Table 2 Water supply and sanitation

	Indicator	Unit	Cambodia 1998	Cambodia 2003	China 1998	China 2003	Indonesia 1998	Indonesia 2003	Lao PDR 1998	Lao PDR 2003	Mongolia 1998	Mongolia 2003	Philippines 1998	Philippines 2003	Thailand 1998	Thailand 2003	Vietnam 1998	Vietnam 2003
W1	Access to Improved Water Services	Percent of Total Population	29	44	75	—	78	—	50	58	60	—	86	—	93	93	41	49
W2	Urban Access to Improved Water Services	Percent of Urban Population	60	72	95	—	90	—	77	85	77	—	91	—	99	95	77	76
W3	Rural Access to Improved Water Services	Percent of Rural Population	24	40	65	—	69	—	45	48	30	—	79	—	92	91	29	26
W4	Access to Improved Sanitation Services	Percent of Total Population	15	22	36	—	55	—	30	—	30	—	83	—	97	98	17	25
W5	Urban Access to Improved Sanitation Services	Percent of Urban Population	49	55	67	—	69	—	67	—	46	—	93	—	100	100	60	68
W6	Rural Access to Improved Sanitation Services	Percent of Rural Population	9	16	21	—	46	—	19	—	2	—	69	—	96	97	3	11
W7	Spending on Water Services	Percent household expenditure	4.3*	3.2*	—	0.8	—	Ranges from 1 to 33*	1.0*	1.6*	4.9*	2.5*	0.8	—	—	—	—	1.4
W8	Average Volume of Water Used	m³ per household per week	8.1	8.3	—	4.4	—	Ranges from 3.8 to 9.6*	7.0	—	7.0	6.0	—	7.0	9.0	8.6	2.1	—

(Continued on the next page)

191

Table 2 (Continued)

	Indicator	Unit	Phnom Penh 1998	Phnom Penh 2003	Sihanoukville 1998	Sihanoukville 2003	Beijing 1998	Beijing 2003	Shanghai 1998	Shanghai 2003	Jakarta 1998	Jakarta 2003	Medan 1998	Medan 2003	Vientiane 1998	Vientiane 2003	Savannakhet 1998	Savannakhet 2003
	Average Water Tariff																	
W9	From Water Utility	Nominal US$/m³	0.21	0.25	—	0.39	0.12	0.35	0.08	0.14	—	0.29	—	0.13	0.02	0.05	—	0.08
W10	From Source 2	Nominal US$/m³, see country notes for source name	—	0.38	—	—	—	—	—	—	—	0.96	—	—	—	14.2	—	14.2
W11	From Source 3	Nominal US$/m³, see country notes for source name	—	50	—	—	—	—	—	—	—	13	—	—	—	139	—	142
W12	Average Sanitation Tariff	Nominal US$/m³	—	—	—	—	—	0.10	0.03	0.08	—	0.23	—	—	No system in place	No system in place	No system in place	No system in place
W13	Percentage of Utility Service Area with 24 hour Supply	Percent	—	100	—	25	96	—	98	100	—	92	—	82	—	50	—	—
W14	Working Ratio	Operating Cost / Operating Revenue	0.5	0.3	—	0.6	1.3	—	1.2	1.1	—	0.8	—	0.8	—	0.8	—	1.0
W15	Staff Ratio	Staff / 1000 Connections	9.0	4.0	—	19.7	27.2	—	1.1	1.1	—	5.3	—	4.6	—	8.8	—	8.4
W16	Collection Rate	Percent	97	100	—	100	99	97	83	95	—	98	—	—	—	59	—	—
W17	Average Revenue Per m³ Produced	Nominal US$/m³	0.16	0.05	—	0.01	0.05	—	0.13	0.15	—	0.14	—	—	0.04	0.08	—	—
W18	Type of Sewerage Treatment	(P)rimary, (S)econdary, or (T)ertiary	No treatment	No treatment	—	—	—	—	—	P	—	—	—	—	No system in place	No system in place	No system in place	No system in place
W19	Type of Water Supply Treatment	(C)onventional, (S)low Sand Filter, (D)esalination, (Ch)lorination, (O)ther	Ch	Ch	—	Ch	C	—	C	C, Ch	C	—	—	—	—	All types	—	All types
W20	Water Volume Billed per Connection	m³	320	381	—	351	2,799*	—	—	552	—	388	—	342	—	675	—	453

		Ulaanbaatar		Darkhan		Manila		Cebu		Bangkok		Chiang Mai		Hanoi		Ho Chi Minh City	
Indicator	Unit	1998	2003	1998	2003	1998	2003	1998	2003	1998	2003	1998	2003	1998	2003	1998	2003
Average Water Tariff																	
W9 From Water Utility	Nominal US$/m³	0.13	0.17	0.12	0.12	0.06 (MWCI), 0.12 (MWSI)*	0.12 (MWCI), 0.29 (MWSI)*	0.48	0.40	0.23	0.29	0.27	0.31	0.16	0.26	0.10	0.18
W10 From Source 2	Nominal US$/m³, see country notes for source name	—	450	—	—	—	2.92	—	—	—	—	—	—	—	—	—	0.66
W11 From Source 3	Nominal US$/m³, see country notes for source name	—	—	—	—	—	—	—	—	—	—	—	—	—	—	—	210
W12 Average Sanitation Tariff	Nominal US$/m³	0.09	0.09	0.03	0.09	—	—	—	—	—	—	—	—	—	—	—	—
W13 Percentage of Utility Service Area with 24 hour Supply	Percent	—	48	—	—	—	88	23	—	100	100	100	100	—	—	—	75
W14 Working Ratio	Operating Cost/ Operating Revenue	1.0	0.9	0.7	0.9	1.2	1.0	0.5	0.5	0.8	0.7	0.6	0.6	0.8	0.7	0.7	1.1
W15 Staff Ratio	Staff/1000 Connections	579*	823*	705*	387*	5.6	4.0	9.2	6.6	5.4	4.8	0.1	0.1	10.0	7.0	6.5	3.5
W16 Collection Rate	Percent	79	90	76	71	97	98	70	62	—	—	—	100	—	—	—	99
W17 Average Revenue Per m³ Produced	Nominal US$/m3	0.06	0.13	0.10	0.09	0.07	0.11	0.28	0.26	0.15	0.21	0.15	0.27	0.06	0.08	0.09	0.11
W18 Type of Sewerage Treatment	(P)rimary, (S)econdary, or (T)ertiary	S	S	S	S	P,S,T	P,S,T	—	—	—	S	—	—	—	—	—	—
W19 Type of Water Supply Treatment	(C)onventional, (S)low Sand Filter, (D)esalination, (Ch)lorination, (O)ther	Ch	Ch	Ch	Ch	C	C	Ch	Ch	S	S	S	S	S	S	C, S, Ch	C, S, Ch
W20 Water Volume Billed per Connection	m³	16,275*	26,284*	18,891*	7,803*	502	548	420	420	668	658	319	310	348	294	648	577

T8: Price of Three-Minute Local Call—Local call refers to the cost of a peak-rate three-minute call within the same exchange area using the subscriber's own terminal (that is, not from a public telephone).

T9: Residential Monthly Telephone Subscription—Residential telephone monthly subscription refers to the recurring fixed charge for a residential subscriber to the Public Switched Telephone Network (PSTN). The charge should cover the rental of the line but not the rental of the terminal (for example, telephone set) when the terminal equipment market is liberalized. In some cases, the rental charge includes an allowance for free or reduced rate call units. If there are different charges for different exchange areas, the largest urban area is used.

T10: Residential Telephone Connection Charge—Installation refers to the one-time charge to apply for basic telephone service for residential purposes. In cases in which there are different charges for different exchange areas, the charge is generally for the largest urban area.

T11: Waiting List for Main Lines—Unmet applications for connection to the PSTN, which have been held over because of a lack of technical facilities (equipment, lines, and so on). This indicator refers to registered applications and thus may not be indicative of the total unmet demand.

T12: Mobile Telecom Revenue per Subscriber—Calculated by dividing total mobile telecom revenue by the number of mobile subscribers. Mobile telecom revenue includes revenues from the provision of all types of mobile communications services such cellular, private trunked radio, and radio paging. The number of mobile subscribers refers to users of portable telephones subscribing to an automatic public mobile telephone service that provides access to the PSTN using cellular technology. This can include analogue and digital cellular systems, but it should not include noncellular systems. Subscribers to fixed wireless (for example, Wireless Local Loop), public mobile data services, or radio paging services are not included.

T13: Income per Fixed Line—Calculated by dividing total fixed line revenue by the number of main lines in operation. The revenue includes nonrefundable connection charges, line rentals, and local and national long-distance, and international call usage charges. It typically includes revenue from public payphones. The treatment of interconnection and settlement payments varies across countries. Most countries include receipts as revenue; some include only billed revenues (not counting any interconnection or settlement payments), while others include net revenues (receipts-payments). A main line is a telephone line connecting the subscriber's terminal equipment to the public switched network and that has a dedicated port in the telephone exchange equipment. This term is synonymous with "main station" or "Direct Exchange Line (DEL)," which are commonly used in telecommunication documents. A main line may not be the same as an "access" line or a subscriber. The definition of access line used by some countries varies. In some cases, it refers to the total installed capacity (rather than lines in service). In other cases, it refers to all network access points, including mobile cellular subscribers. Telephone subscribers would not generally include public telephones that are included in main lines.

T14: Telecom Revenue per Staff—Calculated by dividing total telecom revenue by the total number of full-time telecom staff. The revenue refers to earnings from the direct provision of facilities for providing telecom-munication services to the public (that is, not including revenues of resellers). This includes revenues from fixed telephone, mobile communi-cations, text (telex, telegraph, and facsimile), leased circuits, and data communications services. Some countries include telecommunication-related revenue such as directory advertising and equipment rental or sales. Others include value-added telecommunication services such as the provision of electronic mail or online services. The denominator includes full-time staff employed by telecommunication network operators in the country for the provision of public telecommunication services. Part-time staff are generally expressed in terms of full-time staff equivalents. Some countries do not distinguish between staff working for the provision of telecommunications services and those working in postal services.

Road transport

Rd1: Total Road Network—Kilometer length of the road network. The road network includes all roads in a given area.

- Country Notes
    i. Philippines—National, provincial, city, municipal, and barangay roads
    ii. Lao PDR—Includes 600 kilometers (km) of "special roads" that aren't included in Rd2 through Rd5

Table 3 Telecommunications

	Indicator	Unit	Cambodia 1998	Cambodia 2003	China 1998	China 2003	Indonesia 1998	Indonesia 2003	Lao PDR 1998	Lao PDR 2003	Mongolia 1998	Mongolia 2003	Philippines 1998	Philippines 2003	Thailand 1998	Thailand 2003	Vietnam 1998	Vietnam 2003
T1	Cellular subscribers per 100 inhabitants	People	0.5	3.5	1.9	21.5	0.5	8.7	0.1	2.0	0.4	13.0	2.4	27.0	3.3	39.4	0.3	3.4
T2	Main lines per 100 inhabitants	Main lines	0.2	0.3	7.0	20.9	2.7	3.9	0.6	1.2	4.5	5.6	3.4	4.1	8.5	10.5	2.2	5.4
T3	Total telephone subscribers per 100 inhabitants	People	0.7	3.8	8.9	42.4	3.2	12.7	0.7	3.2	4.9	18.6	5.8	31.1	11.8	49.9	2.5	8.8
T4	Internet users per 100 inhabitants	People	0.0	0.2	0.2	6.3	0.2	3.8	0.0	0.3	0.1	5.8	1.1	4.4	0.8	11.1	0.0	4.3
T5	Telephone faults per 100 main lines	Faults	9.4	7.2	—	—	13.2	20.0	—	—	88.3	20.6	5.2	—	28.6	91.7	—	—
T6	Price of analog cellular three-minute call	US$, nominal	0.60	0.69	—	0.22	0.10	0.10	0.06	0.21	0.63	0.95	0.59	0.46	0.22	0.21	0.35	0.32
T7	Analog cellular monthly subscription charge	US$, nominal	17.0	18.0	6.0	11.8	6.5	7.0	19.1	0.0	45.0	0.0	2.9	0.0	10.9	11.6	16.3	7.0
T8	Price of three-minute local call	US$, nominal	0.09	0.03	—	0.03	0.01	0.03	0.02	0.06	0.02	0.02	0.00	0.00	0.07	0.07	0.09	0.02
T9	Residential monthly telephone subscription	US$, nominal	12.2	2.9	2.7	2.4	2.1	4.0	1.5	1.5	0.9	0.7	11.5	11.1	2.4	2.4	5.1	1.7
T10	Residential telephone connection charge	US$, nominal	183	29	226	—	59	34	91	33	48	52	5	37	81	81	136	52
T11	Waiting list for main lines	Applicants	—	—	—	—	—	—	8,269	5,921	45,373	35,578	—	—	556,305	582,723	—	—
T12	Mobile Telecom Revenue per Subscriber	US$, nominal	—	—	—	—	—	—	353,249	—	—	85,681	—	—	—	—	—	—
T13	Income per Fixed Line	US$, nominal	—	10	203	105	128	146	458	171	219	201	411	231	303	257	226	309
T14	Telecom revenue per staff	US$, nominal	28,481	18,893	56,991	42,750	26,926	54,422	20,226	22,302	6,091	15,870	125,806	127,564	66,882	141,224	7,803	17,908

iii. Mongolia—The Ministry of Road, Transport, and Tourism classifies roads according to national and regional roads only. This figure does not include rural roads.

Rd2: Motorways, Highways, Main Roads, or National Roads— Motorways include roads specifically designed and built for motor traffic, which do not serve properties bordering on it, and which (1) are provided, except at special points or temporarily, with separate carriageways for the two directions of traffic, separated from each other, either by a dividing strip not intended for traffic, or exceptionally by other means; (2) do not cross at level with any road, railway or tramway track, or footpath; and (3) are specially identified by signposts as motorways and are reserved for specific categories of road motor vehicles. Entry and exit lanes of motorways are included irrespectively of the location of the signposts. Highways, main, or national roads include kilometer length of A-level roads. A-level roads are roads outside urban areas that are not motorways but belong to the top-level road network. A-level roads are characterized by a comparatively high-quality standard, either nondivided roads with oncoming traffic or similar to motorways. In most countries, these roads are financed by the federal or national government.

Rd3: Secondary or Regional Roads—Kilometer length of roads that are the main feeder routes into—and provide the main links among— highways, main roads, or national roads.

- Country Notes
    - i. Indonesia—Provincial roads
    - ii. Philippines—Provincial roads

Rd4: Other Urban Roads—Length of roads within the boundaries of a built-up area, which is an area with entries and exists specially identified by signposts as such.

- Country Notes
    - i. Philippines—City roads
    - ii. Mongolia—The national and regional network in Rd2 and Rd3 includes urban roads

Rd5: Other Rural Roads—Length of all remaining roads in a country not included in categories Rd2, Rd3, and Rd4

- Country Notes
    - i. Indonesia—Kabupaten roads
    - ii. Philippines—Municipal and barangay roads

Rd6: Total Paved Roads—Length of all roads that are surfaced with crushed stone (macadam) and hydrocarbon binder or bituminized agents, with concrete or with cobblestones. Aggregate of Rd7, Rd8, Rd9, and Rd10.

- Country Notes
  - i. Lao PDR—Includes 55 km of paved "special roads" not captured in Rd7 though Rd10

Rd7: Paved Motorways, Highways, Main Roads, or National Roads—Length of highways, main roads, or national roads that are paved.

- Country Notes
  - i. Cambodia—Includes national roads 1–7

Rd8: Paved Secondary or Regional Roads—Length of secondary or regional roads that are paved.

Rd9: Paved Other Urban Roads—Length of other urban roads that are paved.

- Country Notes
  - i. Mongolia—A portion of these roads are national roads in urban areas and are included in Rd7

Rd10: Paved Other Rural Roads—Length of other rural roads that are paved.

Rd11: Total Roads in "Good" or "Regular" (Fair) Condition—Total length of roads that are in "good" or "regular" condition. "Roads in good condition" include the following: Paved roads, largely free of defects, requiring only routine maintenance and perhaps surface treatment. Unpaved roads that need only routine grading and localized repairs. "Roads in regular (or fair) condition" include the following: Paved roads with defects and weakened structural resistance. They require resurfacing of the pavement, but without the need to demolish the existing pavement. Unpaved roads that require grading and additional new gravel, plus drainage repair in some places. Aggregate of Rd12, Rd13, Rd14, and Rd15.

Rd12: Motorways, Highways, Main Roads, or National Roads in "Good" or "Regular" (Fair) Condition—Length of highways, main roads, or national roads in "good" or "fair" condition.

- Country Notes
  - i. Indonesia—75 percent of the national and provincial network in "good" or "fair" condition; assumes same percentage across both categories

Rd13: Secondary or Regional Roads in "Good" or "Regular" (Fair) Condition—Length of secondary or regional roads in "good" or "fair" condition.

- Country Notes
  - i. Cambodia—Includes national B and provincial trafficable roads
  - ii. Indonesia—75 percent of the national and provincial network in "good" or "fair" condition; assumes same percentage across both categories

Rd14: Other Urban Roads in "Good" or "Regular" (Fair) Condition—Length of other urban roads in "good" or "fair" condition.

- Country Notes
  - i. Lao PDR—Includes other rural and urban roads
  - ii. Mongolia—These roads are national and regional roads in urban areas and are included in those figures (Rd12 and Rd13)

Rd15: Other Rural Roads in "Good" or "Regular" (Fair) Condition—Length of other rural roads in "good" or "fair" condition.

- Country Notes
  - i. Indonesia—38 percent of the Kabupaten road network is in "good" or "fair" condition

Rd16: Does an institution that advises the Minister on various matters pertaining to management (and financing) of roads, namely a National Roads Board (NRB) or a Road Council/Highways Agency Board exist? No definition needed.

Rd17: Does the Main (National) Road Agency, responsible for the main road network, operate with a report published at least on an annual basis? No definition needed.

Rd18: Main (National) Road Agency Administration Cost—The amount of resources spent by the Main (National) Road Agency in conjunction with its own operation and service per year.

Rd19: Annual Road Expenditure—The total amount of expenditure on new construction and extension of existing roads, including reconstruction, renewal, and major repairs of roads per year.

- Country Notes
    - i. Lao PDR—National roads only
    - ii. Indonesia—Government expenditure only (includes national, provincial, district, and toll roads)
    - iii. Philippines—Includes national and local roads
    - iv. Thailand—Highway department only

Rd20: Capital Investment—The total amount of investment in the road sector to maintain sufficient capacity as well as increase capacity per year.

- Country Notes
    - i. China—Capital investment in highway construction; does not include urban roads, which are under the jurisdiction of the Ministry of Construction
    - ii. Indonesia—Government expenditure only (includes national, provincial, district, and toll roads)
    - iii. Lao PDR—National roads only
    - iv. Philippines—Includes national and local roads

Rd21: Maintenance Expenditure—The total expenditure for keeping roads in working order per year. This includes maintenance, patching, and running repairs (work relating to roughness of carriageway's wearing course, roadsides, and so on).

- Country Notes
    - i. Cambodia—Includes all costs other than capital investment
    - ii. Indonesia—Government expenditure only (includes national, provincial, district, and toll roads)
    - iii. Lao PDR—National roads only
    - iv. Philippines—Includes national and local roads

Rd22: Road Maintenance Requirement—The amount of financing required per year to keep roads in working order. This includes maintenance, patching, and running repairs (work relating to roughness of carriageway's wearing course, roadsides, shoulder, drains, structures, slopes, signs, and so on).

Rd23: Total Daily Traffic—Total number of road motor vehicles that move on a given network per day. When a road motor vehicle is being carried on another vehicle, only the movement of the carrying vehicle (active mode) is considered.

- Country Notes
    i. Mongolia—Calculated by multiplying the average traffic flow over 11,121 km of the road network

Rd24: Daily Traffic on Motorways, Highways, Main Roads, or National Roads—Total average daily road motor vehicle traffic on main/national highways.

- Country Notes
    i. Mongolia—Calculated by multiplying the average traffic flow over 1,720 km of the main national road network [Ulaanbaatar (UB) Darhan, UB-Zuunmod, UB-Lun, UB-Baganuur]

Rd25: Daily Traffic on Secondary or Regional Roads—Total average daily road motor vehicle traffic on secondary/regional highways.

Rd26: Number of Rural People Living within 2 km of an All-Season Road—"With access" means that the distance from a village or household to an all-season road is no more than 2 km; that is, that a walk of no more than 20 minutes or so is required to reach an all-season road. An "all-season road" is a road that is passable by the prevailing means of rural transport (often a pickup or a truck that does not have four-wheel-drive) all year round. Predictable interruptions of short duration during inclement weather (for example, heavy rainfall) are permitted, particularly on low-volume roads.

- Country Notes
    i. Thailand—Percentage of rural villages, not number of people

Rd27: Are there clear and reasonable processes for transport operators to be legally able to deliver different forms of transport service in a competitive manner? No definition needed.

- Country Notes
    i. Cambodia—Bidding processes are in place though real competition is doubtful

Rd28: Are road construction works and road traffic measures subject by law to a thorough appraisal (at least equivalent to the standards required for World Bank investment) of environmental impact and monitoring? No definition needed.

- Country Notes
  - i. Cambodia—Decree is in place though implementation is doubtful
  - ii. Indonesia—Processes in place though implementation is doubtful

Rd29: Is there a government-endorsed plan to improved road safety, which is published and being actively implemented? No definition needed.

- Country Notes
  - i. China—A new road safety law was passed on October 28, 2003, and implemented in May 2004

Rd30: Number of Fatalities from Road Accidents—Number of people who were involved in any injury accident with at least one motor road vehicle in motion on a public road or private road to which the public has right of access, resulting in at least one person killed as a result of the accident and within 30 days of its occurrence. Included are collisions between road vehicles; between road vehicles and pedestrians; between road vehicles and animals or fixed obstacles, and with one road vehicle alone. Included are collisions between road and rail vehicles. Multivehicle collisions are counted as only one accident provided that any successive collisions happen at short intervals. Injury accident excludes accidents incurring only material damage.

Rd31: Are road construction works and road traffic measures subject by law to a thorough appraisal (at least equivalent to the standards required for World Bank investment) of social impact and monitoring? No definition needed.

Rail transport

Rl1: Total Network—Total length of railway route open for public passenger and freight services (excluding dedicated private resource railways). Aggregate of Rl2 and Rl3.

Rl2: Main Lines—Total length of main intercity and other main passenger and freight routes available for public services.

Rl3: Secondary Lines—Total length of remaining passenger and freight routes available for public services.

Table 4 Road transport

		Cambodia		China		Indonesia		Lao PDR		Mongolia		Philippines		Thailand		Vietnam	
	Unit	1998	2003	1998	2003	1998	2003	1998	2003	1998	2003	1998	2003	1998	2003	1998	2003
Rd1 Total Road Network	kilometers	—	38,257	1,278,474	1,809,828	355,363	368,263	22,788	31,210*	49,250*	49,308*	199,950*	202,205*	57,233	63,730	207,264	229,488
Rd2 Motorways, Highways, Main or National Roads	kilometers	—	4,757	123,519	157,644	21,977	27,616	—	7,140	11,063	11,121	28,162	30,434	—	—	15,284	17,295
Rd3 Secondary or Regional Roads	kilometers	—	5,700	189,961	223,425	47,863*	48,905*	—	10,350	38,187	38,187	28,503*	26,926*	—	—	16,403	21,840
Rd4 Other roads: Urban	kilometers	—	0	—	—	—	—	—	1,760	604*	627*	5,767*	7,052*	—	—	45,577	60,353
Rd5 Other roads: Rural	kilometers	—	27,800	920,560	1,371,235	279,523*	291,841*	—	11,360	—	—	137,518*	137,793*	—	—	130,000	130,000
Rd6 Paved roads: Total	kilometers	—	1,648	1,190,086	1,647,412	168,072	211,998	3,544	4,497*	3,572	3,742	39,316	43,754	52,969	61,523	—	—
Rd7 Paved Motorways, Highways, Main or National Roads	kilometers	—	1,333*	123,519	157,644	—	—	3,033	3,771	2,685	2,708	16,029	19,228	—	—	—	—
Rd8 Paved Secondary or Regional Roads	kilometers	—	315	189,961	223,425	—	—	117	228	—	—	5,825	5,606	—	—	—	—
Rd9 Paved Other Roads: Urban	kilometers	—	0	—	—	—	—	394	429	604*	627*	4,048	5,427	—	—	—	—
Rd10 Paved Other Roads: Rural	kilometers	—	—	832,172	1,266,343	—	—	—	14	—	—	13,414	13,493	—	—	—	—
Rd11 Roads in "Good" or "Regular" (fair) Condition: Total	kilometers	—	16,957	—	—	—	197,474	9,532	17,746	1,678	1,802	—	—	57,233	63,730	—	—
Rd12 Motorways, Highways, Main or National Roads in "Good" or "Regular" (fair) Condition	kilometers	—	1,988	—	—	—	20,712*	2,715	5,460	1,283	1,405	—	—	—	—	—	—
Rd13 Secondary or Regional Roads in "Good" or "Regular" (fair) Condition	kilometers	—	3,389*	—	—	—	36,679*	2,691	6,424	396	397	—	—	—	—	—	—
Rd14 Other Roads: Urban in "Good" or "Regular" (fair) Condition	kilometers	—	—	—	—	—	—	4,126*	1,493	340*	353*	—	—	—	—	—	—
Rd15 Other Roads: Rural in "Good" or "Regular" (fair) Condition	kilometers	—	11,580	—	—	—	140,084*	0	4,369	—	—	—	—	—	—	—	—

(Continued on the next page)

203

Table 4 (Continued)

		Cambodia		China		Indonesia		Lao PDR		Mongolia		Philippines		Thailand		Vietnam	
Indicator	Unit	1998	2003	1998	2003	1998	2003	1998	2003	1998	2003	1998	2003	1998	2003	1998	2003
Rd16 Does an institution that advises the Minister on various matters pertaining to management and financing of roads, namely a National Roads Board (NRB) or Road Council, Highways Agency Board exist?	Yes/No	N	N	N	N	Y	Y	N	N	N	Y	N	Y	N	Y	Y	Y
Rd17 Does the Main (National) Road Agency responsible for the main road network operate with a report published at least on an annual basis?	Yes/No	N		N	Y	N	N	Y	—	Y	Y	Y	Y	Y	Y		
Rd18 Main (National) Road Agency Administration Cost	Million US$, Nominal	—	—	—	—	—	—	—	—	0.17	0.21	—	—	319	160	—	—
Rd19 Annual Road Expenditure	Million US$, Nominal	5.0	37.5	—	44,836	426*	—	78*	71*	7.0	17	741*	665*	1,153*	527*	761	1,225
Rd20 Capital Investment	Million US$, Nominal	2.8	29.7	26,190	38,836*	384*	—	73*	52*	5.2	14.9	602*	525*	939	220	710	1,138
Rd21 Maintenance Expenditure	Million US$, Nominal	2.3*	7.7*	—	6,000	43*	—	5*	19*	1.8	2.1	137*	140*	214	307	51.90	87.00
Rd22 Road Maintenance Requirement	Million US$, Nominal	—	—	9,463	14,111	—	475	—	15	—	6.4	—	—	558	518	—	—
Rd23 Daily Traffic: Total	Million vehicle kilometers	—	—	—	—	—	—	—	—	91*	188*	—	—	131,691	140,657	—	—
Rd24 Daily Traffic on Motorways, Highways, Main or National Roads	Million vehicle kilometers	—	—	—	—	—	—	—	—	12*	24*	—	—	45,995	—	—	—
Rd25 Daily Traffic on Secondary or Regional Roads	Million vehicle kilometers	—	—	—	—	—	—	—	—	—	—	—	—	85,697	—	—	—
Rd26 Number of rural people living within 2 km of an all-season road	million people	—	—	—	757	—	—	—	3.2	—	—	—	—	—	43% of rural villages*	—	—

Rd27	Are there clear and reasonable processes for transport operators to be legally able to deliver different forms of transport service in a competitive manner?	Yes/No	Y*	Y*	—	Y	Y	Y	—	Y	Y	Y	Y	Y	Y	N	N	N	N
Rd28	Are road construction works and road traffic measures subject by law to a thorough appraisal [at least equivalent to the standards required for World Bank (WB) investment] of environmental impact and monitoring?	Yes/No	N*	Y*	N	N	N*	N*	N	Y	Y	Y	Y	Y	Y	Y	Y	—	—
Rd29	Is there a government-endorsed plan to improve road safety, which is published and being actively implemented?	Yes/No	N	N	N	N*	N	N	N	N	—	—	—	N	N	Y	Y	Y	Y
Rd30	Number of Fatalities from Road Accidents	People	102	824	78,067	104,372	12,769	13,399	332	430	271	—	—	940	800	12,234	13,116	6,067	11,309
Rd31	Are road construction works and road traffic measures subject by law to a thorough appraisal (at least equivalent to the standards required for WB investment) of social impact and monitoring?	Yes/No	N	N	N	N	N	N	N	N	—	—	—	Y	Y	Y	Y	—	—

205

Rl4: Single Lines—Route length of network consisting of single tracked lines.

Rl5: Traffic Units—Aggregate of Rl6 and Rl7.

Rl6: Passenger Travel—Total passenger travel measured in units of one passenger by 1 kilometer.

Rl7: Freight Coverage—Total freight travel measured in units of 1 metric ton by 1 kilometer.

Rl8: Railway Diesel Fuel Consumption—Fuel used for powering trains and other rolling stock movements.

Rl9: Railway Electrical Energy Consumption—Electrical energy used for powering trains and other rolling stock movements.

Rl10: Is the main national railway company predominantly private (including private concession) rather than publicly owned? Anything above 50 percent is considered predominant.

Rl11: If public, is the national railway company a corporatized commercial entity rather than a government department authority? This step of reform includes (1) the removal of the entity from the direct control that results from being a part of a ministry, and (2) the creation of an independent legal corporation with the goal of behaving like a commercial company (for example, maximizing profits).

Rl12: Is there institutional vertical separation of infrastructure and operations? No definition needed.

Rl13: Are there track access rights for private train operating companies? No definition needed.

Rl14: Passenger Fare Revenue—No definition needed.

Rl15: Freight Tariff Revenue—No definition needed.

Rl16: Other Commercial Revenue—Other revenue may include interest income, scrap sales, real estate, and so on.

Rl17: Passenger Yield—Total passenger fare revenue divided by total passengers/km.

Rl18: Freight Yield—Total freight tariff revenue divided by total tons/km.

Rl19: Is there a safety regulator independent of the railway operating department or authority? No definition needed.

Rl20: Is there a formal safety case or safety plan that is fully documented and regularly updated? No definition needed.

Rl21: Number of Passenger Fatalities—No definition needed.

- Country Notes
  - i. Mongolia—Figure according to the Ulaanbaatar Railway Authority, but this type of data is considered confidential

Rl22: Number of Serious Incidents—See country-specific definitions below.

- Country Notes
  - i. China—Includes derailments, collisions, and incidents involving human casualties
  - ii. Mongolia—Figure according to the Ulaanbaatar Railway Authority, but this type of data is considered confidential
  - iii. Philippines—Incidents include derailment and sideswiping incidents
  - iv. Thailand—Derailment or collision that causes large damage or human casualties
  - v. Vietnam—Vietnam Railways defines "serious rail incident" as an incident that Vietnam Railways is responsible for and that causes huge damages, including human injury

Rl23: Are road construction works and road traffic measures subject by law to a thorough appraisal (at least equivalent to the standards required for World Bank investment) of environmental impact and monitoring? No definition needed.

Rl24: Are road construction works and road traffic measures subject by law to a thorough appraisal (at least equivalent to the standards required for World Bank investment) of social impact and monitoring? No definition needed.

Urban

U1: Slum Population—The definition of a slum varies widely, but they are generally neglected parts of cities where housing and living conditions are appallingly poor. Slums range from high-density, squalid

Table 5 Rail transport

	Indicator	Unit	Cambodia 1998	Cambodia 2003	China 1998	China 2003	Indonesia 1998	Indonesia 2003	Lao PDR 1998	Lao PDR 2003	Mongolia 1998	Mongolia 2003	Philippines 1998	Philippines 2003	Thailand 1998	Thailand 2003	Vietnam 1998	Vietnam 2003
RI1	Total Network	kilometers	750	750	57,584	60,466	4,600	4,600	No rail network	No rail network	2,373	2,373	491	491	4,044	4,044	3,142	3,146
RI2	Main lines	kilometers	650	650	—	—	3,421	3,421	No rail network	No rail network	1,110	1,110	484	484	2,344	2,344	2,632	2,669
RI3	Secondary lines	kilometers	100	100	—	—	1,179	1,179	No rail network	No rail network	1,263	1,263	7	7	1,624	1,624	108	477
RI4	Single lines	kilometers	750	750	37,911	35,796	—	—	No rail network	No rail network	2,363	2,363	454	454	3,892	3,892	2,632	2,669
RI5	Traffic units	Million passenger-km + million tonne-km	119.6	113.8	1,506,000	2,109,839	23,859	23,759	No rail network	No rail network	3,784	8,294	248	138	13,935	14,238	3,911	7,767
RI6	Passenger travel	Million passenger-km	43.9	13.4	343,000	462,279	18,789	18,750	No rail network	No rail network	982	1,039	247	137	11,014	10,251	2,588	5,092
RI7	Freight coverage	Million tonne-km	75.7	100	1,163,000	1,647,560	5,070	5,009	No rail network	No rail network	2,802	7,255	1	1	2,921	3,987	1,325	2,675
RI8	Railway Diesel Fuel Consumption	1000 tons	—	1.8	4,146	5,123	—	—	No rail network	No rail network	33	56	1.7	1.9	105	110	26	46
RI9	Railway Electrical Energy Consumption	million kWh	0	0	7,611	12,121	—	—	No rail network	No rail network	48	63	—	—	—	—	0	0
RI10	Is the main national railway company predominantly private (including private concession) rather than publicly owned?	Yes/No	N	N	N	N	N	Y	No rail network	No rail network	N	N	N	N	N	N	N	N
RI11	If public, is the national railway company a corporatized commercial entity rather than a government department authority?	Yes/No	N	Y	N	N	—	Not applicable	No rail network	No rail network	N	N	Y	Y	N	N	Y	Y
RI12	Is there institutional vertical separation of infrastructure and operations?	Yes/No	N	N	N	N	N	N	No rail network	No rail network	N	N	N	N	N	N	N	N
RI13	Are there track access rights for private train operating companies?	Yes/No	—	N	N	N	N	Y	No rail network	No rail network	No private company	No private company	Y	Y	N	N	N	N

Code	Indicator	Unit																	
RI14	Passenger fare revenue	Million US$, Nominal	—	0.1	3,464	5,764	—	—	No rail network	No rail network	10.9	9.8	2.7	1.5	97.9	97.0	42.7	72.7
RI15	Freight tariff revenue	Million US$, Nominal	—	1.6	10,226	14,761	—	—	No rail network	No rail network	24.3	83.6	0.0	0.0	38.6	50.0	27.8	41.0
RI16	Other commercial revenue	Million US$, Nominal	—	—	1,755	2,689	—	—	No rail network	No rail network	1.5	3.2	2.2	1.7	38.1	61.4	1.9	2.0
RI17	Passenger yield	US$, Nominal	—	0.004	0.010	0.012	—	—	No rail network	No rail network	0.011	0.009	0.011	0.011	0.009	0.009	0.020	0.010
RI18	Freight yield	US$, Nominal	—	0.017	0.009	0.009	—	—	No rail network	No rail network	0.009	0.012	0.122	0.099	0.014	0.013	0.020	0.020
RI19	Is there a safety regulator independent of the railway operating department or authority?	Yes/No	N	N	N	N	N	N	No rail network	No rail network	N	N	N	N	N	N	N	N
RI20	Is there a formal safety case or safety plan which is fully documented and regularly updated?	Yes/No	N	N	N	N	N	Y	No rail network	No rail network	Y	Y	N	N	Y	Y	—	—
RI21	Number of passenger fatalities	People	—	—	—	—	50	72	No rail network	No rail network	0*	0*	—	—	20	7	129	271
RI22	Number of serious incidents	Incidents	—	—	—	15*	125	216	No rail network	No rail network	0*	0*	129*	110*	0*	0*	0*	1*
RI23	Are road construction works and road traffic measures subject by law to a thorough appraisal (at least equivalent to the standards required for World Bank investment) of environmental impact and monitoring?	Yes/No	N	N	N	N	N	N	No rail network	No rail network	Y	Y	Y	Y	Y	Y	—	—
RI24	Are road construction works and road traffic measures subject by law to a thorough appraisal (at least equivalent to the standards required for World Bank investment) of social impact and monitoring?	Yes/No	—	N	N	N	N	N	No rail network	No rail network	N	N	Y	Y	Y	Y	—	—

central-city tenements to spontaneous squatter settlements without legal recognition of rights, sprawling at the edge of cities. UN Habitat's publication "Slums of the World," which defines a slum household as a group of individuals living under the same roof that has one or more of the following conditions: insecure residential status, inadequate access to safe water, inadequate access to sanitation, poor structural quality of housing, and overcrowding.

- Country Notes
    i. Mongolia—Share of households living in ger

U2: Urbanization Rate—Urban population as a percentage of the total population.

- Country Notes
    i. Cambodia—PNH municipality only

U3: Annual Growth Rate of Urban Population—Percentage growth rate of the urban population.

- Country Notes
    i. Cambodia—PNH municipality only

U4–U7: Number of Urban Cities—Urban area defined by densely populated area containing the city proper, suburbs, and continuously settled commuter areas.

U8: Percentage of Housing Stock Built of Materials Lasting 20 Years or More—Materials lasting at least 20 years include cement, brick, iron, tile, and so on.

- Country Notes
    i. Cambodia—Based of roof material only
    ii. Mongolia—Gers not included in housing stock

U9: Percentage of Housing Stock Built and Managed by Public Sector—No definition needed.

U10: Number of Months to Obtain Permits for Land Subdivisions—No definition needed.

U11: Percentage of Solid Waste Collected—Municipal solid waste collected as a percentage of what is generated.

- Country Note
    i. Cambodia—Downtown areas of Phnom Penh only
    ii. Lao PDR—Includes urban residents only

    iii. Mongolia—Best estimate for Ulanbaatar only
    iv. Philippines—Metro Manila only

U12: Percentage of Solid Waste Safely Disposed—Municipal solid waste safely disposed (sanitary landfill, incinerated, and/or recycled) as a percentage of what is generated.

- Country Notes
  - i. Lao PDR—Includes urban residents only
  - ii. Mongolia—Best estimate for Ulaanbaatar only
  - iii. Philippines—Metro Manila only

Finance

F1–F6: Total Expenditure on Infrastructure—Includes available capital and current expenditure on transportation, telecommunications, WSS, power, and other urban (solid waste, housing, and so on) from national government, local government, state-owned enterprises (SOEs), and private sources. The totals presented are simply the sum of the components under F7 through F25. Thus, any figures not available from F7 through F25 are also omitted in the total. Furthermore, the available data in F7 through F25 may be from years other than those specified (denoted by italics) or have omissions/additions themselves (denoted by an asterisk next to the figures in that section). Given these limitations, the figures presented can be interpreted as a broad estimate of the true amount spent on infrastructure.

F7–F11: National Government Expenditure on Infrastructure—Includes capital and current expenditure on transportation, telecommunications, WSS, power, and other urban (solid waste, housing, and so on) from national government unless otherwise specified below.

- Country Notes
  - i. Cambodia—Telecom includes actual (current) expenditures incurred by Ministry of Post and Telecommunications; no figures on capital expenditure available; WSS figures are capital expenditures only; power figures are current expenditures incurred by the Ministry of Industry, Mines and Energy (MIME)
  - ii. China—Although Telecom and WSS expenditures are not available, most expenditures in these sectors come from SOEs

211

Table 6 Urban

		Cambodia		China		Indonesia		Lao PDR		Mongolia		Philippines		Thailand		Vietnam	
	Unit	1998	2003	1998	2003	1998	2003	1998	2003	1998	2003	1998	2003	1998	2003	1998	2003
U1	Slum Population	Percent of urban population	—	72	—	38	—	23	—	66	19*	24*	—	44	3	2	—	47
U2	Urbanization Rate	Percent	22*	19*	33	41	39	43	17	26	50	58	57	61	31	32	23	26
U3	Annual Growth Rate of Urban Population	Percent	4.6*	4.1*	5.5	4.3	4.2	3.7	4.9	4.8	1.3	3.0	3.6	3.2	2.2	2.8	3.7	4.2
U4	Number of Urban Cities with Population above 5 million	Cities	0	0	—	10	1	1	0	0	0	0	0	—	—	1	0	1
U5	Number of Urban Cities with Population from 1 to 5 million	Cities	0	1	—	164	6	6	0	0	0	0	3	—	—	0	3	2
U6	Number of Urban Cities with Population from 500K to 1 million	Cities	1	0	—	274	9	9	0	0	1	1	2	—	—	0	2	4
U7	Number of Urban Cities with Population in Cities under 500K	Cities	35	35	—	212	6	6	5	5	21	21	35	—	—	—	14	19
U8	Percentage of housing stock built of materials lasting 20 years or more	Percent	—	60*	—	—	—	—	7.4	11.6	100*	100*	64	—	—	—	—	—
U9	Percentage of housing stock built and managed by public sector	Percent	0	0	—	—	—	—	0	0	16	12	—	—	—	—	—	—
U10	Number of months to obtain permits for land subdivisions	Months	0.75	0.75	—	—	—	—	3	3	—	—	1	1	—	—	—	—
U11	Percentage of Solid Waste Collected	Percent	55*	60*	79	83	—	—	—	34*	68*	80*	73*	83*	—	91	65	71
U12	Percentage of Solid Waste Safely Disposed	Percent	—	—	—	—	—	—	—	33*	67*	38*	—	61*	—	91	—	—

   iii. Indonesia—Transport figures include transportation, meteorology, and geophysical sector; WSS figures include water and irrigation; telecom figures include tourism, post, and telecom (but most expenditures are on telecom)

   iv. Lao PDR—Road expenditure only

   v. Mongolia—Calculation based on fiscal data and gross domestic product (GDP) composition by sectors; F7 includes telecom

   vi. Philippines—All figures include capital outlays only; power figures include other energy also

   vii. Vietnam—F7 figures include investment by central and local government and SOEs for transport, storage, and telecom; F9 figures include investment by central and local government and SOEs for electricity, gas, and water; investment outlays are the total expenditure to achieve the goal of investment and include expenditure on investigation for construction planning, preparation of investment, expenditure on design and construction, purchase of equipment, and other expenditures

F12–F16: Local Government Expenditure on Infrastructure— Includes capital and current expenditure on transportation, telecommunications, WSS, power, and other urban (solid waste, housing, and so on) from local government (noncentral government) unless otherwise specified below.

- Country Notes
  - i. Cambodia—Available figures are actual current expenditures spent by the provincial department only
  - ii. China—Transport includes urban transport capital construction
  - iii. Indonesia—Transport figures include transportation, meteorology and geophysical sector; WSS figures include water and irrigation; telecom figures include tourism, post, and telecom (but most expenditures are for telecom)
  - iv. Mongolia—Calculation based on fiscal data and GDP composition by sectors
  - v. Philippines—All figures include capital outlays only; power figures include other energy also

F17–F21: SOE Government Expenditure on Infrastructure— Includes capital and current expenditure on transportation, telecommunications, WSS, power, and other urban (solid waste, housing, and so on) from SOEs unless otherwise specified below.

- Country Notes
  - i. China—Telecom and WSS data include capital construction only
  - ii. Lao PDR—Electricité du Laos (EdL) only; 1998 power figure excludes investment (includes operating costs only)
  - iii. Philippines—All figures include capital outlays only

F22–F25: Private Investment in Infrastructure—Includes planned disbursements in assets and facilities based on financial closure year.

- Country Notes
  - i. Vietnam—F22 figures include nonstate and foreign investment outlays for transport, storage, and telecom; F24 figures include nonstate and foreign investment outlays for electricity, gas, and water; investment outlays are the total expenditure to achieve the goal of investment and include expenditure on investigation for construction planning, preparation of investment, expenditure on design and construction, and purchase of equipment

F26: Total Local Government Expenditures—Total local government expenditures as a share of total public expenditures.

- Country Notes
  - i. Cambodia—Current expenditure only

F27: Total Local Government Revenues—Total local government revenues as a share of total public revenues.

Table 7 Infrastructure finance

	Indicator	Unit	Cambodia 1998	Cambodia 2003	China 1998	China 2003	Indonesia 1998	Indonesia 2003	Lao PDR 1998	Lao PDR 2003	Mongolia 1998	Mongolia 2003	Philippines 1998	Philippines 2003	Thailand 1998	Thailand 2003	Vietnam 1998	Vietnam 2003
F1	Total Expenditure on Infrastructure*	Percent of GDP	2.9	2.3	2.6	7.3	3.1	2.7	1.7	4.7	2.7	4.0	5.6	3.6	5.3	15.4	9.8	9.9
F2	Total Expenditure on Transportation*	Percent of GDP	0.7	1.0	0.2	4.0	1.0	1.3	—	1.3	1.1	2.1	1.4	1.2	3.6	3.9	4.5	6.0
F3	Total Expenditure on Telecommunications*	Percent of GDP	1.7	0.4	0.0	0.4	0.8	0.9	0.1	0.3	Included in F2	Included in F2	1.1	0.6	0.1	2.0	Included in F2	Included in F2
F4	Total Expenditure on Water and Sanitation*	Percent of GDP	0.5	0.5	0.0	0.2	0.9	0.3	—	0.2	0.0	0.0	0.1	0.1	0.7	0.5	5.3	3.9
F5	Total Expenditure on Other Urban*	Percent of GDP	—	—	—	—	—	—	—	—	0.4	0.5	0.2	0.6	0.3	0.2	—	—
F6	Total Expenditure on Power*	Percent of GDP	0.3	0.3	2.4	2.7	0.3	0.2	1.6	2.9	1.1	1.3	2.8	1.1	0.5	8.7	Included in F4	Included in F4
F7	National Government Expenditure on Transportation	Percent of GDP	0.3	0.9	—	1.0	0.7*	0.4*	—	1.3*	0.8*	1.5*	1.0*	0.6*	3.6	1.0	3.5*	4.9*
F8	National Government Expenditure on Telecommunications	Percent of GDP	0.9*	0.2*	—*	—*	0.2*	0.1*	—	—	Included in F7	Included in F7	0.1*	0.0*	0.0	0.0	Included in F7	Included in F7
F9	National Government Expenditure on Water and Sanitation	Percent of GDP	0.5*	0.5*	—*	—*	0.4*	0.2*	—	—	—	—	0.0*	0.0*	0.7	0.2	3.5*	3.7*
F10	National Government Expenditure on Other Urban	Percent of GDP	—	—	—	—	—	—	—	—	0.4*	0.5*	0.1*	0.4*	0.3	0.2	—	—
F11	National Government Expenditure on Power	Percent of GDP	0.0*	0.0*	0.1	0.0	—	—	—	0.2	1.1*	1.3*	0.0*	0.0*	0.0	0.0	Included in F9	Included in F9
F12	Local Government Expenditure on Transportation	Percent of GDP	0.1*	0.1*	—	2.6*	0.3*	0.6*	—	—	0.0*	0.0*	0.2*	0.2*	—	—	Included in F7	Included in F7
F13	Local Government Expenditure on Telecommunications	Percent of GDP	0.0*	0.0*	—	—	0.0*	0.0*	—	—	—	—	0.0*	—	—	—	Included in F7	Included in F7

(Continued on the next page)

Table 7 (Continued)

		Cambodia		China		Indonesia		Lao PDR		Mongolia		Philippines		Thailand		Vietnam	
Indicator	Unit	1998	2003	1998	2003	1998	2003	1998	2003	1998	2003	1998	2003	1998	2003	1998	2003
F14 Local Government Expenditure on Water and Sanitation	Percent of GDP	—	—	—	—	0.0*	0.1*	—	—	—	—	0.0*	0.0*	—	—	Included in F9	Included in F9
F15 Local Government Expenditure on Other Urban	Percent of GDP	—	—	—	—	—	—	—	—	0.0*	0.0*	0.0*	0.1*	—	—	—	—
F16 Local Government Expenditure on Power	Percent of GDP	0.0*	0.0*	0.3	0.1	—	—	—	—	0.0*	0.0*	0.0*	0.0*	—	—	Included in F9	Included in F9
F17 SOE Expenditure on Transportation	Percent of GDP	—	—	—	0.3	—	—	—	—	—	—	0.2*	0.3*	—	2.9	Included in F7	Included in F7
F18 SOE Expenditure on Telecommunications	Percent of GDP	—	—	—	0.4*	—	—	—	—	—	—	0.0*	0.0*	—	1.8	Included in F7	Included in F7
F19 SOE Expenditure on Water and Sanitation	Percent of GDP	—	—	—	0.2*	—	—	—	0.2	—	—	0.1*	0.1*	—	0.3	Included in F9	Included in F9
F20 SOE Expenditure on Other Urban	Percent of GDP	—	—	—	—	—	—	—	—	—	—	0.1*	0.1*	—	0.1	—	—
F21 SOE Expenditure on Power	Percent of GDP	—	0.3	1.7	2.5	—	—	1.6*	2.7*	—	—	0.9*	0.6*	—	7.8	Included in F9	Included in F9
F22 Private Investment in Transportation	Percent of GDP	0.3	0.0	0.2	0.1	0.0	0.3	0.0	0.0	0.0	0.4	0.0	0.1	0.0	0.0	1.0*	1.1*
F23 Private Investment in Telecommunications	Percent of GDP	0.8	0.2	0.0	0.0	0.6	0.8	0.1	0.3	0.3	0.2	0.1	0.6	0.1	0.2	Included in F22	Included in F22
F24 Private Investment in Water and Sanitation	Percent of GDP	0.0	0.0	0.0	0.0	0.5	0.0	0.0	0.0	0.0	0.0	0.0	0.0	0.0	0.0	1.8*	0.2*
F25 Private Investment in Power	Percent of GDP	0.0	0.0	0.3	0.1	0.3	0.1	0.0	0.0	0.0	0.0	1.9	0.5	0.5	0.9	Included in F24	Included in F24
F26 Total Local Government Expenditures	Percent of total public expenditure	3.3*	4.8*	71	70	—	—	—	—	35	8	5	16	8	12	—	—
F27 Total Local Government Revenues	Percent of total public revenue	2.1	3.1	78	83	—	—	—	—	34	9	16	21	11	14	—	—

Notes

Executive Summary

1. More precisely, the study's infrastructure coverage focuses on water supply and sanitation, information and communications technology, electricity and gas, and all forms of transportation. The study addresses upstream oil and gas or water resources management only peripherally. It does not specifically cover housing, education, health, or other social infrastructure.

2. For instance, when infrastructure encourages sustainable agricultural resources, or creates alternatives to exploiting forest resources, or provides water and sanitation.

3. The term fiscal space covers all forms of fiscal support, including guarantees and other contingent liabilities, as well as direct expenditures.

Chapter 1

1. Since 1999, the population of the developing countries of East Asia has risen by 4 percent to about 1.85 billion, and the number of people living on less than $2 a day has fallen from 890 million to 636 million, that is, from about one person in two to one person in three. In China, which accounts for 70 percent of the region's population, the headcount of those living on less than $2 a day is down to an estimated 32 percent of the population of 2004, from 50 percent in 1999 (World Bank 2004d).

2. From 4 to 12 percent, excluding oil exports.

3. This is almost as much as the share of global trade represented by trade among North American economies at the time the North American Free Trade Agreement first went into force in 1994.

4. As a measure of the emerging dynamism of China in the trade equation, China's share of the GDP of East Asian developing countries went from one-third in 1996 to one-half only six years later.

5. See http://rru.worldbank.org/investmentclimate/. This is the proportion of firms saying that any of electricity, telecommunications, or transportation are "major" or "severe" obstacles.

6. A perceptions survey of Japanese investors in developing East Asia yielded some interesting findings. For example, Japanese vehicle manufacturers operating in Thailand report that Bangkok traffic congestion has a significant cost-raising impact on the levels of stocks of parts they need to hold. In Vietnam, which has substantial Japanese investment

attracted by high labor productivity and rapid economic growth, 32.9 percent of Japanese firms cite poor infrastructure as their major obstacle. See Nomura Research Institute, Ltd. (2004). See also JBIC (2004).

7. This contrasts with capital-per-worker growth in China of about 10 percent a year since 1990.

8. Measured by the $2 per day poverty line.

9. To give one example of the magnitude of the poverty risk, Spencer (2004) quotes a panel data study from Sichuan which found over a five-year period that, while 30 percent of households fell below the poverty line in at least one year, only 2.4 percent were below the line in all five years, and the average number below the line was only 11–14 percent. See Jones (2004a).

10. Urban areas spreading to envelope rural areas is a close second as a cause of urban growth (World Bank 2004c).

11. The share of agriculture in East Asian GDP has fallen from 28 percent to 13 percent since 1980, while the share of industry and services has risen from 72 percent to 87 percent over the same period (World Bank 2004c).

12. See UTCE/ALMEC (2004a) for a discussion of this issue.

13. The GMS includes Cambodia, Lao PDR, Myanmar, Thailand, Vietnam, and China's Yunnan Province.

14. See, for instance, Rufo and Rufo 2004; Van Hanh, Van Song, Van Duc, and Van Duc 2002; and Xianqiang and Xiurui 2001 for analyses that seek to quantify environmental impacts arising in recent infrastructure undertakings in East Asia. See Uzawa (1994) for a discussion of the environmental impacts arising from Japan's construction of its extensive highway network and several thermal power plants in the 1960s and 1970s.

15. In contrast to the Latin American experience, East Asian private participation in infrastructure tended to be confined to individual greenfield projects with little sector restructuring, rather than privatization of existing assets in the context of sectorwide reforms designed to enhance overall efficiency.

16. An analysis carried out by the World Bank (Yepes 2004) estimates these needs for certain sectors only (see Annex 1 to this Chapter for a methodological explanation). This analysis extrapolates past trends and does not incorporate any normative concept of needs such as the MDGs. It also utilizes efficiency prices (that is, it assumes costs are minimized), so actual expenditures may be significantly higher than these estimates.

17. One exception to this general point is the grant element in official loans and grants, which does provide additional resources. Conceptually, this

can be seen as foreign taxpayers supplementing the resources available from domestic taxpayers, rather than being considered to be financing as such.

18. Development of local capital markets are also seen as a means of mitigating foreign currency risk. If financing is made available in local currency for assets that earn revenues in local currency (which is often the case for infrastructure), the resulting currency match reduces risk. It should be noted that this will not eliminate all currency risk, because domestic currency interest rates will generally reflect expected exchange rate movements—unless capital is completely immobile. It is also worth noting that derivatives markets may provide an alternative hedge against currency risk, although their development tends to lag behind the development of local capital markets.

19. On the basis that up to 80 percent of the costs of delivering water are fixed costs. See Castalia (2004c) for more details.

20. There is a closely related issue of what happens to fiscal space for infrastructure in countries that have been heavily using quasi-fiscal space but decide to reform. For example, if China continues with financial sector reform, and financial institutions consequently cut back on lending for infrastructure projects that are not commercially viable, but have attractive economic rates of return, will the government budget step in to fund those projects?

21. World Bank, Private Participation in Infrastructure (PPI) Database. Note that the PPI Database records total investment in infrastructure projects with private participation, not private investment alone. Investment commitments include expenditures on facility expansion, divestiture revenues, and license or canon fees. For all infrastructure projects with private participation in developing countries, the private sector accounted, on average, for 85 percent to 90 percent of total investment.

22. These are measures of investment in physical infrastructure (for example, roads) rather than in infrastructure service assets (for example, trucks). There are of course important subsectoral differences: private investment is most significant in telecommunications, second comes electricity, third is transport, and last comes water and sanitation.

23. Significantly, private investment in infrastructure in the industrial world seems to have recovered from the 1997 crisis quite quickly. For example, project finance lending (one proxy measure for infrastructure investment trends) reached an all-time high in 2000, because the growth in such lending to industrial countries (which climbed steadily from 1997 onwards) more than offset the post-1997 decline in lending to developing countries (see Sorge 2004).

24. This is one of the principal findings of the *East Asia and Pacific Private Investors in Infrastructure Perception Survey* (2004). The survey

included 50 interviews with infrastructure investors (all operators) active in East Asia (the firms were split roughly 50/50 between those from East Asia and those from elsewhere. This paper is available on http://www.worldbank.org/eapinfrastructure.

25. Here we look at the role of donors in the context of East Asia's funding story. We consider this role more broadly in Chapter 5.

26. ODA includes net disbursements of concessional loans and grants from official sources, as defined by the Development Assistance Committee of the Organisation for Economic Co-operation and Development (OECD). It excludes nonconcessional loans, export credits, and guarantees. No reliable breakdown by sector, to identify the share spent on infrastructure, is available.

27. To the extent that there is a concessional element in donor financing, that concessional element will be an addition to a country's domestic resources.

28. See Clements, Gupta, Pivovarsky, and Tiongson (2004).

29. That is, the data exclude urban roads, unpaved roads, secondary tertiary paved roads, mass transit, ports, airports, gas grids, bridges, and waterways. The analysis therefore excludes substantial infrastructure expenditures.

30. Countries included in the model are China, Indonesia, Lao PDR, Malaysia, Mongolia, Papua New Guinea, the Philippines, and Thailand, which collectively represent 98 percent of the total GDP of the 21 developing countries in the East Asia and Pacific region.

31. For electricity, roads, and railways, we use 2 percent; water and sanitation 3 percent; and telecommunications 8 percent.

32. Countries included are Cambodia, Fiji, Kiribati, the Marshall Islands, Micronesia, Myanmar, Palau, Samoa, the Solomon Islands, Timor-Leste, Tonga, and Vanuatu.

Chapter 2

1. Technological change can have a profound impact on infrastructure provision: It can change the longevity of assets, affect the potential for competition and the challenge of regulation, and alter the balance between incrementalist approaches and lumpy ones. Telecommunications and some parts of transport, for example, have seen some radical technological development in recent decades (for instance, cellular telephony or containerization). Energy has seen some important changes (such as the introduction of combined-cycle gas turbines and advances in gas liquefaction), and may be on the verge of breakthroughs in decentralized and renewable solutions. In water and sanitation, technological change has been more modest.

2. See, for example, Prud'homme (2004), DfID (2002), or Kessides (1996).

3. See Briceno, Estache, and Shafik (2004) for a recent literature survey.

4. At one end of the spectrum of wealth and power, this tension between general and local interests demands safeguarding highly vulnerable groups against dispossession and exploitation. At the other end, it can involve highly advantaged and powerful groups engaging in the phenomenon of NIMBYism (not in my backyard). Infrastructure development runs along a fault line of general versus local interests probably more often than any other sector and, hence, can become highly politicized.

5. This discussion draws on Carruthers, Bajpai, and Hummels (2003), and Fujita and Hisa (2004).

6. Evenett and Venables (2001) show that 40 percent of trade growth in East Asia comes from offering new products and finding new trade partners.

7. To cite just one example, 63 percent of the cost of transporting goods from Chonqing to the west coast of the United States is incurred before arriving at the Chinese port of export (Carruthers, Bajpai, and Hummels 2003).

8. For example, more than 90 percent of the FDI in export-oriented industries in China has gone to the four main coastal provinces. Similarly, the multiplier effect of the textile export boom in Cambodia has been limited mainly to areas easily accessible to the Sihanoukville port. On congestion, a study of Bangkok estimated that moving port-related activities away from the downtown area would result in a 10 percent reduction in peak-hour trips (UNESCAP 2000).

9. Guasch and Kogan (2001) found that inventory holdings in developing countries are two to three times the U.S. level, and estimated that merely halving them would lower production costs by an average of 20 percent, which would bring more producers to market. Uncertainty in delivery schedules may be caused by underdeveloped or poorly maintained road and rail networks, congestion in urban areas where economic activity and population growth have outpaced infrastructure, onerous border procedures, poor security, and unreliable information flows (particularly where information and communications infrastructure does not allow sophisticated electronic data interchange).

10. In many industrial East Asian countries, barely 10 percent of trade-related transport services are contracted to 3PL providers, in contrast to almost one-third of such services in OECD industrial countries (Carruthers, Bajpai, and Hummels 2003).

11. There are various ongoing regional and subregional initiatives in this area, including those under the auspices of the Association of Southeast Asian Nations (ASEAN), Asia-Pacific Economic Cooperation (APEC), the Mekong River Commission, the GMS, and the United Nations Economic and Social Commission for Asia and the Pacific (UNESCAP).

12. This could include protecting rights-of-way for future road or rail development, land banking, and ensuring that land is available for services that require easy access to ports, airports, and so on.

13. The strong links between economic growth and poverty reduction in Vietnam can be attributed, in part, to the peculiar nature of poverty in the country. The poor are not a static group: A high share of the population is clustered around the poverty line and the poverty status of households fluctuates over time (with the exception of ethnic minorities). While this suggests a high vulnerability to shocks, it also implies that small increases in per capita income may be sufficient to lift the poor out of poverty.

14. The elasticity of poverty reduction to economic growth indicates the proportionate reduction in poverty (in percentage points) for every percentage point of GDP growth. See Larsen, Lan, and Rama (2004).

15. Of course there has been far more to Vietnam's success than infrastructure and investment alone. Rural and agricultural strategies, in particular, have played a significant role in supporting both growth and poverty reduction.

16. These impacts have been the subject of a joint government-donor review of infrastructure in Vietnam, as part of Vietnam's Comprehensive Poverty Reduction and Growth Strategy. Projects examined as part of the review included improvements to the National Highway No. 1, the My Thuan bridge and the North-South 500 kV transmission line, in addition to the Ha Noi-Hai Phong northern transport corridor. See GRIPS Development Forum (2003) for details.

17. The authors found that for every billion dong spent on agricultural research, 339 poor people would be lifted above the poverty line. Road investment yields the second largest return, with every billion dong spent on roads lifting 132 poor people above the poverty line. For every billion dong spent on education, 76 poor people were lifted above the poverty line.

18. Between 1998 and 2002, the rate of poverty reduction in rural areas was only 5.4 percentage points against the urban figure of 7.1 percentage points. Poverty among ethnic minorities has decreased by only 2 percent (World Bank 2003b). More than 50 percent of the poor live in three regions (Northern Uplands, North Central Coast, and Central Highlands), which account for only 34 percent of the total population.

19. Of course there has been far more to Vietnam's success than infrastructure and investment alone. Rural and agricultural strategies, in particular, have played a significant role in supporting both growth and poverty reduction.

Chapter 3

1. Mody (1997) gives a detailed account of infrastructure strategies in these six countries.

2. See Kuninori (1997) for a detailed analysis of how Japan approached infrastructure finance.

3. Which is not to say, of course, that at times the short-term fiscal horizon is not more important than the long term. Governments with poor fiscal track records, or recovering from financial crisis, would often do well to concentrate on short-term liquidity.

4. For further analyses of these points see IMF (2004a), Brixi and Irwin (2004), and Easterly and Serven (2003).

5. This section is based on Medalla (2004), except where otherwise indicated.

6. According to the World Bank's 2003 Investment Survey, 33.4 percent of the firms interviewed for the country stated that electricity posed a major or severe threat to business operation and growth; 18.3 percent reported the same of transport (http://rru.worldbank.org/InvestmentClimate/).

7. In 2003, for instance, the financing gap (including loan repayment and capital expenditures, before external financing) of the state-owned generation and transmission company, NPC, increased sharply to P86 billion ($1.6 billion) from P19 billion ($500 million) in 1999, contributing in turn to the country's ballooning public sector deficits.

8. Less than 50 percent of the monitored national road network, for instance, is considered to be in good condition as measured by the International Roughness Index.

9. Recent government data show nationwide averages of access to safe drinking water deteriorated from 81.4 percent in 1999 to 80 percent in 2002, while the percentages for the poorest segment of the population decreased from 71.5 percent to 70.2 percent for the same time period.

10. For instance, following concessioning of local telecommunication services in 1995, telephone mainlines per employee increased from 82 to 181 over a period of six years.

11. Indonesia has more than 400 local governments in *kabupatens* and *kotas* as compared with only 33 provincial governments.

12. Indonesia's fuel subsidies are a good example of the lack of mainstreaming of environmental and social considerations. Although fuel subsidies make good populist politics, they are very poorly targeted (so reduce fiscal space for programs that genuinely help the poor) and exacerbate urban congestion and pollution.

13. This section is based on Liu (2004), except where otherwise indicated.

14. Although by way of context, the average Chinese province has a population about twice that of the whole of Malaysia. China has roughly the same number of provinces as Indonesia, but it has more than five times the total population. Decentralization in China cannot easily be compared with decentralization in smaller countries.

15. This section is based on Webster and Theeratham (2004), except where otherwise indicated.

16. For example, the rise of China as "factory of the world" is causing Thailand to focus more on the high-level service sector. This requires dense, high-transaction business environments with easy accessibility. The desire to create such environments has meant an increased focus on mass transit in the urban core (see Spotlight 1 later in this chapter). In peri-urban areas, manufacturing is becoming increasingly centered in dominant clusters of integrated supply chains (for example, the automotive sector) as a result of competition from China, and infrastructure in peri-urban areas has been reoriented accordingly.

17. Directed lending and government guarantees on loans or bonds have played a significant role in Thai infrastructure financing.

18. MRT (Mass Rapid Transit) is used as shorthand for urban rail systems that carry a mass ridership rapidly. They include metros and Light Rail Transit (LRT) systems that are segregated from other road traffic.

19. See Halcrow Group Ltd. (2004) for a detailed analysis of the tale of three cities.

20. Kuala Lumpur's current population is about 1.3 million people.

21. KL STAR and KL PUTRA were subsequently taken over by the state in 2002.

22. If measured instead from specific project concept to operations the time lapse ranges from 5 years (KL PUTRA) to 13 (MRT2).

23. Hong Kong (China) is an arguable exception. But even in Hong Kong (China), whose high density and prosperous population creates probably the most favorable MRT environment possible anywhere, the MRT system is in effect cross-subsidized from property value appreciation.

24. Some projects were financed in part by state-owned financial institutions, so there may have been some hidden subsidies.

25. All the projects in question had highly overoptimistic projections of ridership—a common bias in MRT planning.

Chapter 4

1. This is not to say that accountability and risk management only operate at this level. For instance, society's leaders are also held accountable (or fail to be held accountable) for the practical relevance of their strategic

vision through their country's national political institutions. Their strategic decisions are deeply determined by avoidance of risk and desire for reward.

2. Sen (1999).

3. We saw earlier how disability advocacy groups got involved in the design of the Bangkok subway during the planning stage, which substantially increased the feasibility of incorporating elevators and barrier-free access (see Chapter 2, Box 2.7).

4. Competitive markets also tend to hold consumers accountable. Where service providers are monopolists they are sometimes obliged to serve even those customers with bad payments records—in essence, subsidizing them out of monopoly profits. In competitive markets, it is harder to impose such an obligation to serve without explicit compensation. Once compensation is explicit, it is more likely to be targeted to specific types of customer, and other customers face a clearer obligation to pay if they are to continue to receive service.

5. Gordon-Walker and Marr (2002). See also Tynan and Kingdom (2005).

6. The system of "inset appointments" in England and Wales allows large users to choose an alternative licensed supplier. Inset appointments allow one company to replace another or the statutory service provider for a specified geographic area. For a comprehensive analysis of level of competition in the water sector in European countries, see, for example, Gordon-Walker and Marr (2002).

7. See Kessides (2004).

8. The IPP/single-buyer model obviously allows for competition for the market (through a bidding process for the IPP concession), although it precludes competition in the market. However, under this model, the government generally decides significant aspects of the technical specifications in an IPP bidding process, often including the type of fuel, which to some extent limits the impact of competition for the market.

9. Usually, the sector structure before the introduction of the IPPs was a vertically integrated state-owned monopoly. The single buyer frequently retains some generation capacity as well.

10. Electricity grids need a central operator to coordinate system balancing, reliability, and ancillary services, and operating cultures cannot easily change overnight from the one prevailing in a vertically integrated utility. Unbundling those operational functions from the control over generation can therefore take time. IPPs can be a transitional step.

11. It is worth noting that single buyers create their own significant risks for generators. If a generator has no choice but to sell power to the single buyer, it faces a risk of contract abrogation with no escape to other

purchasers. This helps explain the length and broad scope of take-or-pay PPAs involving single buyers, as well as the sometimes high prices under such contracts. Unfortunately, long-term PPAs, covering a substantial portion of generated power in a system, make it difficult to move later to a competitive market model without expensive compensation of preexisting contracts.

12. See Kessides (2004) and Hunt and Shuttleworth (1996) for a comprehensive discussion of the merits and demerits of the single-buyer model.

13. Of course, this can also involve regulators holding individual consumers accountable, so that their actions don't negatively affect other consumers (for example, allowing service providers to take action against nonpaying customers so that paying customers don't have to cross-subsidize them).

14. The basic analysis of this section applies whether investors are public or private. However, holding publicly-owned infrastructure service providers accountable for performance is generally more difficult than doing so for private providers, whether through regulation, competition, or other means.

15. See, for example, Kessides (2004).

16. Subsidies paid per connection, or capital grants made to service providers, are examples of one-time payments. Connection subsidies are one type of performance-based subsidy, and are an important example of measuring performance by clearly defined outputs. The funding by donors of subsidies contingent on delivery of outputs has recently become known as output-based aid (OBA), although the term is also used to cover other performance-based subsidies (including those not funded by aid).

17. There are other ways to minimize subsidy risk, including disbursing subsidies into escrow accounts or trust funds, contracts with private providers, or involving an external donor such as through an OBA scheme.

18. See Brixi and Irwin (2004) for a detailed discussion of fiscal institutions to manage infrastructure risk.

19. Even without efficiency gains, solvency could potentially be improved by the transaction if the government's illiquidity would have prevented a pure public investment from being implemented, but private financing overcomes that constraint (as long as the project rate of return is sufficient to exceed the cost of private capital).

20. For example, Guasch (2004) found from a sample of more than 1,000 infrastructure concessions in Latin America and the Caribbean during 1985–2000 that renegotiations occurred in 30 percent of them (this increases to 74 percent for water and sanitation concessions alone). See also Harris, Hodges, Schur, and Shukla (2003).

21. See Kessides (2004) or Coelli, Estache, Perelman, and Trujillo (2003) for surveys of the empirical literature. The analysis is complicated by the variety of risk-sharing arrangements in infrastructure; hence, it is difficult to define "private" and "public" on a comparable basis, and also in the interdependence of performance of different entities in a given network (for example, if private electricity generators rely on a publicly owned transmission company it would sometimes be difficult to assess their performance independently).

22. This case study draws on Maguire and Malinovitch (2004).

23. In all models, however, the government retains responsibility for the delivery of defined core services, such as nurses in hospital and officers in prisons.

24. The survey questionnaire has been prepared for the second meeting of the EAP Forum of Infrastructure Regulators, which was held in Manila on April 5–7, 2004. The survey questionnaire covered 45 regulatory bodies from 21 countries (Australia, Cambodia, China, Fiji Islands, Hong Kong (China), Indonesia, Kiribati, Korea, Lao PDR, Malaysia, Micronesia, Mongolia, Papua New Guinea, the Philippines, Samoa, Solomon Islands, Singapore, Thailand, Tonga, Vanuatu, and Vietnam) and from all infrastructure industries (15 energy regulators, 14 regulators in water and sanitation, 10 regulators in telecom, 1 transport regulator, and 8 multisector regulators).

25. A few significant exceptions are to be acknowledged, namely the Consumer Forum in Malaysia and the Yayasan Lembaga Konsumen Indonesia (YLKI) in Indonesia.

26. Consumer International 2004.

27. Middle-income customers advocating against tariff increases may indeed jeopardize the possibility to expand access.

Chapter 5

1. The term fiscal space covers all forms of fiscal support, including guarantees and other contingent liabilities, as well as direct expenditures.

2. Note that the Corruption Perceptions Index is a general index, and is not infrastructure specific.

3. Taking into account the resource needs of ports, airports, bridges, secondary roads, urban transport, and gas grids, as well as strategic decision to invest in infrastructure ahead of demand, the level of required expenditure may well be higher than 3.6 percent of GDP.

Bibliography

ADB (Asian Development Bank). 2004a. "Nam Theun 2 Hydroelectric Project in Lao People's Democratic Republic." *Summary Environmental and Social Impact Assessment.* http://www.namtheun2.com/gallery/lib_sesia/SESIA%20Final%20Draft%20November%202004.pdf.

————. 2004b. *Water in Asian Cities.* Manila: ADB.

————. 2002. *Report and Recommendation of the President to the Board of Directors on a proposed loan to the Lao People's Democratic Republic for the Greater Mekong Subregion: Northern Economic Corridor Project.* Manila: ADB.

African Forum for Utility Regulation. 2002. Background note on Regulatory Governance, for the Fourth Meeting, Pretoria, South Africa, November 5–7.

Azfar, Omar, Tugrul Gurgur, Satu Kähkönen, Anthony Lanyi, and Patrick Meagher. 2000. "Decentralization and Governance: An Empirical Investigation of Public Service Delivery in the Philippines." IRIS Center, University of Maryland, and World Bank.

Andrews, Charles T., and Cesar E. Yniguez, eds. 2004. *Water in Asian Cities: Utilities' Performance and Civil Society Views.* Manila: ADB.

Aoyama, Shunsuke. 1994. *Japan's Experience in Urban Environmental Management.* Metropolitan Environment Improvement Program: World Bank and UNDP.

APEC (Asia-Pacific Economic Cooperation). 2002. *Deregulating Energy Markets in APEC: Economic and Sectoral Impacts.* Energy Working Group, Asia-Pacific Economic Cooperation Secretariat with Abareconomics.

Australian Council for International Development. http://www.acfid.asn.au/.

Bakovic, Tonci, Bernard Tenenbaum, and Fiona Woolf. 2003. "Regulation by Contract: A New Way to Privatize Electricity Distribution?" World Bank Working Paper Series No. 14, Washington, DC.

Balisacan, Arsenio M., and Ernesto M. Pernia. 2002. "What Else Besides Growth Matters to Poverty Reduction? Philippines." Asian Development Bank ERP Policy Brief Series 5, Manila, February.

Bank Information Centre. http://www.bicusa.org/bicusa/index.php.

Bardhan, Pranab, and Dilip Mookherjee. 2003. "Decentralization and Accountability in Infrastructure in Developing Countries." Boston

University. http://www.bu.edu./econ/Working%20Papers/papers/ Dilip%20Mookherjee/ddinf.pdf

Barnes, Douglas F., and Jonathan Halpern. 2000. "The Role of Energy Subsidies." In *Energy and Development Report 2000*. Washington, DC: World Bank. http://www.worldbank.org/html/fpd/esmap/energy_ report2000/

Briceno, Cecilia, Antonio Estache, and Nemat Shafik. 2004. "Infrastructure Services in Developing Countries: Access, Quality, Costs and Policy Reform." World Bank Working Paper Series No. 3468, Washington, DC.

Calderon, Cesar, and Luis Serven. 2004. "The Effects of Infrastructure Development on Growth and Income Distribution." World Bank Policy Research Paper No. 3400, Washington, DC, October.

Canning, David. 1999. "The Contribution of Infrastructure to Aggregate Output." World Bank Infrastructure Working Paper No. 2246, Washington, DC.

———. 1998. "A Database of World Infrastructure Stocks." World Bank Policy Research Working Paper No. 1929, Washington, DC.

Canning, David, and Esra Bennathan. 2000. "The Social Rate of Return on Infrastructure Investment." World Bank Policy Research Working Paper No. 2390, Washington, DC.

Carruthers, Robin, Jitendra N. Bajpai, and David Hummels. 2003. "Trade and Logistics in East Asia: A Development Agenda." World Bank EASTR Working Paper No. 3, Washington, DC.

CLAIR (Council of Local Authorities for International Relations). 2004. "Local Administration of ASEAN Countries." http://www.clair.or.jp/e/.

———. 2000. "Local Administrative and Financial System in China." http://www.clair.or.jp/e/.

Clements, Benedict, Sanjeev Gupta, Alexander Pivovarsky, and Erwin R. Tiongson. 2004. "Foreign Aid: Grants versus Loans." In *Finance and Development*. Washington, DC: International Monetary Fund. September.

Coelli, Tim, Antonio Estache, Sergio Perelman, and Lourdes Trujillo. 2003. *A Primer on Efficiency Measurements for Utilities and Transport Regulators*. Washington, DC: World Bank WBI (World Bank Institute) Development Studies.

Conan, Herve. 2004. "Small Piped Water Networks: Helping Local Entrepreneurs to Invest." In *Water for All,* ed. Charles T. Andres and Almud Weitz. Manila: ADB.

Consumer International. 2004. "Improving Utilities: Consumer Organizations, Policy and Representation." Speech given by Marilena Lazzarini, CI President, at the World Bank. Washington, DC, May 4.

Crousillat, Enrique. 1998. "Developing International Power Markets in East Asia." World Bank Public Policy for the Private Sector Note 143, Washington, DC.

Dailami, Mansoor. 2004. "Korea PPI Market, Financing Sources, Growth Potential, and New Challenges." Photocopy, World Bank, Washington, DC.

de la Fuente, Angel, and Antonio Estache. 2004. "Infrastructure Productivity and Growth: A Quick Survey." Photocopy, WBIGF, Washington DC.

Demetriades, Panicos, and Theofanis Mamuneas. 2000. "Intertemporal Output and Employment Effects of Public Infrastructure Capital: Evidence from 12 OECD Economies." *The Economic Journal* 110: 687–712.

Deolalikar, Anil B. 2001. "The Spatial Distribution of Public Spending on Roads in Vietnam and Its Implications." Manila: ADB. September.

Devarajan, Shantayanan, Vinaya Swaroop, and Heng-fu Zhou. 1996. "The Composition of Public Expenditure and Economic Growth." *Journal of Monetary Economics* 37 (2–3): 313–44.

DfID (Department for International Development). 2002. "Making Connections: Infrastructure for Poverty Reduction." London: DfID. http://www.dfid.gov.uk/pubs/files/makingconnections.pdf.

Dupar, Mairi, and Nathan Badenoch. 2002. "Environment, Livelihoods, and Local Institutions: Decentralization in Mainland Southeast Asia." Photocopy, World Resources Institute, Washington, DC.

Easterly, William, and Sergio Rebelo. 1993. "Fiscal Policy and Economic Growth: An Empirical Investigation." *Journal of Monetary Economics* 32 (3): 417–58.

Easterly, William, and Luis Serven, eds. 2003. *The Limits of Stabilization.* Stanford, CA: Stanford University Press.

Environmental Resource Management Ltd. 2004. "Contracting Out Utility Regulatory Functions." Case Study. http://rru.worldbank.org/Documents/PapersLinks/2550.pdf.

Estache, Antonio. 2004. "Emerging Infrastructure Policy Issues in Developing Countries." World Bank, Washington, DC. Background paper for the Berlin meeting of the POVNET Infrastructure Working Group, October 27–9.

Estache, Antonio, and Marianne Fay. 1995. "Regional Growth in Argentina and Brazil: Determinants and Policy Options." Photocopy, World Bank, Washington, DC.

Estache, Antonio, and Maria Elena Pinglo. 2004. "Are Returns to Private Infrastructure in Developing Countries Consistent UIT Risks Since the Asian Crisis?" World Bank Policy Research Working Paper No. 3373, Washington, DC.

Evennet, Simon J., and Anthony J. Venables. 2002. "The Geographic Spread of Trade: Evidence From Twenty-Four Developing Countries." Paper presented at the European Research Workshop in International Trade, Munich, June 12.

Faguet, Jean-Paul. 2004. "Does Decentralization Increase Government Responsiveness to Local Needs: Evidence from Bolivia." *Journal of Public Economics* 88 (3–4): 867–93.

Fan, Shenggen. 2003. "Public Investment and Poverty Reduction: What Have We Learnt from India and China." Paper prepared for the ADBI Conference: "Infrastructure Investment for Poverty Reduction: What Do We Know?" Tokyo, Japan, June.

Fan, Shenggen, Pham Lan Huong, and Trinh Quang Long. 2004. "Government Spending and Poverty Reduction in Vietnam." Project report prepared for the World Bank–funded project "Pro-poor spending in Vietnam," by the International Food Policy Research Institute, Washington, DC, and Central Institute for Economic Management, Hanoi.

Fay, Marianne, and Tito Yepes. 2003. "Investing in Infrastructure: What Is Needed from 2000–2010." World Bank Policy Research Paper No. 3102, Washington, DC.

Fernald, John G. 1999. "Roads to Prosperity? Assessing the Link between Public Capital and Productivity." *The American Economic Review* 89: 619–38.

Fritzen, Scott. 2002. "Growth, Inequality and the Future of Poverty Reduction in Vietnam." *Journal of Asian Economics* 13 (5): 635–57.

General Statistical Office of Vietnam. 1996, 1998, 1999, 2000, 2001, 2003. *Statistical Yearbook.*

Global Competitiveness Report. 2004. World Economic Forum. Oxford University Press.

Gomez-Lobo, Andres, Vivien Foster, and Jonathan Halpern. 2000. "Infrastructure Reform, Better Subsidies, and the Information Deficit." World Bank Public Policy for the Private Sector Note 212, Washington, DC.

Gordon-Walker, Simon, and Simon Marr. 2002. "Study on the Application of the Competition Rules to the Water Sector in the European Community." http://europa.eu.int/comm/competition/publications/studies/water_sector_report.pdf.

GRIPS Development Forum. 2003. "Linking Economic Growth and Poverty Reduction—Large Scale Infrastructure in the context of Vietnam's CPRGS." November. http://www.grips.ac.jp/forum-e/.

Gross, Bruce, Christine van Wijk, and Nilanjana Mukherjee. 2001. "Linking Sustainability with Demand, Gender and Poverty." International

Water and Sanitation Centre. http://www.wsp.org/publications/global_plareport.pdf.

Guasch, J. Luis. 2004. *Granting and Renegotiating Infrastructure Concessions—Doing It Right*. Washington, DC: World Bank.

Guasch, J. Luis, and J. Kogan. 2001. "Inventories in Developing Countries: Levels and Determinants, a Red Flag on Competitiveness and Growth." Photocopy, World Bank, Washington, DC.

Harris, Clive, John Hodges, Michael Schur, and Padmesh Shukla. 2003. "Infrastructure Projects: A Review of Canceled Private Projects." World Bank Public Policy for the Private Sector Note 252, Washington, DC. http://rru.worldbank.org/Documents/PublicPolicyJournal/252Harri-010303.pdf.

Hofman, Bert, and Kai Kaiser. 2002. "The Making of the Big Bang and Its Aftermath." Paper presented at the conference "Can Decentralization Help Rebuild Indonesia?" Georgia State University, Atlanta, May 1–3. http://isp-aysps.gsu.edu/fprc/ino/hofmankaiserAtlanta.pdf.

Hunt, Sally, and Graham Shuttleworth. 1996. *Competition and Choice in Electricity*. Chichester, UK: John Wiley and Sons.

IEA (International Energy Agency). 2004. Electricity Information. www.iea.org.

———. 2003. World Energy Outlook. www.iea.org.

IMF (International Monetary Fund). 2004a. "Public Investment and Fiscal Policy." Prepared by the Fiscal Affairs Department. http://www.imf.org/external/np/fad/2004/pifp/eng/PIFP.pdf.

———. 2004b. *World Economic Outlook*. http://www.imf.org/external/pubs/ft/weo/2004/01/

ITU (International Telecommunication Union). Various years. http://www.itu.int.

Jacoby, H. 2000. "Access to Rural Markets and the Benefits of Rural Roads." *The Economic Journal* 110: 713–37.

JBIC (Japan Bank for International Cooperation). 2004. "Survey Report on Overseas Business Operations by Japanese Manufacturing Companies." http://www.JBUC.go.jp/autocontents/english/news/2004/000063/reprot.pdf.

———. 2003. "Impact Evaluation Study on Public-Private Partnerships: The Case of the Angat Water Supply Optimization Project and the Metropolitan Waterworks and Sewerage System." http://www.jbic.go.jp/english/oec/post/2003/pdf/1-02_smry.pdf.

———. 2000. "Eastern Seaboard Development Plan Impact Evaluation." Photocopy, Ex-post Evaluation Report.

JBIC/IDCJ (International Development Center of Japan). 2003. "Impact Assessment of Transport Infrastructure Projects in Northern Vietnam." *Ex-Post Evaluation Report on ODA Loan Projects 2003.* http://www. jbic.go.jp/english/oec/post/2003/pdf/1-03_smry.pdf.

JETRO (Japan External Trade Organization). 2003. "13th Survey of Investment-Related Cost, Comparison in Major Cities and Regions in Asia." http://www.jetro.go.jp/.

JICA (Japan International Cooperation Agency). 2004. "The Study on Integrated Transportation Master Plan for Jabodetabek (SITRAMP)." Photocopy.

———. 2001. "Local Administration and Decentralization." http://www. jica.go.jp/english/.

Kaufmann, Danny, Aart Kray, and Massimo Mastruzzi. 2003. "Governance Matters III: Governance Indicators for 1996–2002." http://www. worldbank.org/wbi/governance/pubs/govmatters3.html.

Kessides, Christine. 1996. "A Review of Infrastructure's Impact on Economic Development." In *Infrastructure and the Complexity of Economic Development,* ed. David F. Batten and Charlie Karlsson. Berlin: Springer-Verlag.

Kessides, Ioannis. 2004. *Reforming Infrastructure—Privatization Regulation and Competition.* Washington, DC: World Bank and Oxford University Press.

Krumm, Kathie, and Homi Kharas. 2004. "Overview." In *East Asia Integrates: A Trade Policy Agenda for Shared Growth,* ed. Kathie Krumm and Homi Kharas, xv–xliv. Washington, DC: World Bank and Oxford University Press.

Kuninori, Morio. 1997. "Financing Japan's Infrastructure: A Blend of Gradualism and Diversity in Financial Instruments." In *Infrastructure Strategies in East Asia.* Washington, DC: World Bank.

Larsen, Theon Ib, Pham Huong Lan, and Martin Rama. 2004. "Vietnam's Public Investment Program and its Impact on Poverty Reduction." Photocopy, World Bank, Washington, DC.

Leipziger, Danny, Marianne Fay, Quentin Wodon, and Tito Yepes. 2003. "Achieving the Millennium Development Goals: The Role of Infrastructure." World Bank Policy Research Working Paper No. 3163, Washington, DC, November.

Maguire, Glenn, and Arseni Malinovitch. 2004. "Development of PPPs in Victoria." *Australian Accounting Review* 33 (2), July.

Manasan, Rosario G. 2004. "Infrastructure and Decentralization." Background Paper for *Philippines AAA,* World Bank, Washington, DC.

Mansuri, Ghazala, and Vijayendra Rao. 2004. "Community-Based and Driven Development: A Critical Review." *World Bank Research Observer* 19 (1): 1–39.

Mellor, Thuy, and Jak Jabes. 2004. *Governance in the Pacific: Focus for Action 2005–2009*. Manila: ADB.

Miller, Nigel J., and Christopher Tsoukis. 2001. "On the Optimality of Public Capital for Long-Run Economic Growth: Evidence from Panel Data." *Applied Economics* 33 (9): 1117–29, July.

Mody, Ashoka, ed. 1997. *Infrastructure Strategies in East Asia*. Washington, DC: World Bank.

MRI (Mitsubishi Research Institute). 2003. "Study on National Land Policy Coordination in Asian Region." http://www.mri.co.jp/E/.

Muzzini, Elisa. 2004. "Consumer Participation in Infrastructure Regulation: Evidence from the East Asia and Pacific Region." Photocopy, World Bank, Washington, DC.

Ng, Francis, and Alexander Yeats. 2003. "Major Trade Trends in East Asia: What Are Their Implications for Regional Cooperation and Growth?" World Bank Policy Research Working Paper No. 3084, Washington, DC.

Panayotou, Theodore, and Zhang Zheng. 2000. *The Cost of Environmental Damage in China: Preliminary Assessment and Valuation Framework*. Bethesda, MD: Aileen International Press for the China Council for International Cooperation on Environment and Development.

Partnerships Victoria. 2001. Public Sector Comparator, Technical Note. http://www.partnerships.vic.gov.au.

Parton, Bennett. 2003. "Saving Utilities During the Asian Financial Crisis." *P3 News* 3 (3).

Peterson, George E., and Elisa Muzzini. 2004. "Decentralization of Basic Infrastructure Service." Background paper for the East Asia and Pacific Decentralization Flagship.

Prud'homme, Rémy. 2004. "Infrastructure and Development." Paper prepared for the ABCDE (Annual Bank Conference on Development Economics), Washington, DC, May 3–5.

Ravallion, Martin. 2003. "The Debate on Globalization, Poverty, and Inequality: Why Measurement Matters." World Bank Policy Research Working Paper No. 3038, Washington, DC.

Reinfeld, William. 1997. "Tying Infrastructure to Economic Development: The Republic of Korea and Taiwan." In *Infrastructure Strategies in East Asia,* ed. Ashoka Mody, 3–26. Washington, DC: World Bank.

Röller, Lars-Hendrik, and Leonard Waverman. 2001. "Telecommunications Infrastructure and Economic Development: A Simultaneous Approach." *American Economic Review* 91 (4): 909–23.

Rufo, Loreta S., and Carlito M. Rufo, Jr. 2004. "Clean Incineration of Solid Waste: A Cost-Benefit Analysis for Manila Resources." Environment and Economics Center for Studies (REECS) Research Report No. 2004-RR7, Quezon City, Philippines.

Sen, Amartya. 1999. *Development as Freedom.* Oxford: Oxford University Press.

Shah, Anwar, Theresa Thompson, and Heng-fu Zou. 2004. "The Impact of Decentralization on Service Delivery, Corruption Fiscal Management and Growth in Developing and Emerging Market Economies: A Synthesis of Empirical Evidence." *CESifo Dice Report* 1. http://www.cesifo.de/.

Sorge, Marco. 2004. "The Nature of Credit Risk in Project Finance." *BIS Quarterly Review* 6 (December): 91–101.

Spencer, Seidman. 2004. "Poverty, Growth and Inequality in Gansu, Sichuan and Yunnan." DfID Draft Paper, China, July.

Tang, Xinpeng. 2004. "Playing Games with Policy: The Image of Project of Fengcheng, Jiangxi." http://www.people.com.cn. July 21.

Transparency International. 2004. *Corruption Perceptions Index.* http://www.transparency.org.

Tuntivate, Voravate, and Douglas F. Barnes. 2000. "Thailand's Approach to Rural Electrification: How Was It Successful?" Draft, World Bank Industry and Energy Department, Washington, DC.

Tynan, Nicola, and Bill Kingdom. 2005. "Optimal Size for Utilities? Returns to Scale in Water: Evidence from Benchmarking." World Bank Public Policy for the Private Sector Note 283, Washington, DC. http://rru.worldbank.org/documents/publicpolicyjournal/ 283tynan.pdf.

UN (United Nations). 2002. *World Population Prospects.* http://esa.un.org/unpp/.

UNESCAP (United Nations Economic and Social Commission for Asia and the Pacific). 2000. "State of the Environment in Asia and the Pacific." Paper no. ST/ESCAP/2087.

U.S. DOE (Department of Energy). Energy Administration Information Database. http://www.eia.doe.gov.

Uzawa, Hirofumi. 1994. "Infrastructure in Japan: Issues and Lessons." Background paper for the *World Development Report 1994.* World Bank, Washington, DC.

van den Berg, Caroline. 2002. "Viet Nam: Evolving Management Models for Small Towns Water Supply in a Transitional Economy." World

Bank Water and Sanitation Program Working Paper No. 27003, Washington, DC.

Van Hanh, Nguyen, Nguyen Van Song, Do Van Duc, and Tran Van Duc. 2002. "Environmental Protection and Compensation Costs for the Yali Hydropower Plant in Vietnam." Economy and Environment Program for Southeast Asia (EEPSEA). http://web.idrc.ca/ en/ev-29440-201-1-DO_TOPIC.html.

Vietnam Development Report-Governance. 2004. Joint Donor Report to the Vietnam Consultative Group Meeting, Hanoi, Vietnam, December 1–2.

Warford, Jeremy, and Yining Li, eds. 2002. *Economics of the Environment in China.* China Council for International Cooperation on Environment and Development.

Webster, Douglas. 2004. "The Need for Inter-Jurisdictional Co-operation in Extended Urban Regions." Photocopy, World Bank, Washington, DC.

————. 2001. "On the Edge: Shaping the Future of Peri-Urban East Asia." Photocopy, World Bank, Washington, DC.

Wen, Jiabao. 2004. *Report of the Work of the Government.* http://english.people.com.cn/ 200503/14/eng20050314_176792.html.

World Bank. Forthcoming a. *Decentralization Flagship.* Washington, DC: World Bank.

————. Forthcoming b. *Philippines AAA.* Washington, DC: World Bank.

————. Forthcoming c. *Vietnam AAA.* Washington, DC: World Bank.

————. 2005a. *China Quarterly Update.* Washington, DC. February. http://www.worldbank. org.cn/English/Content/cqu-en.pdf.

————. 2005b. *Global Economic Prospects, Trade, Regionalism and Development.* Annual Report. Washington, DC: World Bank. http.//www.worldbank.org.

————. 2004a. *Averting an Infrastructure Crisis—Indonesia. A Framework for Policy and Action.* Washington, DC: World Bank.

————. 2004b. *China Brief.* Washington, DC: World Bank. April.

————. 2004c. "East Asia and Pacific Urban Business Directions." World Bank Urban Development Working Papers No. 5., Washington, DC, September.

————. 2004d. *East Asia Update.* Washington, DC: World Bank. November. http://siteresources.worldbank.org/INTEAPHALFYEAR-LYUPDATE/Resources/EAPupdatefinalNov04.pdf.

————. 2004e. *East Asia Update.* Washington, DC: World Bank. April. http://siteresources.worldbank.org/INTEAPHALFYEARLYUPDATE/Resources/550192-1100799330039/EAP+Regional+Overview+ Apr04.pdf.

————. 2004f. "Public Policy for the Private Sector." World Bank Private Sector Development Vice Presidency Note 274, Washington, DC, September.

————. 2004g. "Vietnam Public Expenditure Review: Managing Public Expenditure for Poverty Reduction and Growth." Photocopy, World Bank, Washington, DC.

————. 2004h. *World Development Indicators.* Washington, DC: World Bank.

————. 2004i. *World Development Report 2005: A Better Investment Climate for Everyone.* New York: Oxford University Press.

————. 2003a. "Combating Corruption in Indonesia." World Bank Poverty Reduction and Economic Management Unit Report 27246, Washington, DC.

————. 2003b. *Infrastructure for Poor People: Public Policy for Private Provision,* ed. Timothy Irwin and Penelope Brook. Washington, DC: World Bank.

————. 2003c. "Vietnam Development Report 2004—Poverty." World Bank Poverty Reduction and Economic Management Unit Report 27130-VN, Washington, DC, November.

————. 2003d. *World Development Report 2004: Making Services Work for Poor People.* New York: Oxford University Press.

————. 2003e. *World Development Indicators.* Washington, DC: World Bank.

————. 1997. *Clear Water, Blue Skies: China's Environment in the 21st Century.* Washington, DC: World Bank.

————. Investment Climate Surveys. Various Years. http://rru.worldbank.org/InvestmentClimate/.

————. Private Participation in Infrastructure (PPI) Database. http://ppi.worldbank.org.

World Economic Forum. 2003. *Global Competitiveness Report.* New York: Oxford University Press.

————. 2001. *Global Competitiveness Report.* New York: Oxford University Press.

World Energy Council. 2001. *Energy Markets in Transition: The Latin American and Caribbean Experience.* London.

Xianqiang, Mao, and Guo Xiurui. 2001. "Improving Air Quality in Chinese Cities by Substituting Natural Gas for Coal: Barriers and Incentive Policies." Beijing: Institute of Environmental Sciences. http://www.eepsea.org.

Yepes, Guillermo. 1990. "Management and Operational Practices of Municipal and Regional Water and Sewerage companies in Latin

America and the Caribbean." World Bank Discussion Paper, Infrastructure and Urban Development Department, Washington, DC.

Yogita, Mumssen. 2004. "Output-Based Aid in Cambodia—Private Operators and Local Communities Help Deliver Water to the Poor." Washington, DC: Global Partnership on Output-Based Aid. November. http://www.gpoba.org/documents/OBApproaches_Cambodia_Water.pdf.

Yuan, Lee Tsao. 1997. "Infrastructure Geared to International Economic Activity: Singapore." In *Infrastructure Strategies in East Asia,* ed. Ashoka Mody, 69–83. Washington, DC: World Bank.

Yusuf, Shahid, Simon J. Evenett, Kaoru Nabeshima, Marc Shotten, and Douglas Webster. 2001. "East Asia's Urban Regions: A Strategy for the Coming Decade." Photocopy, World Bank, Washington, DC.

Background Papers

Asanuma, Shinji. 2005. "The Role of Planning and Coordination in Asia's Infrastructure Development."

Besant-Jones, John. 2004. "Lessons from Experience of Power Sector Reform."

Brixi, Hana Polackava, and Timothy Irwin. 2004. "Fiscal Support for Infrastructure in East Asia and the Pacific: Toward a More Effective and Transparent Approach." Background paper for the Infrastructure Flagship.

Burgess, Steven. 2004. "Rural Infrastructure and Governance."

Castalia. 2004a. "Integrity in the Provision of Infrastructure: The Way Forward in Control of Corruption and Accountability."

———. 2004b. "Pacific Infrastructure Review."

———. 2004c. "Sector Note on Water Supply and Sanitation."

Civil Society Perceptions. 2004. Background survey for the Infrastructure Flagship. http://www.worldbank.org/eapinfrastructure.

East Asia and Pacific Private Investors in Infrastructure Perception Survey. 2004. Background survey for the Infrastructure Flagship. http://www.worldbank.org/eapinfrastructure.

EMBARQ, the World Resources Institute. 2004. "Rapid Motorization in China: Environmental and Social Challenges."

Fujita, Yasuo, and Hisa Shoichi. 2004. "Shifting Trade Patterns—How Will They Impact Infrastructure Needs in the East Asia and Pacific Region?"

Halcrow Group Ltd. 2004. "A Tale of Three Cities: Urban Rail Concessions in Bangkok, Kuala Lumpur, and Manila."

Jones, Stephen. 2004a. "Contribution of Infrastructure to Growth and Poverty Reduction in East Asia and the Pacific."

———. 2004b. "Regional Integration through Cross-Border Infrastructure: Framework Paper."

Liu, Zhi. 2004. "Planning and Policy Coordination in China's Infrastructure Development."

Medalla, Felippe. 2004. "Policy Coordination, Planning and Infrastructure Provision in the Philippines."

Nomura Research Institute, Ltd. 2004. "Private Sector Perceptions of Challenges and Opportunities by Japanese Infrastructure Users." Background paper for the Infrastructure Flagship.

Structured Credit International Corp. 2004. "Role of the Financial Sector: Channeling Private Savings to Infrastructure Investments in East Asia and the Pacific."

Takamine, Yutaka. 2004. "Infrastructure Services and Social Inclusion of Persons with Disabilities and Older Persons in East Asia and the Pacific."

Ure, John. 2004. "Telecom Note." Background paper for the Infrastructure Flagship.

UTCE/ALMEC (UTCE Ltd. and ALMEC Corporation). 2004a. "Infrastructure Development and Service Provision in the Process of Urbanization."

———. 2004b. "Infrastructure Development and Service Provision in the Process of Decentralization."

Warford, Jeremy. 2004. "Infrastructure Policy and Strategy in the East Asia and Pacific Region: Environmental and Social Aspects."

Webster, Douglas, and Patharaporn Theeratham. 2004. "Policy Coordination, Planning and Infrastructure Provision: A Case Study of Thailand."

Yepes, Tito. 2004. "Expenditure on Infrastructure in East Asia Region, 2006–2010."

Index

Page references containing *b* refer to text appearing in boxes, *f* refers to figures, *t* refers to tables, and *n* refers to footnotes.